FRENCH SOCIALISM AND SEXUAL DIFFERENCE

French Socialism and Sexual Difference

Women and the New Society, 1803–44

Susan K. Grogan

*Lecturer, Department of History, Victoria University of Wellington
New Zealand*

First published 1992

Published by
MACMILLAN ACADEMIC AND PROFESSIONAL LTD
Houndmills, Basingstoke, Hampshire RG21 2XS
and London
Companies and representatives
throughout the world

ISBN 0-333-52530-2

Printed in Hong Kong
British Library Cataloguing in Publication Data
Grogan, Susan K.
French socialism and sexual difference: women and the new society, 1803-44.
1. France. Socialism. Role of women, history
I. Title
335.00944

In loving memory of
Josephine Mercy Foley (1920–87)

Contents

Acknowledgements

Like many first books, this one began as a doctoral thesis and has incurred debts of gratitude spanning a decade. My affection for the early nineteenth century French socialists was first nurtured by Dr John Hooper of Murdoch University, Western Australia. I thank him for that, as well as for providing valuable criticism of drafts of this work, as teacher and later as colleague. Dr Robert Stuart of the University of Western Australia also has a long acquaintance with this book, which has benefited from his critical comments and friendly advice. My colleagues at the Victoria University of Wellington, New Zealand, have also contributed in various ways to the completion of this project. I thank Dr David Mackay in particular for reading and commenting on parts of the text. My special gratitude is extended to Ms Jacqueline Matthews, who shares my interest in this subject and has generously shared her insights with me. Her expertise in the French language has also been most valuable, though the responsibility for translation and interpretation naturally remains my own. I also thank Mrs Gloria Biggs, Mrs Kristin Downey and Mrs Barbara Cleverley for typing the manuscript, and solving many of my word-processing problems.

As all scholars based in the Antipodes know, a project such as this cannot survive without the specialised assistance of Library staff, especially in the Reference and Inter-loan departments. I have been fortunate to have had such assistance at Murdoch University Library; the Reid Library, University of Western Australia; and at the Victoria University of Wellington Library. The staffs of the Bibliothèque de l'Arsenal and the Bibliothèque Marguerite Durand in Paris, and the Goldsmiths' Library at the University of London, were also particularly helpful.

It is customary for authors to thank their families at this point, and I shall be no exception. The project has imposed on their lives in many ways yet I have had their unfailing, if sometimes bemused, support. Now that it is complete I hope they experience the satisfaction, or at least relief, which their contributions warrant.

1
Introduction

The place of woman in early nineteenth-century French society was fraught with contradictions. She was worshipped as 'Muse and Madonna' of the society,[1] but was legally a non-person. She was the symbol of Truth and Justice, of Liberty and the Republic, yet she was simultaneously exploited and despised. In fact, the idealisation of 'Woman' as abstract entity contrasted dramatically with the subordinate position of real women in the economic, political and civil structures of their society. Since men dominated those structures and created the images, the contradictions between them illustrated men's ambivalence towards women. However, the ambiguities in women's position also reflected the uncertainties of a society which had undergone (and continued to experience) major political upheavals, and which faced the disruptions of incipient industrialisation. New patterns of economic and political life required and created new patterns of identity; new ways of relating to others in the society. For conservatives seeking 'order', liberals seeking 'progress', and socialists seeking a radical restructuring of society, defining women's place in society, and constructing models of femininity which justified it, were crucial undertakings.

Charles Fourier, the Saint-Simonians and Flora Tristan – amongst the most important figures in French socialism in the first half of the nineteenth century – all shared the belief that the subordination of women was unjust, and a hindrance to the construction of a more perfect society. They argued for immediate changes in the status and treatment of women, and assigned them specific roles in transforming the social system. The socialists' theories on women were based in part on their observation of women's inferior position in their own society, but they also made assumptions about women's nature which were widely shared at that time. These assumptions about female 'otherness' shaped their speculations about ideal female roles in the future. Socialists deliberately strengthened and extended the concept of sexual complementarity, employing this concept as the basis for a new

1

social order, and in particular, for the liberty of women. Their theories aimed to turn all women into free and productive members of the new society, in order to achieve the social and moral benefits which this would produce.

WOMEN'S LIFESTYLES: WORKERS AND BOURGEOISIE AT THE TURN OF THE NINETEENTH CENTURY

Socialist calls for women's liberty reflected their critiques of the lifestyles of women in early nineteenth-century French society. Women dependent on wages lived very different lives from women of the wealthy classes, but the exploitation of both groups demonstrated to socialists the injustices and inefficiencies of the existing order. The working woman, subject of concern to socialists and conservatives alike at this time, faced contracting earning opportunities. The processes which restricted women's employment in craft production had accelerated during the eighteenth century, as legislation and pressure from male workers gradually excluded them from lucrative areas of work and skilled occupations.[2] Women in the old commercial and craft centres, including Paris, were increasingly confined within a narrow range of jobs in textile production, garment-making and street-trading, although they were represented in all industrial sectors. Midwifery and domestic service also remained important female occupations.[3]

The growth and mechanisation of the textiles industry at this time drew heavily on a pool of under-employed rural women, offering them domestic outwork or drawing them into the mills in emergent spinning towns. Their appeal to employers lay, above all, in their cheapness, since they were paid little more than children and rarely more than half the male wage. Outwork allowed costs to be minimised because the worker bore most overheads herself, although many women with children found this the best way of combining their domestic and wage-earning duties. Women's maternal responsibilities were invoked to justify the payment of a supplementary wage (rather than a living wage, or a wage commensurate with output), and to force the acceptance of intermittent work. However, women's reproductive role did not protect them in the factories, where they laboured in dangerous and debilitating conditions.[4]

The inadequacy of women's wages and earning capacity was

dramatically illustrated by the upsurge in prostitution in the early nineteenth century, particularly in the capital. The hardships caused by revolution, war and economic crisis led to an explosion in the numbers of prostitutes in Paris, and a system of supervision and registration was introduced in 1802 in an effort to contain them. By mid-century there were 34 000 registered prostitutes in Paris, working in about 200 official brothels. However, the registration system accounted for only a small proportion of working prostitutes, whose real numbers were much higher than the official figure.[5]

Prostitution was the subject of considerable public debate in French society at that time. Many were offended by the public scandal which it occasioned, while socialists regarded it as the ultimate indictment of the contemporary social order. The publication in 1836 of Doctor Parent-Duchâtelet's study, *De la Prostitution dans la Ville de Paris*, highlighted the economic causes of prostitution. It demonstrated that most Parisian prostitutes lacked education and were normally employed in the lower levels of the garment trades.[6] Many had come to Paris from nearby areas in search of employment, and they resorted to prostitution as a result of 'lack of work and misery, the inevitable result of insufficient salaries'. 'One can only reproach them', Parent-Duchâtelet argued, 'for not having had the courage to die of hunger.'[7]

'Insufficient salaries' affected the entire working class in the early nineteenth century. Wages declined in all trades by an average of 22% by 1830, while the cost of consumer goods rose about 60%.[8] Increasing numbers of families required aid in order to survive. During this period the 'dangerous classes', the 'barbarians in the midst' of the civilised bourgeoisie, were born.[9] This was not a time when working women could have adopted the domestic ideal offered to bourgeois women, had they desired to do so. As Groppi has remarked of the popular classes, the woman at home, unless engaged in some form of domestic production or outwork, was an unemployed woman.[10] Housework was quickly completed where families had few possessions and lived in one or two rooms. Besides, many tasks could not be done at home because the facilities were lacking. Clothes were washed in public laundries or in a nearby river; a communal well provided water, limiting both cooking and cleaning; in the towns bread was purchased, not baked at home, where a large pot over an open fire provided the only cooking facilities. Daily chores were therefore communal chores for women of the popular classes. They were performed in a social context incompatible with bourgeois notions of private household management.[11] Nevertheless, the domestic ideal could provide a focus of aspiration, since it was associated with a degree of domestic comfort. Working-class leaders adopted the model as the century progressed, and it sometimes appealed to working women because it promised an end to laborious, exhausting and poorly remunerated employment. Still, working women's support for the domestic ideal was by no means universal.[12]

Domesticity was more influential amongst bourgeois women, in many cases shaping both the ideal and the reality of their lives. To the early socialists, bourgeois women's lifestyles illustrated some of the worst abuses of contemporary society. These women were criticised as idle consumers, and their status as merchandise on the marriage market was also condemned. Bourgeois marriage was first and foremost an alliance between families, although the likely happiness of the couple was not necessarily ignored.[13] Young women were carefully chaperoned to introduce them only to suitable men, thus minimising the risk of a *mésalliance*. The argument that they were not well-equipped to judge the suitability of a partner was justified given the sheltered conditions in which girls were raised, and the considerable age gap between brides and grooms suggests that men were in a stronger position than women to play a decisive part in the selection of their partners.[14]

The appropriate role of the bourgeois wife was laid out in the large number of books which explored this issue in the early nineteenth century. Many of these were written by women of aristocratic or bourgeois background, and attempted to define an honourable role for women of the wealthy classes in a changing society. They praised domesticity, arguing that the role of 'wife–companion' gave women dignity and significant moral influence over their husbands.[15] It offered them a degree of independence and social status which the spinster never attained.[16] However, the domestic ideal also stressed effacement, dependence and public invisibility for women, and accepted that domestic harmony required patriarchal authority within the home. The Civil Code of 1804 legitimised male power. It denied women equal legal status with men, and ensured their economic dependence by restricting women's property rights. Bourgeois women did not share the political power increasingly concentrated in the hands of bourgeois men during the nineteenth century.[17]

The role of the *bourgeoise* was defined as familial, but women's participation in the family business was often crucial amongst shopkeeping and industrial families on the way up. This direct and public involvement was uncommon amongst women of the *haute bourgeoisie*, and female withdrawal from active participation in business generally accompanied the family's rise up the social scale.[18] Conformity to the domestic ideal was thus more pronounced amongst the wealthier sectors of the bourgeoisie, and in the professional sector where women lacked the education to share their husbands' work.

The domestic ideal placed special emphasis on motherhood. This role was praised and respected, although mothers had few guaranteed parental rights. Bourgeois women generally had only one or two children in the early nineteenth century, limiting the size of their families in order to provide abundant attention and substantial inheritances to each of their offspring. In wealthier families, where the fragmentation of inheritance was not a cause for concern, larger numbers of children were more common.[19] Children were generally lavished with love and affection, but bourgeois mothers offset this by a zealous inculcation of the virtues of self-discipline, thrift and hard work.[20] The mother-educator had responsibility for her sons' instruction only for the first six or seven years, but girls' education often rested entirely in the hands of their mothers. They strove to instil in their daughters the simplicity, self-discipline and devotion to others which were regarded as the most desirable qualities for a well brought-up woman. These qualities, supplemented by some general knowledge, the polite accomplishments, and practice in household management, would produce a marriageable daughter. The mother's task was then complete.[21]

The family was idealised by the bourgeoisie as a place of emotional and psychological refuge. In France, this was essentially a reaction to the traumatic experience of the French Revolution.[22] From the perspective of the bourgeoisie, the popular revolution had almost destroyed the social fabric, and the re-establishment of a stable society required particular attention to the family, the nucleus of society. The role assigned to the bourgeois woman was valued, therefore, and it was primarily a moral one. She instilled accepted values in her children and exercised moral influence over her husband. She also created a world of order and regularity within the home, in contrast with the disordered world of the masses.[23]

The middle-class mother thus established a model of family life to be imitated by, or imposed upon, the lower classes.

Family relations amongst the urban working classes diverged from the bourgeois pattern in a number of ways, and the bourgeois model was not easily enforced. Workers usually chose their own partners, but financial considerations were often important for them too. Women's inadequate wages made partnership with a male worker a matter of survival, yet a competent tradeswoman was also a desirable partner for a working man. In theory, greater equality was possible in workers' relationships, because partners were freely chosen and closer in age than was usual amongst the bourgeoisie. Socialists often praised the moral superiority of working-class marriages on these grounds. However, workers' memoirs indicate that the patriarchal family model survived at this level of society as well.[24] Workers' family lives were diverse, like those of the bourgeoisie, and for many unskilled, migrant and casual workers family life was an unaffordable luxury.[25] The attitudes of working men towards their wives and children were influenced by the codes of behaviour of the various trades and occupations. Carpenters, for instance, had a reputation as good family men and considerate husbands, whereas tailors and rag-dealers were contemptuous of their wives and preferred the company of their workmates. There were exceptions, but the peer group exerted pressure on men to conform to its norms.[26]

Women frequently held a significant level of power within working-class families. They were often partners in decision-making as well as in business, and in many cases controlled the family finances.[27] Bourgeois moralists and social critics sought to reinforce this power, envisaging women as purveyors of bourgeois moral order amongst the working classes. The image of the clean-living, thrifty and teetotal worker, taking home his wages to a domestic wife, socialising at home rather than at the *cabaret*, was the model they sought to enforce. As agents of social control within the working-class home, wives would subdue their husbands and keep them out of the public places: the places where grievances were aired and discontent festered, and hence where strikes and revolution were born.[28]

During the July Monarchy the bourgeoisie became increasingly concerned that workers were living in common-law unions rather than legal marriages. These unions were often stable and long-term partnerships, which were not formalised because of the complexities and expense of meeting the legal requirements for marriage.[29] However, to the middle-class mind, workers' failure to marry illustrated both the sexual depravity and disorder of the masses, and the decline of the family.[30] The failure of working-class mothers was singled out for attention. The increase in illegitimacy rates was viewed with alarm, since it was feared that mothers who gave birth to such children lacked the moral capacity to instil in them the appropriate social virtues. Illegitimate births had been increasing since the mid-eighteenth century, partly due to the rising proportion of common-law unions. In large cities such as Paris and Lyon, between a third and a half of all children were illegitimate in the early nineteenth century.[31] Furthermore, about 33 000 foundlings a year came into State custody in France in the 1815–30 period.[32] To bourgeois observers, these figures illustrated an absence of parental (and especially maternal) feelings amongst the workers. They denounced the *mère dénaturée* whose abandonment of her child flouted the laws of nature, although the laws of economics, so revered by the bourgeoisie, generally lay at the heart of a woman's decision to surrender her infant.[33] Bourgeois social policy in the early nineteenth century therefore focused on enforcing familial sentiment amongst the masses by offering limited home assistance to needy mothers. This, they hoped, would ' . . . reawaken . . . in the breasts of mothers who wished to abandon [their children] a maternal feeling that had been cooled . . .'.[34]

There were vast discrepancies between the lives of the majority of women in early nineteenth-century France, therefore, and the idealised roles of wife and mother deemed proper for them. Women's lifestyles were thus the subject of major debate. Their roles were seen as crucial, not only to men's comfort and happiness, but to the survival and welfare of the nation. The construction of normative models of femininity assumed increasing importance in order to justify and enforce the allotted gender division. Religion, philosophy and science were called upon for this purpose.

DEFINING 'WOMAN': IDEOLOGY AND IMAGERY

Images of 'woman' played an important part in the negotiation of power between the sexes, at a time when traditional forms of authority were under attack, and a new social order was being created. Patterns of domestic life were deeply affected by the late eighteenth-century challenge to religious and monarchical power in France, and the attempts over succeeding years to base political relations on a social contract between theoretically equal citizens. Since the hierarchical family had provided a model for relations in the State, patriarchal authority in the home was threatened by its condemnation in the political sphere. The redefining of political bonds thus entailed a redefinition of sexual relations, and this in turn required a reconsideration of the nature of each sex, and a reinterpretation of the differences between them.[35]

The eighteenth century marked a turning point in the perception of womanhood. 'Woman's place' was no longer defined (in theory, at least) solely by the teachings of Catholicism. The insights of Nature and Reason were also brought to bear on this subject and science, in particular, made possible the 'unveiling' of woman.[36] As a result the earlier model of woman as imperfect man was replaced by a concept of the specificity of female nature. Woman was defined as 'other' than man in every respect, and in her 'otherness' theorists observed the unmistakeable signs of her destiny and social role. However, the newfound uniqueness and perfection of woman were not seen as justifying her social equality with man. Rather, the notion of 'incommensurability' was used to deny the application of 'natural rights' to woman.[37] By defining woman as 'other', therefore, late eighteenth- and early nineteenth-century theorists found a new justification for preserving hierarchy in sexual relations, and for excluding women from public life. Their images of 'woman' provided the intellectual context in which socialist theories on women were framed.

Images of Woman in the Catholic Tradition

The Catholic religion had long maintained a polarised view of women, which emphasised their potential as agents of evil and as models of Christian virtue.[38] The first tradition derived from the Genesis account of woman's secondary creation, her role in the Fall, and her subsequent punishment by God. All women bore the stigma of Eve the temptress. Furthermore, women were defined as representatives of 'the flesh' and sexuality, which were despised and mistrusted. This view therefore emphasised women's natural and Divinely-ordained subordination to men.[39] A selective reading of the Scriptures and a heavy reliance on the Church Fathers justified the Church's defence of female subordination, and alternative egalitarian accounts of gender relations in both the Old and New Testaments were ignored.[40]

The view of woman as a physical and moral threat to man was alive and well in the first half of the nineteenth century. Influential figures in the French Church expressed their suspicion of women, and their preference for a way of life from which women were excluded. Frédéric Ozanam, founder of the Saint Vincent de Paul Society, advocated virginity or late marriage, arguing that ' . . . man surrenders much of his dignity the day he chains himself to the arms of woman'.[41] Abbé Jean-Joseph Gaume, writer and key advocate of devotion to Mary, was more hostile. He described woman as 'corrupt and corrupting', and demanded the revival of the ancient practice of ritual purification after childbirth.[42] His condemnation of woman as 'a foul spider [who] spreads her seductive power over the whole expanse of the earth like a vast web' was designed to justify female subordination, as well as suggesting that male hostility to women had deep psychological causes.[43]

The mistrust of woman exhibited in Catholic teaching, and in the attitudes of some clergymen, contrasted with the significant position assigned to Mary in the Catholic tradition. Michaud suggests that the cult of Mary performed an exorcistic function, countering the sexual and moral threat which real women posed. It was therefore compatible with repressive attitudes to women.[44] The early nineteenth century witnessed a dramatic upsurge in devotion to Mary, especially after 1830. This was the age of apparitions, the Virgin appearing to Catherine Labouré in Paris in 1830; to the children of La Salette in 1846; and later to Bernadette Soubirous at Lourdes in 1858.[45] The Miraculous Medal, supposedly requested of Labouré by the Virgin herself, had twenty million wearers by 1837. Confraternities dedicated to Mary expanded rapidly; pilgrimages to sites of the Virgin's appearances and to churches dedicated to Mary were popular; and religious orders under her protection multiplied.[46]

Mary was the model presented to women for imitation, because her submission to the Divine will had enabled her to play a role in redemption and to counter the sin of Eve. The idealisation of Mary thus made possible the idealisation of women who modelled themselves on her image. Like Mary, woman became an angelic and saving figure in the life of man. Chateaubriand, a leading

figure in the nineteenth-century Catholic revival, made this connection in his *Génie du Christianisme*. Mary was portrayed as the
archetypal woman, the epitome of beauty and innocence, exhibiting 'the sweet virtue of her sex'. Above all she was virgin and
mother, 'the two most divine states of womanhood'.[47]

The potential benefit to women of a feminised Catholicism lay,
therefore, in its glorification of the Christian wife and mother.
Chateaubriand wrote fervently:

> The Christian wife is not a mere mortal: she is an extraordinary,
> mysterious, angelic being . . . Without woman, [man] would be
> primitive, uncouth and alone . . . woman adorns him with the
> flowers of life, as the vines of the forest adorn the trunk of the
> oak tree with their perfumed garlands.[48]

However, Chateaubriand also emphasised woman's innate physical and moral weakness and her capacity to transmit her failings to
others. Being 'born of woman', rather than created by God as
Adam had been, was man's true 'fall'.[49] His attitude to women,
therefore, conformed with that of another conservative Catholic
theorist, Joseph de Maistre. In de Maistre's opinion, the weakening of the power of the Church and the advocacy of women's
liberty promised 'shameful licence', 'universal corruption' and the
collapse of the State.[50] Apart from religious celibacy, women's only
valid roles were those of wives and mothers, subject to the control
of their husbands. Despite women's 'mysterious' and 'angelic'
qualities, therefore, male authority within the family was regarded
as essential for social order. The early nineteenth-century Church
proved reluctant to accept change, rejecting the ideas and learning
of the new age, and supporting the Restoration and its values.[51]
Similarly, by condemning women to subservience and domesticity,
the Church attempted to maintain the hierarchical gender order of
the past without any amendment.

'Enlightened' Views of Woman

The systematic study of human nature by eighteenth-century
'Enlightenment' philosophers provided an alternative source for
ideas on women's nature and social roles. Several influential texts
on women were produced by the *philosophes*. Montesquieu's *Per-
sian Letters* was widely read throughout Europe; while Rousseau's

Emile was 'devoured' by women readers in the period before the Revolution.[52] Diderot wrote an essay *On Women*, although it was not published in his lifetime; and the question of woman's nature and place in society was also discussed by such writers as Laclos, Helvétius, D'Holbach and Condorcet.[53]

Enlightenment writers generally emphasised the natural differences between the sexes, and the more powerful determinism of biology in the lives of women. Sexual difference was regarded as a total distinction, extending from the physical to the intellectual and moral spheres. According to Rousseau, the original reproductive differences between the sexes had assumed new dimensions as society progressed. Perfectly adapted for her reproductive role, woman had not needed to develop the faculties which denoted 'civilised' man: reason, memory and imagination. As a consequence woman had become increasingly different from man over time, rather than closer to him.[54]

Femininity was frequently portrayed as a less perfect condition than masculinity by the *philosophes*. Diderot believed that woman's physical 'limitations' made her a prey to her biology and a permanent invalid, and Montesquieu held a similar view. Rousseau claimed to defend the particularity rather than the inferiority of woman. The sexes were separate and distinct states of being, and comparison between them was meaningless.[55] However, he also stressed the limiting impact of women's physiology on their social roles.[56] This essentialist perspective was rejected by other *philosophes*, such as Helvétius, d'Alembert and Condorcet, who attributed sexual difference largely to environment and education. According to this view, both women and men could be shaped and improved, though not necessarily made equal.[57] Condorcet's insistence on woman's potential for rational development ran counter to the dominant emphasis on difference and complementarity.[58] According to most of the *philosophes*, the great social danger lay in sexual confusion and inversion.[59]

In defining woman's difference from man, Rousseau identified her as the representative of Nature, locating her outside history and outside the processes of social development.[60] The concept of woman as 'Nature' served a variety of purposes in Enlightenment writings, and was not incompatible with an alternative view of woman as 'Culture'. In the latter role, woman was portrayed as a civilising influence within the home and society. She oversaw the moral education of her children and tamed the lower instincts of 'natural' man.[61] The definition of woman as 'Nature', however, had both positive and negative ramifications. As 'Nature', woman embodied the virtues of simplicity, spontaneity and innocence. She thus symbolised the new morality which emphasised innate human goodness, and whose legitimacy was independent of religion. The 'natural' woman, defined in opposition to the superficial and false society woman, became a model of virtue and a source of moral regeneration for society. However, woman's closeness to Nature also had a negative sense. Woman as 'Nature' represented the uncontrolled and disorderly. She was the embodiment of ignorance and superstition, the defender of tradition, the creature of instinct. 'Nature' was therefore a tool of social criticism, open to a variety of meanings, and its association with women served the broader political purposes of its wielders.[62]

The question of whether women were capable of developing their reason, and whether it was socially desirable that they do so, was addressed at length by the *philosophes*, as they sought to establish appropriate roles for women in society. As Lloyd points out, possession of reason forms one of the basic criteria for personhood in the Western philosophical tradition.[63] The argument of several *philosophes* that women lacked full rational power therefore justified their status as dependent beings who belonged in the care of men. Diderot regarded women as pre-rational, and contrasted female 'mystery' with male logic.[64] Although Rousseau had argued against drawing comparisons between the sexes, he maintained that women's reason was of a lower order than that of men. They possessed a 'practical' rather than 'theoretical' reason; one adapted to means not ends; one incapable of original thought. Education would never make women men's intellectual equals, therefore, though it would threaten women's natural qualities and deter them from fulfilling their duties.[65] The intellectual realm thus remained safely the preserve of men and women's exclusion from intellectual pursuits was justified.

The *philosophes* emphasised that woman's whole being was designed for maternity.[66] Extrapolating from a potential function to an obligatory social role, they argued that motherhood was women's moral destiny, and that their rejection of this role carried serious personal and social consequences.[67] Rousseau was the most celebrated advocate of the maternal role, and his writings featured amongst the most influential works on women in this period. Contemporaries attributed the fashionable return to breastfeeding in the 1770s largely to his advocacy, though Diderot also emphasised its desirability on both medical and moral grounds.[68] The role of motherhood was defined in positive terms, and Rousseau emphasised its nurturing and educative aspects. Mothers formed citizens, instilling the appropriate social virtues. The importance of their role thus stemmed from its moral component, since the basis of society and of its virtues lay in the family.[69] However, by confining women entirely to the maternal role, the theories of Rousseau, and other *philosophes*, offered no place to women outside a nuclear family structure. Rousseau was unambiguous on this point, defining a woman without a husband and children as sexless, with no reason for existence.[70] Woman did not exist for herself as an independent being, as man did, but only in relation to man. Although Rousseau sought to idealise woman as 'mother', and to insist on the incommensurability of the two sexes, his concept of female nature assumed its inferiority to male nature, which was inherently self-sufficient.

With the exception of Condorcet, the *philosophes* defended the subordination of women to men. Female weakness and the physical constraints imposed by motherhood prevented their full participation in communal life, according to the *philosophes*. Women were naturally dependent on men, and hence necessarily submissive.[71] Rousseau located the transition to sexual hierarchy at the dawn of history, when woman supposedly proved less adaptable than man to the demands of an increasingly complex social life, and chose to focus on her childrearing role. The hierarchical family unit, in which woman was subordinate to man, was therefore natural and just. However, despite the 'naturalness' of the female condition, both Rousseau and Montesquieu highlighted the need to shape girls for submission and dependence from childhood.[72]

Enlightenment arguments about the 'naturalness' of female dependence were accompanied by the claim that their subordination was necessary for the security of the State. For Montesquieu, woman represented the anarchic forces of sensuality. Her confinement signified and achieved the control of the passions, and the public good justified the restriction of liberty which this entailed.[73] For Rousseau, even women's virtues became vices if transported into the political sphere. The exclusive quality of maternal love, for instance, was incompatible with the social ties of citizenship.[74] Female domestic subordination was therefore a precondition for the healthy functioning of the male public sphere. Its separation from the domestic world, defined as feminine, allowed the 'spirit of virile discipline', which characterised the State, to flourish.[75] Women's exclusion from public life thus freed men for the role of citizenship undistracted by sensual and familial temptations.

The submission of women to their husbands was also a symbol of the just hierarchy which was necessary in the State. The submissive wife, representation of domestic order, provided a model for the acceptance of the rule of law, and the subordination of self-interest to the general good. Montesquieu argued that this hierarchy was not inconsistent with the 'true equality' desirable in a Republic, which allowed for authority to be exercised between equals. Woman's formal equality was thus reconciled with the power to be exercised by man 'as magistrate, as senator, as judge, as father, as husband, as master'.[76] The concept of women's free consent to male authority disguised their subordination in Enlightenment visions of society. It suggested women's acceptance that their subordination was just. 'Freely-consenting' women, rather than despotic men, thus became responsible for female subordination.[77] Male authority was defended in these theories by a variety of strategies, therefore, and in this respect Enlightenment thought demonstrated its continuity with the Catholic view of woman's place.

Medical Experts Examine Women

Doctors provided another source of authority on the nature and social roles of women in the late eighteenth and early nineteenth centuries. They relied mainly on authorities such as Rousseau for their ideas about women, and produced a 'medical philosophy' rather than an empirical science.[78] However, where learned examiners of female physiology had formerly seen only beings similar to men, they now noticed fundamental differences which permeated every fibre of woman's being. Doctors thus reinforced the philosophers' pronouncements on the uniqueness of woman, who was no longer a lesser, inadequate man but a radically different embodiment of the human species. As 'experts' in the study of bodies and their healthy functioning, doctors were ideally suited to reveal and interpret the significance of sexual differences. Their proclamations about women thus extended beyond physiology to the social and moral realms.[79]

The expanding science of anatomy aided the exploration of sex differences from the eighteenth century.[80] Skeleton, muscles, tissues, nerves and fibres were all subjected to scrutiny, and confirmed physicians' views of the specificity of the female. Doctors emphasised two physiological characteristics of women: their weakness and *sensibilité*. 'Weakness' was never clearly defined, let alone measured, but it referred to a general lack of muscular development in women, and to a perception that the female body was soft, delicate and fragile.[81] In both respects, a normative (and idealised) male physiology was the point of reference, as physicians attempted to construct a female image which contrasted with it.[82] Women's *sensibilité* was more carefully delineated by physicians, although their findings reflected conviction rather than clinical observation. Women's superior *sensibilité* described an acute responsiveness to sensory inputs, so that women were dominated, even overwhelmed, by sensory 'messages'. Doctor Cabanis explained:

The speed and the liveliness of activity in the nervous system are the measures of the general sensibility of the subject . . . Woman is more sensitive and more unstable because the structure of all her organs is softer and weaker . . . The greater the sensibility and the freer and more rapid the messages, the more too this influence must produce sudden, varied, extraordinary phenomena.[83]

According to this theory, women's brains were subjected to an incessant battery of sensations. They were less able to process all the messages received and translate them into concepts. Despite the fact that a sensationalist theory of knowledge was predominant in the late eighteenth century, then, women's sensory superiority was not interpreted as a sign of superior rational potential. Instead, women's sensibility defined them as intuitive rather than rational; lacking in concentration; incapable of the higher intellectual functions of reflection, analysis and synthesis; incapable, finally, of creativity and genius.[84]

The allocation of sensibility rather than rationality to women indicated their destiny within society, and established the basis of their relationship with men. According to the physicians, sensibility gave women a superior capacity for tenderness and compassion which, in the view of doctors like Roussel and Virey, indicated their destiny of motherhood.[85] In reaching this conclusion the doctors were influenced by their understanding of women's sexual and reproductive biology. The uterus remained the female organ *par excellence*, although it was gradually displaced by the ovaries after the discovery of ovulation in 1827, and more especially, after the discovery of spontaneous ovulation in some mammals in 1843.[86] Doctors argued that the female body was totally sexualised by nature in order to ensure and facilitate the reproductive function. The uterus, ovaries and breasts, and also woman's natural delicacy and dependence, marked her out for motherhood. Maternity was not only a biological imperative, then, but a social and moral imperative for women. Doctors ignored the fact that family limitation was increasingly being exercised by French couples, as the falling birthrate attests.[87] They omitted birth-control from their treatises and described abortion as an entirely accidental phenomenon, probably to avoid becoming a source of information on such practices. At a time when the demands of maternity showed some potential for reduction, therefore, doctors were keen to lock women securely into that 'predestined' role.[88]

The focus on the breast in the eighteenth-century medical literature reflected doctors' admiration for the maternal role, and symbolised the links they established between the biological, social and moral realms. The breast represented physical motherhood, and doctors such as Roussel made breastfeeding a physical and moral duty for women:

> The care of infants is the destiny of women; it is a task which nature has assigned to them . . . If reasons concerning the organisation and natural sequence of her functions oblige every woman who is not too ill to breastfeed, the moral reasons which appear to compel this are no less significant. . . .[89]

There was some truth in the claim that infants not fed by their own mothers were in jeopardy. However, medical arguments emphasised the moral rather than the physical benefits of maternal breastfeeding: infants would absorb moral principles with their mothers' milk.[90] For this very reason, however, other doctors were reluctant to make maternal suckling an infallible law, since it could also become a vehicle for transmitting undesirable passions and vices to the child.[91]

In denoting the nurturant role of woman, the breast also defined the female role as a private and familial one.[92] The configuration of women's bodies thus marked out the social spaces they were to occupy, just as the physiological features of male sexuality indicated to doctors men's destined social prominence:

> Since man's whole being seeks to expand, to extend, since the heat and vigour of his sex impose this law of expansion on him physically as well as morally, everything, in woman, must somehow unite to contain, to gather her affections, her thoughts and actions in the home for the reproduction and education of the family. It is not our institutions, it is nature which proclaims this truth, that a wife is only in her element, in the place which is most respectable, even most happy for her, when she is where her essential duties call her . . . If she abandons it, her virtues, lacking their purpose, become vices which are rarely forgiven.[93]

Doctors stressed the pitfalls for women who evaded their sacred duty in the home and sought fulfilment in other realms. In particular, they warned against intellectual pursuits for women. The cultivation of reason would necessarily entail the weakening of sentiment, argued Cabanis, and hence destroy the grace and charm which constituted femininity. Woman's beauty would fade, and since (as he argued) 'women's happiness will always depend on the impression they make on men', unhappiness would surely follow.[94] Cabanis and Roussel agreed that women who rejected their 'maternal' role or protested against it were depraved.[95]

Like Cabanis, Virey argued that women's subordination to men was natural and inescapable:

> [Woman] does not live for herself, but for the multiplication of the species, in conjunction with man; that is the only goal which Nature, society and morality allow. It follows that woman is a being naturally subordinate to man by her needs, her duties, and especially by her physical constitution . . . If woman is weak in her very constitution, Nature has thus sought to make her submissive and dependent in the sexual union . . . she must therefore bear the yoke of constraint without complaining, to preserve peace in the family by her submission and her example.[96]

He criticised women for resisting dependence, and 'seeing in even the most deserved submission only the shackles of slavery'.[97] Women lacked the rational strength to recognise their own legitimate subordination, he claimed, but of course if they had possessed that level of rationality their subordination would no longer have been warranted. For the leading French doctors of the early nineteenth century, however, the construction of a particular model of femininity which stressed female specificity and biological determinism, served to justify a patriarchal family structure. The veneer of 'science' reinforced restrictive views about women's place in society. Like theology and philosophy, science emphasised women's 'special' nature, and defined as 'natural' women's confinement to the home and their subordination to men.

French socialists shared some of the assumptions made in the religious, philosophical and medical discourses on women in this period. It is significant, for instance, that pre-1848 socialist writings on ideal female roles did not appeal to the models of the French Revolution, which would have provided a precedent for redefining women's place.[98] No doubt the early socialists wished to avoid raising the spectre of female disorder and social chaos, which many of their contemporaries associated with women's entry into the public sphere during those years. The silence of the socialists on the activities of Revolutionary women was also consistent with their attempts to define a set of 'female' roles which were essentially different from those of men, and thus a reflection of women's different nature.

While the weight of religious, philosophical and medical opinion on female nature justified a restricted domestic role for women, however, a number of French socialists employed the concept of women's special nature in order to advocate a non-domestic role for women. Charles Fourier, the Saint-Simonians and Flora Tristan were strong defenders of this position, making it central to their visions of a new social order. Women would take their places alongside men in all areas of life. Both public and private life would be transformed and the barriers between them lowered. They rejected the widespread insistence on separate spheres, although they generally accepted the distinctiveness of male and female natures. Their understanding of sexual difference and its social significance, therefore, provides a counterweight to the dominant ideology of their day. For these socialists, sexual difference pointed the way to a new society which avoided the repressive features of the emergent world of separate spheres. Their attempts to transform sexual difference into a concept of liberation for women and for society, and the theoretical and practical difficulties this posed, are considered in the following chapters.

2
Charles Fourier and the Nature of Women[1]

Charles Fourier was the founder of a feminist tradition within French socialism. His condemnation of the injustices of contemporary society incorporated a critique of the subjection of women, and in the ideal world of Harmony which he envisaged the 'liberty' of women would be guaranteed. Women would live, love and work with the same independence as men. These ideas had a major impact on Fourier's contemporaries and successors, although few accepted his proposals unequivocally. Prominent figures within the socialist tradition such as Flora Tristan, Karl Marx and Rosa Luxemburg reiterated or paraphrased his famous saying:

> . . . as a general proposition: *Social progress and changes of [social] Period occur by virtue of the progress of women toward liberty, and the decline in the social Order occurs by virtue of the decrease in women's liberty. . . .*
>
> In short, *the extension of the privileges of women is the general principle of all social progress.*[2]

Numerous studies of Fourier and of early French socialism have also reproduced this maxim to illustrate Fourier's feminist radicalism. He has even been credited with inventing the term 'feminism' itself.[3]

Fourier's concern about the position of women and his arguments for their 'liberty' reflected his vision of a universe structured by dualisms and oppositions, which needed to be kept in balance. The suppression of one of a pair of contrasted elements distorted the system entirely, and needed to be redressed for the correct functioning of the cosmos. The contrast between 'the feminine' and 'the masculine' was one of the most important dualisms, according to Fourier. It had important implications for women, since it established a sometimes limited view of their nature and potential roles in Harmony, making his legacy for feminism a mixed one. In addition, however, sexual difference represented a range of other fundamental polarities. Fourier's writings on 'the feminine' were not always propositions about real women, but his ideas about women shaped his views on the operation of 'the feminine' at the social and cosmic levels. Perfected gender relations – revitalised, reordered and loving – were necessary for social harmony, but they also stood as metaphor for Harmony itself. Concepts of sexual difference provided a language through which Fourier's vision of social and cosmic equilibrium, based on the harmony of opposites, could be expressed.

Fourier's commitment to the 'liberty' of women would probably have seemed as extraordinary to the citizens of Besançon, where he was raised, as his renowned fantasies about humans evolving tails, and the seas turning into lemonade.[4] The capital of the Franche-Comté, in the far east of France, was not noted as a centre of advanced thought, let alone as a home of feminism. The influence of the Catholic Church remained strong there, and Fourier regarded his home town as the archetype of the small-minded provincial centre.[5] Nor did Fourier's own background point to his emergence as a radical theorist and inspired visionary. He was born into commerce, not the intelligentsia; destined for life as a cloth merchant, not another Newton (as he liked to imagine himself). Indeed, as the only son and heir to a wealthy textile family his future seemed predictable and rather pedestrian. However, the young Charles showed few of the aptitudes or interests of the aspiring bourgeois. As a child he collected atlases, grew a wide assortment of flowers in his bedroom, and loved music, drawing, geography and arithmetic.[6] These interests continued into adulthood, and were reflected in the ideal world of Harmony which he later developed.

Despite Fourier's lack of interest in commerce, family pressure prevailed, and in 1789 he was apprenticed to a Lyon cloth-merchant. Not surprisingly, the Revolutionary period made a strong impression on this young man. He lost the bulk of his inheritance during the siege of Lyon in 1793, when the goods he had purchased to establish his own import business were confiscated. He was imprisoned and narrowly escaped execution for taking part, apparently under duress, in the defence of that rebellious city. Conscripted into the Revolutionary army in 1794, Fourier was discharged for ill-health eighteen months later.[7] These years left him with an abiding impression of social disorder, but a deep distrust of violent solutions. Although he had perhaps come to terms with the prospect of a business career in 1793, his misadventures disillusioned him. Fourier's disgust with commerce was reinforced as he witnessed the 'anarchy' of free competition, boldly displayed in the profiteering, speculation and inflation of the Revolutionary period.[8]

During the 1790s, Fourier's journeys within France as a travelling salesman enabled him to observe French lifestyles and economic operations at first hand. This further persuaded him of the need for social reorganisation. In particular, Fourier became convinced that the poverty which plagued his society was due largely to the inefficiencies of the household system of production. Many of his ideas about the ideal social roles of women reflected his determination to transform this economic system. However, in his view, the 'anarchy' of the free-market system, and the dehumanisation of factory production, were not the means to improvement. Besides, changes to the economic system were only one part – albeit a very important part – of the total reorganisation of society which Fourier sought.

By 1799 Fourier believed he had found the key to this reorganisation in the 'law of passionate attraction': supposedly the social counterpart to Newton's law of gravitational attraction.[9] This 'law' established that the satisfaction of the innate human passions would produce social harmony, which was the Divine plan. However the repression and curtailment of these drives resulted in social disorder, because they found an outlet in harmful actions.[10] Individual freedom was the motive force within the system of 'passionate attraction', since Fourier argued that a natural equilibrium would result if all individuals were free to develop their talents and potential to the full. As prime targets of social repression in contemporary society, women would benefit significantly under the new Harmonic order, and Fourier made specific provision for ensuring their liberty.

Fourier identified twelve basic passions, different combinations of these producing 810 personality types.[11] The ideal community would compromise 1500 to 1600 individuals who exhibited as full a range of passional combinations as possible. They would form a communal group, the phalanx, and reside in a communal establishment known as a phalanstery. Each phalanstery would be a largely self-supporting and primarily agricultural community, though craft production and the arts would also be important. Phalansterians would spend their time in a number of freely-chosen occupations, performing only duties that they liked, and never spending more than two hours at a single task to prevent boredom. Enthusiasm for work would also be maintained by a mixture of competition and co-operation, and by the high rewards for labour, capital and talent which would be possible in this system of plenty. The sexual drive, along with the other human passions, would play a role in making work attractive. Sexual incentives and rewards were envisaged for both sexes, but Fourier emphasised the sexual roles of women in his system.

Many of Fourier's ideas were controversial but his theories on women were amongst the most hotly debated, both during his own lifetime and after his death. His writings are exceedingly complex. They interweave parody and incisive social criticism with fantastic portraits of an ideal and imaginary world. Fourier's extensive use of neologism, his abandonment of many of the conventions of writing, and his fondness for bizarre tables and charts, make the reader's task a complex but intriguing one. So, too, does his refusal to privilege any particular discourse over the others, so that the discussion of the sex life of planets, or the analogic qualities of melons, for instance, is neither more nor less significant to his overall theory than his critique of contemporary commerce.[12] This diversity and complexity has provoked enormous debate about the 'meaning' of Fourier's works which has raged since his own lifetime. Some have sought to see in him a social scientist whose writings outline workable economic and social reforms. Others have emphasised the imaginative elements in his writings and his ideas on sexuality, pronouncing him the father of surrealism, or the precursor of Freud rather than of Marx.[13] His writings continue to speak in a number of different voices and to make possible a number of different readings.

To some extent, however, Fourier presented his ideas publicly in an increasingly circumspect form as he struggled to gain acceptance for his doctrine. He first outlined his proposals in 1808, in a work entitled *Theory of Four Movements and of the General Destinies: Prospectus and Announcement of the Discovery*. Women occupied a central place in this book since their experiences denoted the progressive or regressive character of each era. Furthermore, amorous customs were defined as the 'mechanical pivot', the essential starting point for social change. Fourier thus emphasised the need to transform sexual relations and restore to women their original sexual liberty, and he speculated on the types of amorous relations which would prevail in the future.[14] New economic roles for women were portrayed as effects rather than causes of social change. The book was so heavily criticised that Fourier abandoned his studies for several years. He finally completed his 'great treatise' in 1819 but it was never published in full. In particular, the sexual aspects of his theory remained largely unknown until 1967 because Fourier became increasingly aware of the need for self-censorship, and began to be more discreet about the amorous innovations he envisaged:

> The details of this amorous code would fill several long chapters but the hypocrisy of our morals has forbidden me to publish them. That is why everything that deals with the accords of love has had to remain very incomplete. It's not that the theory is faulty but morality makes the going difficult.[15]

The devotees that he attracted in the 1820s and 1830s also encouraged the suppression of any controversial material.[16]

However, Fourier never abandoned his commitment to sexual liberation for all, or his belief in the importance of women's amorous roles in Harmony. These were discussed at length in his private notebooks, and continued to be referred to in his publications. Instead, he sought a rationale for social change which had more hope of persuading his contemporaries. Increasingly, therefore, he emphasised reforms affecting domestic economy, industry and agriculture. Modifications to marriage and to women's amorous roles were portrayed as the result of economic and social progress, rather than as causes of and prerequisites for all other change. This admission gave a new emphasis and rationale to Fourier's published writings on women. In his later works the primary focus shifted from speculation about a new role for women in an ideal, imaginary world, a role focusing on their propensity for love, to a description of the practical benefits resulting from a new role for women in the real world, a role conceived principally in economic terms. In line with this more pragmatic approach there were several unsuccessful attempts by Fourier's followers to establish a trial phalanstery, though Fourier condemned them for failing to conform to his blueprint. He spent considerable energy trying to convert the powerful to his ideas, but the rich benefactor whom he hoped would finance his experiments had still not appeared when Fourier died in 1837.

CHARLES FOURIER'S CONCEPT OF THE NATURAL WOMAN

Fourier's writings emphasised the difference between femininity and masculinity, which he regarded as opposite and counteracting forces. As the embodiment of 'the feminine' women were charged with asserting its potential and bringing its influence to bear on society, but their oppression by men prevented this from happening. By recognising and allowing free development to women's talents, therefore, his system would restore the 'natural' balance between the masculine and the feminine. This would ensure women's happiness and make possible social harmony, a harmony which relied not on sexual equality but on sexual equilibrium.

Fourier enumerated the 'vices' of women, and examined their personal failings in considerable detail. This served, first of all, to justify their liberation, for women were deformed by the process of constraint and coercion imposed on them from infancy. This process was designed to keep women in a state of ignorance and to stifle their natural talents, in order to ensure that they accepted their subordination.[17] It was therefore an essential feature of 'civilisation':

> . . . each social period must shape its young to revere the dominant stupidities . . . thus the civilised Order must stupefy women from childhood in order to make them conform to the philosophical dogmas, to the slavery of marriage, and to the humiliation of succumbing to the power of a husband. . . .[18]

Men's deference toward women who fitted the desired model ensured the survival of the system, because conformity was the only avenue to social acceptance for women. If civilisation required stupefied and oppressed women, however, creating a new society would require the re-fashioning of women. Fourier proposed to do this, although he insisted that he was not re-shaping women to meet his own criteria but rediscovering and liberating the 'natural' woman. Yet his confident type-casting of women rested uneasily beside his assertion that their nature had been deformed by upbringing. If the superficial aspects of femininity could not be trusted to reveal its essence, on what did Fourier base his definition of the 'nature' of woman?

According to Fourier, the 'civilised' order suppressed the natural potential of women in two main areas. Firstly, it inhibited their access to sexual fulfilment. The institution of monogamy, requiring premarital chastity and fidelity within marriage, thwarted women's capacity for love. The double standard of morality was designed to ensure women's conformity to the monogamous system, while condoning men's deviation from it. Since women were forced to resort to deceit in order to find sexual and emotional fulfilment, their dominant characteristics became hypocrisy and pretence. Furthermore, the frustration of women's physical needs hampered the development of their interest in 'sentimental' love. The 'civilised' woman was therefore completely devoted to sensual and physical forms of fulfilment.[19]

Women's capacity to wield power and authority was also denied in the 'civilised' order. Only by the exercise of their 'charms' could women excel or take control. Women's manipulation of men, in Fourier's view, resulted from impeded ambition as well as impeded sexuality. Their capacity for intrigue and their competitive spirit – both virtues for Fourier – were diverted into control by stealth, rather than finding their intended outlet in the search for individual power and excellence. Women's widely condemned tendency to fritter away their time at dances and the theatre was a sign of frustration to Fourier, showing their need to compensate for empty and unfulfilled lives.[20]

This picture of the 'civilised' woman was drawn from the lifestyle of the privileged classes. It echoed contemporary criticisms of manipulative and sexually-dominating women, interfering in politics with disastrous results.[21] No doubt Fourier had read such accounts, although he never mixed in those elevated social echelons. The pundits' attacks defined politics as an illegitimate and unacceptable field for women. Women's reputed sexual excesses provided an explanation and an analogy for their political unreliability, so the sexual confinement and political exclusion of women were both justified. However, Fourier's discussion subverted such accounts. For him, the harmful effects of women's subterfuge justified empowering them both sexually and politically, offering them legitimate outlets for those capacities. His criticism of women became a device for attacking 'civilisation' (a term of abuse for his own society) and proposing an alternative form of social organisation. It provided a critique of the forces and systems which produced such women, including the philosophers who formulated society's beliefs and practices:

> And when [philosophy] harps on the vices of women, it criticises itself; it produces those vices itself by a social system which, suppressing their faculties from childhood and throughout their lives, forces them to resort to deception in order to surrender to nature.[22]

Like woman, 'civilisation' was deformed and unnatural. It was subject to arbitrary laws and controls which hindered its development, and exhibited all the ill-effects of constraint. The empty-headed, frivolous woman, interested only in appearances and ignorant of her true role, resembled only dimly the 'natural' woman he envisaged in the future, when the true potential of the feminine sex would come to fruition. Similarly, 'civilisation' bore little resemblance to the wonders of Harmony. Fourier's presentation of a certain image of 'woman' thus served a broader purpose in justifying his undertaking. Furthermore, the inescapable imperative of 'nature' became a force to be understood if society's ills were to be comprehended and overcome. Fourier presented himself as the person capable of understanding nature, and hence of understanding 'woman'.

Fourier's concept of the 'natural' woman relied upon a distinction between 'feminine' and 'masculine' natures. This distinction was not simply an anatomical one. Rather, 'masculinity' and 'femininity' described combinations of physical, emotional and intellectual traits which might be possessed by either males or females. Since Fourier believed that gender was not automatically determined by sex, he favoured identical treatment of male and female infants in Harmony, in order to determine whether they possessed 'feminine' or 'masculine' personalities:

> Amongst the *lutins* [children aged 2 and 3] the two sexes are not distinguished by different clothing, such as skirts and trousers; that would jeopardise the unfolding of potential and risk falsifying the proportion of the sexes in each function . . . [T]he girls would be separated from the boys; and they should be left together at this age, so that the *extra-sexual* inclinations, male

inclinations in a little girl, feminine leanings in a little boy, can emerge unrestricted, due to the combined presence of the two sexes in each workshop, at each task.[23]

Fourier clearly recognised the process of sex-role socialisation to which children were currently subjected, but he also suggested that differences between the sexes were innate: the ideal system would simply allow those differences to 'emerge'. Rather than regarding personality traits as gender-free, he defined each as masculine or feminine, apparently on the basis of observation and experience. This inhibited a re-thinking of the processes by which gender categories were assigned. Traits which were most commonly found in 'civilised' females were defined as 'feminine', and therefore indicated 'feminine' personalities. Consequently, according to Fourier's calculations, most females were likely to possess 'feminine' personalities in Harmony, as they did in 'civilisation'.

Fourier believed that 'masculine' and 'feminine' personalities were well established by the age of nine, when the children of Harmony would take their places within the 'Little Bands' or the 'Little Hordes'. These groups therefore demonstrate a number of characteristics which Fourier defined as feminine and masculine, and hence as typifying females and males. The Little Bands comprised those children with an appreciation for finery, good manners and things of beauty. They would take care of the flower beds and the ornamentation of their surroundings, as well as censoring bad language and promoting refinement. They would also be devotees of literature and the arts. The Little Hordes, on the other hand, would attract those children given to more active pursuits, and to dirty and unrefined occupations. Such children gloried in less pleasant but necessary tasks such as cleaning up rubbish and removing insect pests.[24] Drawing once again on his observation of 'civilised' norms, Fourier argued that 'if the majority of male children enjoy uproar and dirt, we see the majority of little girls favour finery and good manners'. He therefore anticipated that boys would outnumber girls by 2:1 in the Little Hordes, with a reverse ratio in the Little Bands which would thus be 'feminine in the majority'. The only male children to join that group would be the 'young intellectuals' with a taste for study, and the 'young effeminates who, from the age of nine, are disposed to indolence, to the life of the Sybarite'.[25] Although Fourier proposed to remove the processes of sex-differentiated socialisation in early childhood, then, he still anticipated that the majority of little girls would exhibit 'feminine' personalities, since he believed that 'feminine' traits were innate in most females. Fourier thus proved unable to carry his insight into the social construction of gender difference to its logical conclusion. However, his identification of a 'feminine' personality (inclined to sedentariness and indulgence of the senses) in contrast with a 'masculine' personality(characterised by activity, vigour and a lack of sensuality) established sets of contrasting and opposite human traits. Fourier regarded the antithesis between them as a creative tension which could be made beneficial for society.

Fourier's concept of 'the feminine' had a physiological base. He contrasted the 'weak' sex with the stronger masculine sex,[26] and based a number of other differences between the sexes on this foundation. The criteria by which 'strength' and 'weakness' were defined were never laid down explicitly, but in identifying the 'strong' Fourier apparently had in mind those with the capacity to perform hard physical labour, the kind of labour which he believed should be the province of men. Women also performed extremely hard work in Fourier's society, as they do today, but this suggested to Fourier that the 'civilised' division of labour was absurd, rather than that his theory was flawed:

> . . . in industry . . . man has invaded even the occupations of sewing and the pen which require attention to detail, while we see women exhaust themselves in laborious rural work. Isn't it scandalous to see strong fellows thirty years old hunched in front of a desk, and hairy-armed chaps serving coffee, as if there weren't enough women and children to attend to the details of the office and the household?[27]

Fourier's understanding of 'strength' also obscured the fact that female physiology displays considerable capacity for strength and endurance in ways which differ from the male pattern. Childbirth provides an obvious example. But Fourier was oblivious to such considerations. Although he regarded pre-pubescent children as a third 'neuter' sex, Fourier likened women to children rather than to men because of their shared physical 'weakness'. This 'weakness' had facilitated the subordination of both groups in a social system based on physical force, he believed, and thus explained their rebellious inclinations.[28] The similar (but not identical) culinary tastes of women and children, who preferred lighter and sweeter dishes than men, also suggested different constitutional 'strengths', although this was not spelled out by Fourier.[29] However, the differences he envisaged between 'men's work' and 'women's and children's work' explicitly reflected his view of their different physical capacities. The 'femininity' of the Little Bands was underlined by their work roles, which would comprise 'all functions of mind and body which do not require physical strength'.[30]

This formula suggested a link, in Fourier's theory, between physical capacity and intellectual ability: a curious argument for someone who admitted his own unimposing physical stature.[31] However, Fourier did not explain which functions of mind do require physical strength. Nor was he consistent in his argument, for he also stated that intellectual and physical capacity were unrelated and thus defended the intellectual potential of women.[32] Nevertheless, Fourier did not define male and female intelligence as identical. 'Civilised' women, deprived of the opportunity for scientific study, understood instinctively rather than rationally, hence their ability to understand Fourier's theories.[33] Fourier's insistence on sexual differentiation and rivalry also led him to anticipate differences in the intellectual capacities of men and women in Harmony, where female intellectual potential would be recognised and developed. Girls would have a head start in intellectual development, even in the scientific field, since feminine personalities (and thus the majority of girls) were naturally studious:

> From the age of 9 we will see attraction make a mockery of our prejudices against the instruction of women, and it is certain that in the assemblies of the final [childhood] stage, 8½ to 15 years, the girls, already having a liking for scientific studies, will shine more than the boys, who will be rather distracted from [studies] by the arduous duties of the little hordes in which the masculine sex predominates.[34]

Once boys began to take study seriously, however, they would outstrip girls, despite the natural studiousness of the feminine sex. It was surely no accident that this change in dominance took place at the age of puberty. In Fourier's view puberty was a crisis and its impact was particularly serious for girls, since love began to exert an overwhelming and unrestrained influence on their lives. 'Civilised' educators had found no way to establish 'counterweights to the influence of love, which comes along at 15 or 16 years to distract and preoccupy young heads, especially the women, making them neglect the little that they have learnt of the arts and sciences . . .'.[35] However, since Fourier predicted that girls' intellectual role would diminish after menarche, he apparently accepted the impossibility of 'inoculat[ing] women's reason' against the impact of the biological crisis.[36] Growing up, for boys, was associated by Fourier with their entry into intellectual life, and their diversion from the largely physical preoccupations of the Little Hordes. For girls it was conceived as an abandonment of the life of the intellect for a life dominated by the body and the emotions.

At adulthood, therefore, the typical Harmonian man and woman illustrated the contrast between reason and feeling which determined their anticipated social functions. The contrast between the 'masculine' sciences and the 'feminine' arts highlighted this division:

> . . . nature distributes the aptitude for the sciences and the arts to the 2 sexes in equal proportions, except in the allocation of areas; the taste for the sciences being more particularly given to men and that of the arts more especially to women, in approximate proportions of men, 2/3 to the sciences, 1/3 to the arts; women, 2/3 to the arts, 1/3 to the sciences. . . .[37]

This assumption reflected Fourier's desire to emphasise the differences and subsequent rivalry between the sexes:

> Wouldn't the law of contrasts, one of the principal ones in the system of nature, be excluded from education if women did not have a superior aspect? They will be sure of achieving fame in the culture of the arts which will be recognised as more suited to their faculties when an appropriate education has developed them from childhood.
> Nature generally gives young girls the taste for finery, so stupidly spent amongst us on playing with dolls, in order to dispose and attract them to the culture of the arts.[38]

However, the allocation of women to predominance in the arts has added significance when Fourier's understanding of the characteristics of these two fields is taken into consideration. He regarded science as the key to all knowledge, the realm in which things could be known with certainty, and believed that his own theories were thoroughly scientific. The arts, on the other hand, were the non-rational domain of human endeavour, according to Fourier. They had a prized and respected role in Harmony as a major source of pleasure for the senses, and as providers of community enjoyment. By consigning women to dominance of the arts he was not confining them to a despised or insignificant sphere. Nevertheless, in arguing that most men were destined for the sciences and most women for the arts, Fourier accepted the view that men were the rational sex, the discoverers of knowledge, and women the emotional sex, who represented and re-created beauty. This type-casting again associated masculinity with intellectual power, and femininity with the emotions. Typically, men were envisaged creating new knowledge by rational means, while women reproduced instinctive insights in some artistic form.

Fourier's definition of women as weak and emotional underlined the physiological basis of his concept of female nature. This was further reinforced by his views on female sexuality. Women were not simply 'the weak sex' for Fourier, they were 'the sex', the group defined by their sexuality. By assigning sexuality as a female characteristic this label implied that men were not hostage to their biology in the same way as women. Their sex was a peripheral characteristic, one which they utilised as they chose, while for women sexuality was a state of being.

Like a number of other contemporary theorists, Fourier argued that women's physiological need for sexual fulfilment was extremely powerful, and that without it they became ill and even died:

[The law] condemns a woman who, driven by an urgent need . . . admits a man to her bed for carnal or animal love. So we often see women whose parents let them suffer and die sooner than grant them satisfaction in this matter, and indeed, a young girl who is languishing, suffering for want of that pleasure which nature commands for her, certainly warrants an exception. It would be so easy to make an arrangement with a responsible young fellow who would promise discretion and the customary measures to prevent pregnancy which public opinion condemns.[39]

Fourier criticised both prolonged virginity and obligatory monogamy, which he believed turned young women into 'denatured beings continually consumed by desire', their instincts masked but not altered.[40] He believed that few women were suited to a monogamous pattern of sexual relations, since perpetual fidelity was contrary to the nature of both sexes, and he cited as evidence women's reputed willingness to engage in orgies or change partners when the opportunity arose.[41] Fourier's writings on female sexuality thus emphasised the vast gulf between professed sexual mores and patterns of sexual conduct in his society. For him, this disparity highlighted the absurdities of the 'civilised' system rather than the need to repress women's sexuality. However, a mechanism to contain women's rampant sexual instincts was needed, since they were less capable than men of controlling their sexual drive and subordinating it to the demands of honour, friendship and family loyalty:

> The sweetest, the most virtuous woman becomes a tigress as soon as, in her own interests, someone crosses her in some matter of love. The very appearance of opposition, even the best intentioned opposition, makes her hate all those for whom she had some affection. The most ancient sentiment of honour, friendship, family feeling, cannot restore the balance. In women, love is a torrent which sweeps all before it. . . .[42]

The personal consequences of sexual deprivation for women were overshadowed by its social consequences. The 'torrent' of female sexuality could not be denied. If provision was not made for it to run its course, it would burst through all obstacles as a river bursts through a dam wall, destroying all in its path.

Fourier's views on the irrepressible power of female sexuality owed something to the received wisdom of his day, but they were also based on his own experiences with women. As his biographer has argued, Fourier was not always the recluse that he became in old age. He had many lasting friendships with women, exchanged romantic verses with those who took his fancy, and apparently had a number of affairs.[43] His belief in the demanding sexual appetites of women was expressed in his earliest published writings, but it was considerably strengthened during his residence at Talissieu, where he lived in the household of his nieces and nephews from December 1815 until early 1817. Two of his nieces had a reputation for their sexual exploits, and this was confirmed by Fourier's observations. He was amazed by the extent of their amorous adventures, and even attempted to draw on their sexual experience in constructing his sexual theories. He claimed to find their sexual behaviour less offensive than their lies and feigned innocence, but the young women's blatant sexual indulgence was finally too much for Fourier. Adopting a 'civilised' demeanour he demanded at least more prudence for the family's sake. The confrontation over this issue finally led to his departure from Talissieu,[44] and it heightened his commitment to finding the 'counterweights' to sexual liberty, which were particularly necessary for women. The significance of the Talissieu experience is also suggested by his subsequent emphasis on regulating the sexual practices of the young. The problem of dealing with the sexuality of young women was discussed on several occasions,[45] and the need for decorum and restraint in their sexual relationships became a recurrent theme. The 'typical' young person of Harmony would be quite unlike the 'profligates who swear like troopers' that he had observed at Talissieu.[46]

A further example of Fourier's belief that female sexuality was irrepressible was provided by his emphasis on female adultery. Although he deplored the prevalence of male debauchery in his society, and reminded men that they could not expect fidelity if they were not prepared to be faithful themselves, he dwelt at length on female infidelity, on the need of husbands and fathers to supervise women, and on the ineffectiveness of that supervision. Fourier regarded female adultery as more serious than male adultery, defining the foisting of illegitimate children upon an unsuspecting husband as the greatest crime of marriage.[47] Furthermore, female adultery required a greater degree of hypocrisy, he argued, because the wife showed increased eagerness for her husband's affections 'so as to hide the affair from him and place herself beyond suspicion in case of pregnancy':

> This consideration alone forces the lady to seek the favours of
> the husband at the very time that she wishes to give herself to
> the lover. She fears that he will make a blunder so, prudently,

she does not surrender to the lover until she has received as security the favours of the husband. . . .[48]

The adulteress/cuckold was thus the pattern of marital infidelity that Fourier usually described. The 'Table of Cuckoldry' appeared several times in his writings, described with up to eighty variations, while an outline of the three ways in which women could be the victims of infidelity was described only once.[49] The 'Table of Cuckoldry' was a scornful attack upon male stupidity, but it also demonstrated Fourier's conviction that women's need for sexual fulfilment and variety could not be denied. From the age of puberty women would seek to satisfy this need, moral precepts and vigilant fathers notwithstanding.

Fourier's writings on female nature highlighted its distinctive features in contrast with male nature. Woman's physical weakness, emotional strength and dominant sexuality indicated the roles which she should play in society, and distinguished her roles from those of men. Gender difference was a fundamental structuring mechanism within society, in Fourier's view, and would remain so as society progressed. The distinction between weakness and strength, between emotion and reason, expressed the interplay between opposing tendencies within human nature which needed to be balanced and harmonised for individual happiness and social order. The characterisation of 'the feminine' relied heavily on Fourier's perception of female biology, and tied woman more firmly than man to physical imperatives. In this sense woman was identified as Body to man's Spirit. However, the contrast between the 'feminine' and the 'masculine' was also a contrast between quiet gentility and vibrant energy; between refinement and vulgarity; between culture and crudity. The masculine would be civilised, or rather 'Harmonised', by the influence of the feminine. Simultaneously, therefore, woman represented Culture to man's Nature. Strength of emotion both drew her towards the fullest expression of her natural impulses, and enabled her to elevate the natural to higher planes. The task that Fourier set himself was to ensure that women were enabled to fulfil the tasks they had been assigned by Nature.

SEXUAL DIFFERENCE AS A SOCIAL AND COSMIC FORCE

Fourier believed that the laws of passional attraction governed the entire cosmos. Humanity was not the superior and isolated pinnacle of creation, according to this theory, but one link (a very significant one, of course) in the chain of created existence. The human passions affected the entire cosmos and were reflected in it. It was therefore possible to 'read' the universe, to see the passions exhibited there, and to learn of the properties of those passions from their cosmic manifestations.[50] Conversely, a human being was a 'mirror of the universe', and the qualities of the macrocosm could be observed by studying the microcosm. Aspects of the life of a human person (such as the 'phases' of childhood, youth, maturity and old age, and the 'transitions' of birth, puberty, menopause and death) indicated corresponding features in human social existence and in the life-span of the universe.[51]

The idea that a network of immutable laws governed the cosmos had significant implications for Fourier's theory of human relations. Since the macrocosm and the microcosm obeyed the same laws and followed the same pattern, Fourier supposed that gender and sexual function were features of every order of being. Masculinity and femininity were not simply human attributes, but cosmic forces with a calculable range of qualities and effects. Each balanced the other, thus maintaining a state of social and cosmic equilibrium. The sexes were polar opposites even in the literal sense, since the North Pole was masculine and the South Pole feminine.[52] This cosmological theory provided the basis for Fourier's distinction between the male and female spheres of life. In Harmony the affairs of men and women would be conducted separately, and the counteraction between them was the essence of social stability.

Fourier regarded his cosmological theory as a scientific one, but his attempt to employ the scientific method had consequences which he apparently did not foresee. The patterns and relationships which he detected in the cosmos reflected his perceptions of human life. By searching the cosmos for evidence about human relationships, therefore, he produced a theory which confirmed his original presuppositions. The manner in which he classified the human passions, and established the laws of their relationship to each other by observing the cosmos, exemplifies his method and his assumptions.

The four affective passions which Fourier identified were ambition and friendship, the 'major' passions, and love and devotion to family, the 'minor' passions. Simone Debout has pointed out that the terms 'major' and 'minor' were derived from music:

> Friendship, ambition, the major octave, indicate sharpness, vigour and relative simplicity, love and family attachment, analogous to the minor keys have a more soulful resonance, something both gentler and more intense. They reach the inmost feelings of each person and maintain their mystery. The terms major and minor therefore do not indicate a hierarchy.[53]

Fourier frequently used these terms in a musical context in the *New Amorous World*. In his discussion of analogy, for example, Fourier stated his intention of using musical terminology and proceeded to distinguish between the major scales and the minor scales, with their 'vibrations', 'transitions' and modulations.[54] However, we need to examine the rationale by which Fourier linked the 'major' and 'minor' keys with masculinity and femininity respectively; the relationships he established between these two branches of the passions; and the assumptions about men and women that these links implied.

Fourier was unequivocal in associating the minor key with women and the major key with men. He referred to them quite explicitly as *le sexe mineur* and *le sexe majeur*.[55] By this he meant that women were particularly associated with the passions and activities comprising the 'minor' key, and men with those comprising the 'major' key:

> The major mode includes the relations exclusive to the masculine sex, the minor mode those exclusive to the feminine sex. . . .[56]

> Thus we see the minor or feminine sex more passionate in Love and in maternal tenderness, while the major or masculine sex is stronger in the two branches of Honour and Friendship. . . .[57]

The distinction between major and minor was most frequently used to differentiate between friendship and ambition, on the one hand, and love and family attachment on the other, but Fourier also employed it in other contexts: to distinguish between science and the arts, wisdom and virtue, and gastronomy and love. In each case his perception of masculine and feminine capacities and inclinations was reasserted through this distinction.

This becomes clear in Fourier's discussion of the system of social honours which he envisaged for Harmony. 'Sanctity' and 'heroism' would be achieved in both the major and minor orders. In the major sphere, the award of 'sanctity' would be made to those outstanding in gastronomy, and that of 'heroism' to those outstanding in the sciences. The corresponding awards in the minor order were reserved for those demonstrating prowess in love, and excellence in the arts. Gastronomic excellence was described as 'wisdom', and amorous excellence as 'virtue'.[58] Hence the major/masculine sphere was the realm of wisdom, gastronomy and science; the minor/feminine sphere was the realm of virtue, love and artistic achievement.

Having established the composition of the major and minor spheres, Fourier examined their relationship to each other, and defended the need for 'masculine' predominance over the 'feminine' element. The major passions should enjoy a 'slight edge' over the minor passions, he argued. They should 'take precedence, to *set the lead for the other 2 . . .*':

> . . . Love and family attachment, so harmful today, so estranged from the laws of Honour and Friendship, will have to comply with these constantly in Harmony so as to leave to the two majors the superiority of 1/21 in the general balance . . . to assure to Honour and Friendship that precedence in rank, that authority over relationships which all well-bred souls would wish to bestow on them.[59]

Fourier's defence of the superiority of the major/masculine passions thus relied partly upon an appeal to 'civilised' norms and good breeding. More importantly, however, the typology reasserted Fourier's fear of the 'feminine' passions with their potential disruptiveness. Although Honour and Friendship were never clearly defined, Fourier implied that these 'masculine' passions provided a basis for broader social loyalties than their 'feminine' counterparts. The contrast between the feminine and the masculine was a contrast between disorder and order, between private and public loyalties; hence the superiority of the masculine.

The superiority awarded to the 'major' passions also rested on Fourier's claim that they were more 'spiritual' than the minor ones:

> The differences between major and minor stem from the influence of the two principles, material and spiritual, called BODY AND SOUL. The groups of family attachment and love belong to the minor order, because the material principle is dominant there, especially in that of family attachment which is firmly governed by the material element, since one cannot break the ties of blood . . . The group of love, although strongly governed by the material principle is not its slave: the spiritual principle is sometimes dominant in the bond of love . . . Thus this group is the nobler of the two minors.
>
> The group of friendship is almost entirely devoid of the material [element]; . . . so it belongs to the major order . . . The group of ambition or the corporative bond is dominated by fame and self-interest. It is influenced by riches or industrial matter, which is more noble than corporal [matter]; on these grounds . . . it belongs to the major order, where the spiritual principle is dominant.[60]

The major passions were more 'spiritual' because they were more closely associated with God, 'the active and moving principle'. The 'minor' passions, by contrast, were associated with 'Matter, the passive or moved principle'.[61] Fourier's cosmological theory thus associated the 'feminine' with passivity and the 'masculine' with activity. It linked the 'feminine' with matter, nature and bodily function, and the 'masculine' with mind, the soul and spiritual function.

Fourier believed there was abundant evidence that the predominance he gave to the major passions was correct. Evidence could be drawn from analogies in various orders of creation. In music, first of all, Fourier claimed that there were more major chords than minor ones, and that the ascending octave was stronger and louder than the descending one. The major passions would therefore be predominant during ascending Harmony (the period leading up to Harmony), and the minor passions during descending Harmony (the period of decline, from Harmony to extinction). The natural world also indicated the most suitable relationship between the major and minor orders in several ways. It produced twenty-one males to twenty females, by Fourier's calculations, showing that the balance should favour the masculine side in ascending Harmony. This 'natural' sexual imbalance would be reflected in the composition of each phalanx, for the 810 personality types would be represented by 395 women and 415 men, not 405 bisexual couples. Fourier explained this by pointing out that Harmony was characterised by counterbalances, not equality, and that some passions of the 'major' order developed between two men rather than between a man and a woman. Apparently none developed only between women.[62]

The cosmos provided further evidence justifying the predominance of the 'major' passions within the human realm, according to Fourier. Defining the ringed planets as the major/masculine ones, he argued that males of most species, 'from the insects to the stars', were equipped with *ornements* which indicated their superiority. Despite the fact that the priority of the major/ masculine elements was attributed to their 'spiritual' qualities, then, Fourier nevertheless employed a phallic analogy: male physical attributes reinforced that 'spiritual' superiority. Fourier also continued this line of reasoning in deciding that the north pole of a planet was the masculine/major one; that consequently the north poles of planets produced male generative fluid and the south poles female fluid; and that the *couronne fécondante* would form initially at the north pole of the earth. Besides, the magnetic needle pointed north, demonstrating that the 'northern or major aspect should be our starting point'.[63]

Fourier's pattern of thinking was rarely straightforward and never simple, and his definition of the major and minor orders was not merely a male/female distinction. Love had both physical and spiritual forms; both men and women in Harmony would develop all four of the affective passions, and because of the 'law of exceptions', some women would excel in the major sphere as some men would excel in the minor sphere. For this reason each title which could be gained had both masculine and feminine forms.[64] It was even possible for an individual to excel in each sphere consecutively:

> One can accumulate these four honours. The first two: minor heroism and minor sanctity being the attributes of youth and the other major two demanding knowledge which one only attains

with maturity. One can thus compete alternately for these four awards.[65]

But Fourier's hierarchy of the passions did assume that the 'major' passions represented the 'spiritual' aspects of life. They were linked with knowledge gained by experience, more commonly possessed by men who were connoisseurs of good food as well as of scientific knowledge. They were also the passions of maturity. The minor passions, by contrast, were the youthful, immature passions and were linked in Fourier's theory with the physical aspects of life. They were attributes, present innately rather than acquired by personal effort. They were more commonly found in women, whose expertise lay in the arts and in the 'virtue' of love: 'the domain of unreason'.[66]

Despite the complex origins and varied applications of these concepts, then, there was a 'natural' hierarchy between the major and minor orders which reflected a number of conventional perceptions of the two sexes. The major/masculine realm was an intellectual one; the minor/feminine realm an emotional one. The 'masculine' characteristics of ambition and friendship were to predominate over the 'feminine' attributes of love and devotion to family within the individual and the community, as the masculine dominated the feminine in the cosmic order. The reversal of this relationship during declining Harmony, when more females than males would also be produced, would herald the deterioration and ultimate collapse of the social order: a utopian variation, perhaps, on the theme of 'the world turned upside down'. This formula had significant implications for the pattern of social relations in Fourier's ideal society, since he believed that the majority of women were feminine in personality. It provided a limited and inadequate basis for the social recognition of 'feminine' potential, and for transforming women's roles in society. The social dominance of males over females was condemned by Fourier, but it would be replaced by the dominance of the masculine over the feminine. The superiority of masculine rationality and the subordination of feminine emotion were reaffirmed.

3
Charles Fourier and the Roles of Women

Fourier envisaged a wide variety of roles for women in his ideal society, where they would be completely free and encouraged to develop their natural talents. Life in the phalanstery would be organised communally and women's family role would disappear. They would participate in society as individuals, taking part in all occupations and sharing in all the financial and social rewards of the new system. Fourier's advocacy of public roles for women contrasted with the domestic ideal which was to gain prominence in the early nineteenth century. His model differed partly on economic grounds, since he emphasised the need for all citizens to play a productive role. However, he also insisted on the vital interaction between the forces of 'masculinity' and 'femininity', rather than their assignment to 'separate spheres'. The separation of love and work, of sentiment and reason, ran counter to Fourier's emphasis on the role of love and emotion in stimulating production. This concept necessitated the presence of women in the industrial order of Harmony.

Despite these innovations, Fourier predicted women's superiority in the 'new world of love', and men's superiority in the 'new industrial world'. This allocation of roles was intended to achieve a balance between the 'masculine' and the 'feminine' and place them in a relationship of creative opposition. His concept of 'feminine' and 'masculine' roles reflected his views on 'feminine' and 'masculine' natures, and his belief that the social roles of the sexes had a natural basis. Fourier's emphasis on the sexual roles of women highlighted the pivotal function of sexual relations in his restructured society. Since the entire universe was marked by sexual difference, the establishment of harmony in the sexual order represented and made possible a new social order characterised by satisfaction of the needs of all, and concern for the well-being of others. The liberty of women was crucial to both these objectives.

WOMEN'S DOMESTIC ROLE AND THE FAILINGS OF 'CIVILISATION'

According to Fourier, the organisation of women's labour in the private household exemplified the failings of the domestic economy, and of the 'civilised' order in general. It demonstrated society's inability to recognise and develop talents, and therefore to maximise productive potential. An absurdly inefficient system of production and distribution, based on coercing people into roles for which they were unsuited, resulted in widespread poverty, unhappiness and social disorder. By detailing the inadequacies of the current socio-economic system, Fourier hoped to persuade his readers to support the alternative which he proposed.

In 'civilisation' women were required to fill a servile but essential function: 'skimming the stew, washing the children, and mending the old trousers of the true republicans'.[1] The 'civilised' woman was destined to be a housewife and mother. In Fourier's view most women had neither the capacity nor the inclination for this role, but were forced into it by the demands of the household system:

> 1st the needs of small children; 2nd illnesses which in civilisation are at least ten times more common than they will be in Harmony, and the total care of which falls to women; 3rd the poor quality of fabrics which quadruples the amount of sewing necessary; 4th far too many pregnancies; finally so many other aspects of domestic complication, especially private kitchens.[2]

Women rebelled against their imposed role by fulfilling it poorly, while the natural talent for housewifery possessed by one woman in six was under-utilised. It was spent on the duties of a small household, rather than in running a larger establishment.[3] The 'civilised' system provided no means for advancement, even for the woman of outstanding domestic skills. Time and talent were clearly wasted in this system.

Fourier also condemned the promotion of motherhood as an ideal and obligatory role for women. He dismissed the influential theories of Rousseau on this issue:

> Zeal for the care of children is not a virtue, whatever a certain engraving of 1798 may say; it is an inclination, a liking which

nature distributes in a proportion which must be respected. We must believe that God has been able to calculate the necessary dose, and if we only find a quarter of women and men inclined towards this role it is an indication that it will only require that number in the order ordained by God. So we should neither condemn the failure of the three-quarters who have no inclination for this kind of duty, nor extol as virtuous those who, in performing it willingly, are only yielding to pleasure and attraction.[4]

According to this analysis, childcare was not an exclusively female occupation, and nor should it be obligatory for women. Fourier believed that the devotion to children which many women exhibited was due to two factors: social expectations and lack of alternatives. Maternal devotion was 'a diversion from boredom, from the emptiness which the domestic life leaves in their souls'. It was a 'last resort of idleness'.[5]

Fourier was particularly critical of women of the privileged classes, whom he believed were especially indulgent towards their children. He associated this problem with breastfeeding. Whereas Rousseau had extolled the virtues of maternal nursing, Fourier denounced its 'crimes':

> If there were courts and criminal laws on the faults committed during childraising, on the imprudent acts of which the child is victim, I estimate that nine-tenths of rich women who nurse their own children would have to be sentenced harshly. . . These mothers only make a point of giving [the child] a thousand harmful illusions, which are a slow poison for him and which kill the majority of rich children . . . So rich women are murderers of their children, creating a host of faults in them, while the peasant woman forced to take care of twenty jobs, and having only half an hour morning and evening to devote to breastfeeding, does not raise the child to satisfy his whims nor to develop more of them than nature gives him.[6]

This attack on rich mothers reflected Fourier's intolerance of idleness and its harmful effects: busy women who were usefully occupied had no time for indulging their children. It also countered the emergent ideal of domesticity which urged women to absorb themselves in their children. By contrasting the backwardness of children raised at home by wealthy mothers, with the achievements of those raised at public expense in a communal system, Fourier tried to project an appealing model for change.[7] His criticism of contemporary women's domestic and maternal incompetence was thus at least partly strategic, designed to encourage the adoption of the social system he proposed.

Fourier's critique of women's domestic roles was also quite selective. In particular, the portrait of the inadequate housewife did not acknowledge women's 'productive' role within families of the artisanal and labouring classes. The family economy incorporated a clearly-defined sexual division of labour, but it assumed women's involvement in income-earning activity. Wives and children of artisans assisted in the production process, and sold the goods produced by the family workshop. They also engaged in domestic production, often for one of the female branches of the textile industry. In Lyon, for instance, where Fourier could have observed the family economy of the working population in operation, Garden estimates that more than 20 000 women were employed in the silk industry in the late eighteenth century, others working in the broad range of female trades in the town.[8] Married women combined this work with their duties as wives and mothers, but wetnursing was common because of the difficulties of caring for infants whilst operating a loom.[9] For peasant women, who remained in the majority at that time, the dividing line between 'productive activity' and 'housewifery' was equally as unclear. They ran the household, like their urban counterparts, but they also performed income-earning labour in 'female' branches of farm work, and earned income in domestic textile production.[10] Their role as wetnurses to the women of nearby towns is also well known.[11] Many women would not have recognised themselves, then, in Fourier's critical portrait of domestic wives. He had little to say about women's roles in paid employment though he did lament men's incursion into the female trades.[12]

But it was precisely the complexity of women's roles which drew Fourier's criticism. Women's domestic duties interfered with 'productive' tasks, to which they were able to devote themselves only intermittently. Fourier defined domestic functions as unproductive, not because they did not create social value, but because they absorbed the efforts of most women when they might have been performed communally by a few. Much of women's labour was wasted because tasks such as cooking, laundry and childcare were organised inefficiently in a system based on private households. By Fourier's calculations, women's productive contribution to society was only one-fifteenth that of men.[13] He regarded this as one of the crucial weaknesses of the current social system and a major reason for establishing a new form of social organisation. In his view, it provided a persuasive economic argument for change.

Fourier's emphasis on women's incompetence in their 'civilised' roles may also have been designed to make his theories more acceptable to men. This strategy helps to explain the detailed attention to female inadequacy in his later works, as he attempted to convince his readers of the practical benefits to be gained by adopting his system. However, the attempt to combine an appeal for male support with a commitment to the liberty of women resulted at times in contradictory attitudes, since the two objectives were not compatible. Thus Fourier emphasised the authority of the husband and father even in the new system of communal childraising:

> But if a mother, in coming to the nursery to feed or see her child, was giving her child bad habits . . . her child would be taken away from her, and her husband would become very angry with her. For this would be a three-fold disgrace, the expense of individual education, the loss of the wife's labour, and the ruining of the child's health and progress.[14]

Similarly, he made the alteration of moral standards subject to the unanimous approval of husbands and fathers, although this contradicted the main aim of the reform, namely the liberation of women.[15] In Harmony, women would not have husbands in the 'civilised' sense of the word, so the patriarchal model was irrelevant. However, Fourier viewed men as capable of making rational decisions on matters in which women were swayed by emotion. The demands of love and attachment to family could not be allowed to override the greater good of the community. The dominance of masculine over feminine, which Fourier had defended in principle, thus implied male authority over women, even in Harmony.

THE SOCIAL ROLES OF WOMEN IN HARMONY

In Harmony, every woman would 'support herself by devoting herself to attractive work in about thirty Series'.[16] Women would enjoy complete freedom in choosing their occupations and would play a significant role in such fields as medicine and teaching, which were closed to them in 'civilisation'.[17] Nevertheless, Fourier predicted that women would generally choose to fill roles similar to their 'civilised' roles, and would compete unsuccessfully with the 'masculine' sex in the industrial order. His presuppositions reflected his view of women as 'the weak sex', who were destined by nature for delicate and non-strenuous work, for the adornment of society, and for setting the moral tone of the community. The distinctiveness of 'feminine' nature ensured the distinctiveness of 'feminine' roles and their contrast with those of the 'masculine' sex.

The significance of sexual difference in the industrial order of Harmony was indicated by Fourier's proposal that men and women should work alongside each other in all occupations:

> Although each branch of industry is particularly suited to one of the sexes, like sewing for women and ploughing for men, nevertheless nature desires combinations, sometimes of a half, and in some occupations of a quarter; she desires at least one-eighth of the other sex in each function. Thus while the cellar is the particular domain of men, the series of cellar-keepers must contain one-eighth of women who will support the work of white, sparkling, sweet wines, and other types which women like. . . .[18]

'Nature', to whose secrets Fourier once again claimed privileged access, authorised women's participation in previously male areas, but individual tasks in each occupation were defined as masculine or feminine. Men and women would work together, but they would perform tasks which were in keeping with their different capacities and inclinations. The 'law of exceptions' would produce some individuals with 'extra-sexual' capacities, but sexual difference would tend to separate and distinguish the functions of the sexes. The intermingling of the sexes which Fourier proposed served to emphasise sexual difference and give it added importance.

This was evident in Fourier's discussion of women's agricultural and industrial occupations in Harmony. He envisaged a limited role for them in agriculture, stipulating that 'women rarely participate except as assistants in *l'ordre massif*, which comprises the strenuous occupations . . .'.[19] While typical men's work included forestry, irrigation and ploughing, 'women's and children's work' included the care of the cow sheds, the poultry and the kitchen gardens.[20] Women would generally work closer to the phalanstery than the men, and even the female Hordes would 'undertake the unpleasant tasks in the kitchens, apartments and laundries', rather than outdoors or in the fields.[21] This definition of women's agricultural roles resembled the pattern of women's work in rural France at that time, when women were responsible for the domestic animals, and for a number of tasks performed in close proximity to the farmhouse.[22] In Fourier's view, physical weakness would limit women's participation as agricultural workers in Harmony's primarily agricultural economy.

The characteristics of 'feminine' nature also indicated to Fourier the types of careers for which they were well suited, and in which they would tend to specialise in Harmony. Firstly, he believed that seven-eighths of women would be attracted to tasks traditionally performed by the housewife. In his view, such jobs as cooking and sewing were women's 'natural destiny', as heavy agriculture was men's.[23] The division of labour, indoors as outdoors, would be determined by physical strength, so men would take care of any heavy domestic work in Harmony. But this criterion ensured a range of domestic tasks suitable for women of all ages, while limiting those tasks suitable for adult males:

> Cooking, as a sedentary function which requires little physical strength, is particularly suitable for women, although men monopolise it in all the large civilised towns; but what haven't they taken over, even sewing which is the essential attribute of the feminine sex? In Harmony [the feminine sex] will be more numerous in the kitchens than the masculine sex, which will confine its activities there to the tasks requiring vigour, and will leave whatever remains to the women and children, without exclusive allotment, because everything is free in Harmony; but since the kitchens of a phalanx will require a system of heavy machinery . . . men will have their particular jobs there, and while they will share in the finer details of preparation, they will

not be tempted to steal from women and children the tasks which nature has specially reserved for these two sexes.

Thus it will be fitting for men to be trained in the finer points of kitchen work during childhood; they will abandon it at adolescence, but they will have acquired the necessary knowledge, and will have acquired it at the age when it is appropriate to practise the little tasks compatible with physical weakness.[24]

Fourier's view of women's physical limitations thus shaped his belief that household occupations would continue to be performed predominantly by women, even when those households became communal establishments. One aspect of the 'civilised' sexual division of labour would therefore be maintained in Harmony. However, Fourier envisaged household functions as an area where women could excel, and where feminine talent would rival masculine supremacy.

Women's opportunity to become experts in cuisine or household management was made possible partly by their release from maternal obligations. According to Fourier's calculations, maternal 'virtue' would be reduced to one-twelfth the level required by the 'civilised' order, and its decline would be conducive to socialised childraising.[25] By attracting women away from motherhood to other occupations, Fourier proposed to increase their economic productivity and their happiness. When they had 'thirty industrial groups to investigate with the opportunity for advancement and reward', when they had 'useful and exciting intrigues' to occupy their attention, they would have no time to think about children.[26]

While the 'civilised' emphasis on motherhood would disappear, however, women would continue to play the major role in child-rearing in Harmony. Fourier estimated that 'about an eighth' of women had a natural inclination for this function, as did a small minority of men. The younger the children, in Fourier's view, the more likely they were to be cared for predominantly by women. Women were preferable amongst those working with two and three year-olds, while the care of children less than two would be entirely a female occupation, 'with rare exceptions'. Consequently, the Series of *nourrices* or nurses was assigned to women, despite Fourier's criticism of breastfeeding and his commitment to the development of artificial feeding.[27]

Fourier regarded child-care as an inferior occupation, 'for in general women who passionately love caring for small children

. . . are rather limited types incapable of distinguishing themselves in occupations of a higher order'.[28] Girls aged seven to nine years would assist the women, since a number of them showed a keen interest in babies.[29] Fourier appears to have regarded this interest as innate, rather than seeing it as a result of socialisation and role modelling. Only a minority of less capable women would fill this role in Harmony, therefore, but childcare would remain an occupation for 'the weak sex' since it was 'very lucrative and not tiring work'.[30] Its unstrenuous nature made it 'women's work', in Fourier's terms, and the fact that it was well rewarded reflected Fourier's belief that caring for babies was a necessary but unpleasant task. Fortunately for men, perhaps, 'nature' had assigned it largely to women.

The relative inferiority of 'feminine' industrial achievements was reflected in Fourier's estimates of worker productivity in Harmony. Fourier claimed that the performance of any Series would depend upon its competitive spirit:

> . . . the Series which is most strongly motivated by intrigues, the one which would make the greatest financial sacrifices to satisfy its pride, will be the one which will create the most perfect and valuable products . . . but if it has few rivalries, intrigues and alliances, little pride and enthusiasm, it will work [without ardour] . . . and its products like its earnings will be very inferior to those of a Series with strong rivalries.[31]

He also emphasised the competitiveness of women, arguing that they had been more strongly endowed than men with 'the passion of gambling and intrigue'. Since women would be more competitive than men and equally as industrious, we might expect that the Series composed predominantly of women would out-perform those composed mainly of men.[32] However, Fourier insisted upon the greater productivity of men:

> [In the combined order] individual production is estimated at:
> MAN, 12; WOMAN, 9;
> CHILD, 7, from 5 to 15 years. TOTAL, 28.[33]

Women's productivity would thus make an enormous leap from one-fifteenth that of men to three-quarters that of men, according to Fourier's calculations, but he did not believe that women could close the gap completely. He did not explain how he arrived at his calculation of their respective outputs. Since women and men performed different tasks and produced different goods, comparisons of their productivity would be difficult. Nor did he explain how women's enthusiasm for industrial rivalry would be maintained if male predominance was inevitable. The differences were probably based on Fourier's assumptions about women's inferior physical strength, or their limited power of reason: the factors which denoted their 'femininity'. While emotional and artistic people had their uses in Harmony, their talents were not those associated by Fourier with industrial or agricultural productivity.

The industrial limitations of the 'feminine' sex were also reflected in Fourier's estimates of the rewards which would accrue to male and female workers in Harmony. He stressed the importance of providing women with well paid work to stimulate their ambition and productivity, and even proposed affirmative action: reserving one-half of jobs in lucrative fields for women. Similarly, he proposed giving women equal access to positions of status and power. Each Series would elect office bearers in proportion to the numbers of each sex that it contained,[34] and women office-holders (like men) would have authority in their own right. They would no longer acquire power simply through marriage:

> Women perform their own functions, and are not invested with meaningless titles, as amongst us, where madam president presides over nothing, madam marshall commands nothing. In the combined Order, where marriage does not take place, one does not acquire honours by sleeping with someone; one only bears the title for the functions which one performs, and when a woman is named the colonel or the banner-carrier . . . we will see her command the Series on parade, or carry the banner, or head the committee in a meeting related to her functions.[35]

However, this separation of male and female affairs enabled the preservation of distinctions between men and women, for women office-bearers would have less extensive duties and would therefore receive 'less lavish remuneration'.[36] Again, Fourier did not explain his reasoning, but his system distinguished between 'masculine' and 'feminine' tasks, with the former being more highly regarded and better rewarded.

While women could never compete successfully with men in the agricultural sphere they would come to the fore in the artistic sphere, where their celebrity and earnings would help to compensate for their lesser achievements in masculine-dominated occupations. Fourier regarded the Arts as particularly compatible with women's nature. Women such as Madame de Sévigné and Madame de Staël had already provided a glimpse of 'the destiny of the weak sex' in the field of literature.[37] They would also excel in all aspects of 'general ornamentation', and the beautifying of the community. This included painting, and the care and adornment of the agricultural altars where they would tend the flowers and shrubs. Women's association with these tasks reflected not only their assumed artistic talents, but the decorative role they themselves were destined to play within society. They not only created objects of visual and sensory appeal, but exerted such an appeal themselves. The Arts formed part of 'the sensual domain', and the artistic field was thus an area where 'the feminine sex' would predominate.[38] Fourier also stressed the moral role of the Arts, and his definition of the Arts as a 'feminine' career was compatible with his concept of the moral role of women and girls in the community. Their 'feminine' virtues of good manners and refinement countered the roughness and crudeness of the 'masculine' sex.[39]

Fourier rejected domesticity as the ideal female pursuit, then, and assigned all roles to men and women on the basis of aptitude. However, by drawing on 'civilised' norms for his understanding of women's aptitudes Fourier inhibited his re-assessment of their potential. Since he valued physical strength, defined as a 'masculine' attribute, the opportunities for 'the weak sex' in the industrial order of Harmony were inherently limited. There was an underlying paradox within this approach, for Fourier's principle of free development contrasted markedly with his attempts to classify and predestine future lifestyles. He sought to ensure the development of individuality from infancy, and attempted to set out the guidelines by which individual differences could be recognised and fostered. He also claimed to have developed a mathematical model by which the precise numbers of those exhibiting each personality profile might be determined. This methodology resulted in a tension between Fourier's ideal of women's 'liberty', and his assumptions about their potential roles as liberated beings. The traditional female occupations, reorganised to meet the requirements of the new society, remained most suited to women in Harmony. Furthermore, women were assumed to be emotional rather than rational in character, indicating their suitability for a set of roles requiring strength of 'sentiment'. This trait, along with the dominant sexuality of the 'feminine' sex, indicated to Fourier the areas in which women would rise to prominence in Harmony.

THE SEXUAL ROLES OF WOMEN IN HARMONY

Women's 'feminine' nature would become an advantage in the amorous order of Harmony. The emotional superiority and sexual precocity of the 'feminine' sex would open a range of amorous careers to women, providing the opportunity to compensate for their lesser achievements and earnings in industry. 'Feminine' superiority in matters of love ensured that contrast and complementarity would be maintained between the masculine and the feminine spheres, and between masculine and feminine potential. So while Fourier criticised the 'civilised' system in which women's sexuality provided their only means to power and wealth, he defined 'the functions of love' as one of women's major methods of social advancement in Harmony.[40]

The typical woman of Harmony would have a sexual but not a reproductive role, since Fourier anticipated that many women would be sterile in future. A combination of diet, exercise and sexual activity, he predicted, would make women 'more suited to pleasure, but much less to conception'.[41] Fourier argued that this new woman would be a work of 'nature', but his projections about that nature enabled the deployment of female sexuality in society in new ways. He maintained a polarised view of women as sexual beings. They were portrayed as virginal and pure, tantalising objects of desire, or as sexually available and generous with their favours. In either case, female sexuality was envisaged as a potentially dangerous force, which needed to be channelled and regulated. Fourier ridiculed the philosophers' attempts to achieve this objective by enforcing monogamy and chastity, and set out to discover the means by which women's sexual needs could be satisfied without creating chaos. In Harmony female sexuality would be harnessed and become a powerful unifying force in the community. It would become a source of satisfaction and contentment within society, and an incentive or reward for industrial prowess. Satiety would provide the basis for sexual order, and sexual order would make possible social order.

Individuals would join a variety of amorous Series in Harmony as their circumstances and inclinations altered, so they would always be able to find a mode of sexual fulfilment which met their changing needs. Unlike 'civilisation', which only reluctantly made provision for those who were not faithful by nature, Harmony would legitimise a range of amorous choices. This would be particularly beneficial for women, who were more repressed under the 'civilised' arrangement:

> . . . people will immediately begin to think sensibly about the social politics of love; they will realise that since, in this passion as in any other, characteristics are arranged in genera, species and varieties, man is a fool to demand from all women uniformity of character in love, a uniformity required in the present situation which would insist, according to law and morality, that all women be faithful, and have no other desire than to skim the stew.[42]

The sexual roles available to both women and men in Harmony would extend from virginity to promiscuity. However, variations between their projected sexual roles reflected Fourier's perceptions of the difference between 'masculine' and 'feminine' natures.

Fourier regarded sex as the basic mechanism for creating and reinforcing social bonds, so he believed that sexual infidelity could serve an important social function.[43] The starting point for his theory of sexual relations, therefore, and the aspect which he considered to be unique, was his rejection of monogamy:

> What has led all the civilised philosophers astray on the future of love is that they have always thought about forms of love limited to the couple; consequently, they have only been able to reach the same result, egoism, the inevitable outcome of love confined to the couple; so in envisaging unlimited developments it is necessary to begin with the collective exercise [of love] and I will adopt no other course.[44]

The 'civilised' system of sexual relations was based on 'exclusive physical possession and the exclusion of the most worthy, perhaps the most devoted lovers'. Harmony would facilitate a system of male and female infidelity: 'a [sexual] possession which is un-limited in number, extending to all those who are worthy because of the intensity of their passion'.[45]

The value of infidelity, according to Fourier, lay in its ability to extend and reinforce the bonds uniting the community. 'Mono-gynes', who took only one lover, aspired simply to belong com-pletely to the loved one. In Fourier's view, this attitude was both banal and anti-social, and ignored the jealousy and frustrated desire left in its wake.[46] He anticipated that some people would remain 'monogynes' in Harmony, but most would become 'polygynes' and take a variety of sexual partners. Their infidelities would serve a useful social purpose:

> [Since] polygynes mostly have the characteristic of preserving friendship after love, their infidelity supports virtue completely, for a female polygyne who has changed lovers 12 times and who is still friendly with the 12 while saving her love for the 13th, has formed, by this infidelity, 12 bonds of friendship which would not exist if she had been faithful.[47]

Inconstancy would also extend the bonds of family relationships. It would end 'family egoism' and assist the distribution of wealth, as Harmonians remembered former lovers in their wills. Whereas monogamy created 'universal discord amongst people',[48] there-fore, infidelity would create a network of affectionate ties which cut across boundaries of wealth and nationality. Sexual bonds would contribute significantly to social harmony.

Fourier stressed the interaction between the major and minor orders, between politics and love. 'Industry, pleasure and social politics' all went hand in hand.[49] The situation of women provided a special example of the connections between the sexual and political realms. Fourier pointed out that women's oppression had both sexual and political forms. Their sexual subordination was essential to their political powerlessness, and their sexual libera-tion would be a first step towards their total emancipation. Furthermore, because sex relations were inherently political, the condition of 'the sex' was a gauge of the political condition of a society. Change in the sociopolitical sphere was proportionate to change in the gender order.[50] Fourier also compared sexual depri-vation and its social consequences to starvation:

> . . . the sense of taste, the need for subsistence is the barometer of the people; . . . if they are hungry the people and the troops rise up and overthrow the government, and still the law allows no guaranteed minimum in subsistence . . . even less will it allow a [guaranteed] minimum of pleasure; because it seems less important; that is incorrect and, although a person can survive without sex and not without food . . . the need for tactile pleasure definitely causes as many social disorders as the need for subsistence.
>
> Certainly the two senses rebel in very different ways. In the event of privation that of taste revolts openly, that of touch works silently and its ravages, though less obvious are even more inevitable. . . .[51]

Meeting the community's sexual needs was as important for preserving social peace as providing its subsistence.

All forms of sexual activity would be legitimate in Harmony. Some people might enjoy sex as part of a trio, which would 'redouble' the bonds of friendship between the three.[52] Similarly the orgy, the 'infinitely large' bond of love, would strengthen emotional bonds between those who took part:

> The participants in these activities feel very strongly that a special bond exists between them, a type of attraction which they cannot define and which gives their souls a wonderful stability . . . They regard their collective union as sacred, as an alliance of a special type, a bond which produces effects very different from love, for it eliminates jealousy.[53]

At the opposite end of the amorous spectrum, the legitimation of the 'manias' or sexual obsessions was designed to bring together those attracted by rarer sexual practices. Fourier stressed the social utility of minority tastes. They were 'one of the means which nature has devised to maintain and incorporate into the series those whom exclusive love tends to alienate . . .'. Consequently the 'manias' would be encouraged methodically amongst the very young in Harmony.[54] Even incest would have its place, since Fourier was determined to authorise 'whatever multiplies bonds and does good to many people without harming any'. However, Fourier distinguished between different degrees of incest and recognised the need to prevent pregnancy.[55]

A variety of sexual roles would be available to both men and women in Harmony, but Fourier believed that women had a particular talent for the affairs of love. They would excel and assume command in this realm as men excelled in the industrial realm. He therefore assigned women to the major roles in supervising and directing the affairs of love. They would predominate as 'Ministers' and 'Matrons' in the amorous order, or as 'Pontiffs' who took charge of amorous affairs in the industrial armies:

> After the magnificent Daytime battles over gastronomic perfection, in the evenings they will have no less immense amorous concerts which will join each man and woman in enjoyable and conspiratorial relations with all the individuals of the most numerous army. Thus the role of great Pontiff of the army will be a ministry as magnificent for women as the role of general in chief is for men. It will take clever feminine minds to direct this immense exercise capably, in a well ordered fashion. This will be the triumph of the old women so mistreated today and deprived of the functions of amorous management to which nature calls them.[56]

Women would also be predominant within the corporation of 'fairies' who assisted the pontiffs in the administration of love. Their task was to study the sexual characters of the citizens of Harmony, to advise on the selection of partners, and to organise the orgies. They would be skilled in 'the algebra of love or the calculation of the accidental sympathies in love':

> . . . this is the art of matching the passions of a crowd of men and a crowd of women who have never met each other; in order to see to it that each of the hundred men perceives straight away for which of the hundred women he will experience *composite love*, a perfect moral and physical compatibility. . . .[57]

Women's particular insight in matters of love enabled them to judge the rapport of other couples. Love would be *l'affaire principale* in Harmony, but it would be the particular business of women.

The usefulness of women's strong sexuality was also demonstrated by the role which Fourier assigned to the virgins in Harmony. Young people would join the corps of vestals at puberty, but many would depart before reaching the maximum age of 19 or

20 as the delights of sex proved more appealing than the honours
of virginity. Fourier's theory made explicit provision for male as
well as female virginity, and he regarded this concept as very
progressive. As he pointed out, demanding abstinence from girls
and not from boys was unjust and impractical.[58] Nevertheless,
Fourier persisted in the view that female virginity would be more
common: 'It is normal that women maintain the role of virginity
longer; besides, they have more enticements for persisting in
it . . .'.[59] Although Fourier argued that women were superior in
love, that the sex drive was dominant in women, and that the
opportunity for satisfying that drive would exist in Harmony, he
nevertheless anticipated that girls would outnumber boys by two
to one in the Series of vestals, while the Series of damsels (adolescents who were sexually active) would be composed predominantly of males.

Male virginity was portrayed as circumstantial, or as the means
to an end. The *vestels* would comprise those boys who were
uninterested in amorous affairs because they were too busy, or
those with a particular objective such as winning the favours of a
vestale or being chosen by a princess to father heirs.[60] Girls would
also be attracted towards virginity by its potential rewards.[61] However, the appeal of virginity to girls, in Fourier's account, lay in the
honour and renown they could achieve for their beauty and accomplishments. The *vestales* would be the recipients of devotion
and affection which stemmed from their virginal state itself, because female virginity was a desirable quality in its own right:

> If the *vestales* hold pride of place, it is because nothing com-
> mands our esteem better in young girls of 16 to 18 years than an
> unquestionable virginity, a real and unfeigned modesty, an
> ardent devotion to useful and charitable works, an active pursuit
> of suitable studies and of the fine arts.[62]

Their status stemmed in part from their youth and beauty, but it
also had a sexual dimension. Fourier's portrayal of the *vestales*
emphasised the appeal of female sexual innocence. Although he
criticised the importance 'civilised' men placed on being the first
'possessor' of a woman,[63] he emphasised the sexual desirability of
the *vestales*, and male hopes (or fantasies) for first possession. The
virgin herself was the prize, the desired one, although able to
choose who would win her. Thus Fourier argued that women

preferred sexually-experienced men as lovers,[64] but he emphasised men's desire for virginal partners, and based the industrial system of Harmony upon male competition to 'possess' female virgins.

Male and female virginity served different purposes in the projected society of Harmony. The major role assigned to the males by Fourier was that of 'putting children on the wrong scent in matters of love'.[65] Fourier explained:

> If all the youths . . . took a mistress at 16, moved suddenly from the [children's series] to the ranks of the damsels, and abruptly abandoned the morning work sessions, this general defection of the men would arouse some awkward guesswork . . .: [the children] would conclude from this occurrence that the court of gallantry and the [affairs of] love are therefore brimming with attraction; soon the children of 15 and then those of 14 and 13 would seek to anticipate the time fixed for this transition.[66]

It was therefore necessary for some boys (as well as girls) to remain in the corps of virgins, which had links with the children's Series and not with the courts of love. However, the *vestels'* function in hiding the mysteries of sex from children required that they themselves be informed about those mysteries. Each day they would lock away any animals on heat before the Little Hordes began their duties in the stables.[67] Apparently the *vestales* would be kept in ignorance of such matters to safeguard the sexual innocence which was their major appeal.

The main role of the *vestales* lay in assisting the recruitment of the industrial armies and inspiring their performance as they carried out all major public works. Those who sought the favours of a virgin applied for the title of suitor, and the suitors put themselves to the test in the industrial campaigns. There would be some women amongst the suitors, vying for the favours of the *vestels*, but Fourier emphasised that the majority of the virgins would be female and the suitors male.[68] This division was also suggested by the heavy nature of much of the industrial work. The *vestales* assessed the work performance of their suitors, their skill in the public games, and their courtesy and manners in the festivals. The number of suitors diminished as the campaign progressed, until each virgin selected a partner and consummated the union.[69] Under this system, possession of a virgin would be the reward for the outstanding industrial 'soldier'. Fourier surmised that there would be no shortage of willing workers, as young people vied for a place in the industrial armies and a chance to carry off the prizes.[70] From their position of honour the *vestales* therefore exerted a major influence on the industrial productivity of the community, and through their role as desired sex objects the force of love was diverted to the creation of wealth.[71]

Fourier asserted that the sexual desirability of the *vestales* would enable them to influence the sexual conduct of the men in Harmony, and thus to ensure that truth and honour prevailed in sexual relations. This was one part of their significant political role, for as guarantors of the fundamental virtues of Harmony they ensured its safety as the vestal virgins had safeguarded Rome.[72] Men's eligibility for the title of suitor depended upon their record of amorous good conduct:

> This title is sought and obtained on the deliberation of the corps of vestals, gathered in a synod at which the female dignitaries of the court of love assist. The conduct of a man is scrutinised when he applies to be a suitor; infidelity is not considered a crime, for it has its uses in Harmony; but one examines whether, in his different amorous liaisons, he has always shown proof of deference for women and loyalty towards them.[73]

The *vestales* would also make non-sexual or 'sentimental' love attractive by demonstrating the glory which practitioners of such love enjoyed. Nevertheless, the importance and utility of female virginity in Harmony lay in its latent sexual appeal. The *vestales'* role was the ambiguous one of creating sexual desire, and diverting it into non-sexual channels, either work or sentiment, with the promise of sexual rewards in the future.

Fourier's theory of virginity therefore rested upon and emphasised the sexuality of women. The innocence of their 'sentimental' relations with their suitors may have been designed to foster 'sentimental' love, but the charm of such relationships lay, at least in part, in the sexual expectation with which they were imbued. Women's role as virgins demonstrated Fourier's belief in the power of female sexuality, and the uses to which it might be put in a well-organised society. The innocence of the virgins served only to highlight their sexual appeal, and the dominant sexuality of female nature.

A further example of the usefulness of female sexuality in the Harmonic order was provided by the *bacchantes*. They played an important role in the industrial armies, along with the 'pontiffs', 'fairies' and virgins. Fourier outlined the composition of these armies:

> . . . we would find more young legions of men and women than necessary (for the armies of Harmony require a third [of their members] as *bacchantes, bayadères, facquiresses, paladines, héroines* and in other occupations, not including those of the court of love). . . .[74]

The female members of the armies would thus be drawn largely from the amorous Series, rather than from the industrial Series. Unlike the vestals, these groups would not be celibate. They played a role as industrial workers, but also had the task of providing sexual rewards and comforts for the soldiers. For instance, the role of the *bacchantes* would be one of 'charity', healing the sorrows of unrequited love. Each morning the *bacchantes* would inform rejected suitors of their misfortune: 'they endure the first shock, the cries of treachery and ingratitude; and, to console [rejected suitors] they lavishly employ their eloquence and their charms'.[75] Male *bacchantes* would perform a similar role for the smaller number of unsuccessful female suitors but Fourier emphasised the largely female composition of the group. Through the role of the celibate Series such as the virgins and the non-celibate Series such as the *bacchantes*, therefore, Fourier contrived to make female sexuality a useful commodity in Harmony. Women's sexual talents would contribute significantly to the creation of a satisfied, productive and united community.

Despite Fourier's general support for uninhibited sexual freedom, he also sought to contain sexuality in Harmony by providing distractions and alternatives. This idea was put forward in his first work, but appears to have been significantly reinforced by his experiences at Talissieu. The boundary between 'freedom' and 'anarchy' was blurred in his nieces' sexual lives. In the manuscripts written after this episode, and published later as *The New Amorous World*, he developed in detail the 'counterweights' to sexual liberty.

His aim was to ensure that the citizens of Harmony controlled their sexual desire and were not dominated by it, and he contrasted the sexual anarchy of 'civilisation' with the order prevailing in Harmony. By ensuring the sexual satiety of the Harmonians, and especially of sexually-demanding women, Fourier aimed to guarantee the reign of 'sentimental' or celibate love.[76] Sentiment depended not on physical ties but on 'spiritual' bonds, so it would unite the community even more securely than sex. Paradoxically, therefore, the world of sexual liberty was also a world in which 'sainthood', or social status, was achieved by sexual self-denial.

Fourier's emphasis on sexual restraint was well demonstrated by his portrayal of the damsels. This Series comprised adolescents who were just beginning their sexual careers. They lacked the talent, beauty and strength of character of the virgins, but compensated for their sexual precocity by their delicacy in love.[77] Fourier contrasted their sexual moderation with the scandalous behaviour of 'civilised' newlyweds, who 'believe that they have performed feats of domestic valour if they wear themselves out in bed until 9 o'clock in the morning celebrating the sacrament'.[78] In Harmony love would stimulate people to work better, rather than distracting them from it. According to Fourier, the many pleasures and diversions of life in the phalanstery would counterbalance the 'amorous fire' of 15 to 30 year old people. If 'attraction' was not sufficient to ensure a sensible attitude to love-making, other measures would place pressure to conform on young people. In an authoritarian vein Fourier announced that they would be allowed little time to indulge in sex, being 'continually directed into useful activities' among groups of people. They also faced the prospect of being ridiculed, especially by the vestals, and being exiled from the court of love.[79] The needs of the group must take precedence over personal desire:

> In short, couples of young lovers like all the other corporations of Harmony, must foster the initial source of attraction, internal and external wealth. They would diverge from both, if they spent their days in an indolence which, by enervating them, compromised vigour or internal wealth, and distracted from industry, the path to external wealth or riches.[80]

Thus, although the damsels lacked the innocence and self-control of the virgins, they would ensure that love did not override social duty. Sex was a means to an end, not an end in itself, and could only be socially beneficial if its power was controlled.

Fourier's concept of amorous 'sanctity' was also designed to ensure the predominance of social duty over egotistical sexual indulgence, and to increase social cohesion. The path to 'sanctity' required a series of trials in which the candidate exhibited various forms of sexual altruism. The first requirement for those seeking to enter the path of sanctity, for example, was the 'initiative':

> . . . this consists of a welcome to the 3 elderly choirs of the opposite sex in the *Tourbillon*: a young man who wishes to enter the career of sanctity firstly owes . . . amorous tribute to all the ladies [of the rank of] Reverend, Venerable and Patriarch who do not all accept it. It is the same for a young girl. . . .[81]

Other trials required candidates to participate in various forms of heterosexual, homosexual and 'celadonic' or celibate love,[82] irrespective of their own sexual desires.

One of the highest forms of sanctity was exhibited by the 'angelic' couples. They shared a chaste love for each other, while each one directed the sexual liaisons of his or her partner.[83] Unlike egotistical lovers, their motto was 'all for others and nothing for me, except what they wish to give me'.[84] They were thus the epitome of sexual self-control. To be admitted to the angelic ranks demanded a record of 'prowess in sanctity', that is, in sexual charity, and a noviciate during which the candidates offered themselves as a sexual gift to the elders to satisfy them physically and spiritually.[85] Sexual love thus assumed a purifying function, for it was by abandoning themselves totally to the sexual demands of others, and restraining their own sexual preferences, that they became angelic. They were then capable of rising above egotistical sensuality to experience a 'sentimental ecstasy'[86] which surpassed immediate gratification:

> [The angelic role] has the pleasure of transcendent celibacy or the superior degree of pure love, a kind of mental eroticism which raises the participants above physical desires while creating for them a rapturous diversion which defers desire until another phase of the passion.[87]

The sexual 'liberation' of the body, which was placed at the disposal of others, freed the spirit to pursue 'pure love', or love which transcended physical pleasure. Like Christian saints, Fourier's saints required self-control and the conquest of the flesh. However, that conquest was achieved by sexual service to others, rather than by abstinence.

Fourier believed that respect for supra-sexual love could only flourish when sexual need was fully gratified. This view had particular relevance for women, whose sexual needs were more compelling. Fourier emphasised that only ensuring the full physical satisfaction of women would encourage them towards sentiment, the 'noble portion' of love:[88]

> When a woman is well provided with all the necessities of love, indulging in love with complete freedom with a wide assortment of well-built fellows, with orgies and bacchanalia, both simple and composite, then she will be able to find in her heart ample room for sentimental fantasies[.] [S]he will provide herself with several very refined arrangements and liaisons of this kind and counterbalance physical pleasures.[89]

The sexual system of Harmony, with its infinite variety of sexual possibilities, would provide 'full liberty' to women, and thus facilitate and encourage their pursuit of sentiment.

One means for ensuring that women were well provided with love was through lesbianism. Fourier believed that women were much inclined towards this kind of love, and in the imaginary scenes of *The New Amorous World* he made lesbians of 'all or almost all of the ladies of Gnide'.[90] His belief in women's inclination towards sapphic love stemmed from his view of female nature, as well as his observation of contemporary women:

> One can already see that women in their state of liberty of perfectibility like those of Paris, have a strong leaning towards sapphism . . . this sex is more inclined than the other towards monosexuality. Well, in a new order where all feminine mistrust and enmity has ceased, where the mechanism of the series of assemblies and other passional balances has made all the present jealousies of women disappear . . . it will not be surprising that all or almost all of them will engage in an intimacy which is already so widespread in the places where they are more organised.[91]

Fourier denied that lesbianism would be balanced by widespread male homosexuality. The laws of Harmony stressed contrast and 'equilibrium' rather than similarity, and the natural inclinations of women indicated to Fourier their predominance in this form of love. He summarised his view: 'Minor more loving than major: *inde* not as many Pederasts – equilibrium not equality . . .'.[92]

Lesbianism was important for the smooth functioning of the Harmonic community, as an abbreviated note in *The New Amorous World* suggests:

Sapphism: source of equilibrium – if women very satisfied amongst themselves, very loving, will be sought after more by more attentive men who are already becoming worried. Sapphism: perfection . . .(*sic*).[93]

He did not explain why sapphism was 'perfection', but the context suggests that lesbianism provided the ideal mechanism for the amorous reforms that Fourier sought to achieve. It would largely satisfy the sexual needs of women, thus stimulating their pursuit of sentiment. Furthermore, women's satisfaction with lesbian love would induce a more genteel attitude in the men who sought women's affections. Lesbianism would thus contribute towards uplifting the moral tone of the community, and promote the honourable sexual relations which Fourier sought to establish. Women's superiority in love would no longer be dangerous. Their physical needs satisfied, they would devote themselves to sentiment.

In defining appropriate sexual roles for women in Harmony, Fourier reasserted the gender difference which he had emphasised in defining their nature, and in outlining their social roles. Complementarity, not equality, remained crucial to his system. The 'feminine' expressed the emotional, sensual, artistic potential within human nature, counterbalancing the rational and physical power of the 'masculine'. Fourier thus gave prominence to sexual and cultural pursuits in Harmony, as well as to industrial and scientific ones. The force of the 'feminine' would be represented in every Series and occupation in Harmony. Its interaction with the 'masculine' would have a creative and beneficial effect at the inter-personal level and at the social level, as the two forces enlivened each other. Gender difference acted as a 'magnetic force' within human society, attracting and repelling, energising the circuit of human possibilities. By fostering a gender divide and incorporating it within the system of social and sexual roles in Harmony, Fourier attempted to exploit the meanings and possibilities of sexuality to the full. Those possibilities included the creation of a wealthy and harmonious community: the ultimate achievement of sexual and social liberation.

4

The Saint-Simonians Discover 'Woman', 1803–1829

Fourier's main rival as theorist and prophet of the new society in the early nineteenth century was Henri, Comte de Saint-Simon.[1] A man of noble birth, he had fought alongside Washington during the American Revolution and, like Fourier, had had a narrow escape from the guillotine during the French Revolution. Like Fourier, too, he sought to understand this cataclysmic event, and to uncover the basis for a new form of social organisation to replace the discredited *ancien régime*. He dedicated himself to achieving 'the perfection of civilisation', the 'golden age of humanity', which he insisted lay in the future, not in the past.[2] Although Saint-Simon died in 1825 a movement inspired by his ideas flourished during the late 1820s and 1830s, and the Saint-Simonians can be described as the first socialist organisation in France. The movement attracted a diverse group of participants, bourgeois and labouring class, male and female, all welcoming the prospect of a new society.

In the late 1820s, the definition of women's nature and place in society became crucial to the Saint-Simonian project, although originally it had not been singled out as having special importance. The Saint-Simonians discovered 'woman' as a creature set apart from man, different in nature, destined for roles which were inscribed within her very being. The distinctiveness of gender characteristics justified a projected sexual division of labour, and the opening of new social roles to women. However, in addition, it defined the parameters for appropriate female identity and action, closing off options and implicitly establishing what was 'unnatural' and inappropriate for women. While Saint-Simonian proposals to alter relations between the sexes had radical elements, therefore, they also prescribed the limits to change, and thus contained the radical potential inherent within such a project.

The broader meanings associated with gender by the Saint-Simonians help to explain their portrayal of women, and their idealised pattern of relations between the sexes. Sexual difference became a way of marking contrasts among natural and social phenomena, as well as among human attributes, characteristics and roles. Saint-Simonian theory, at this stage the work of men alone, re-evaluated the feminine and insisted on its positive character and social significance. Like Fourier, the Saint-Simonians stressed the antithetical relationship between masculine and feminine. Sexual complementarity thus offered a vision of a world in which opposites were reconciled and divergent forces were harmonised.

EARLY SAINT-SIMONIAN THEORIES ON WOMEN

While Fourier's proposed agricultural communities disavowed the increasing importance and sophistication of industry, Saint-Simon welcomed the emergent industrial world. The new order would be dominated by technicians, scientists and bankers, he predicted. They would replace the inefficient and corrupt system of the past with a centrally planned and managed economy, rather than one based on the divisive principles of *laissez-faire*. Society's watchwords would be efficiency, progress, technological advance, productivity. The parasites who had dominated the *ancien régime* would give way to a new elite drawn from the productive forces in society. Hierarchy would be based upon merit, although this concept was restricted by the notion of innate natural capacities. A greatly increased productive effort would increase wealth, and end the misery of the 'largest and poorest class'. In his final years Saint-Simon became convinced that only a new religious faith, a 'New Christianity', would ensure that the needs of all were met by the new society. He therefore proclaimed his doctrine as the completion of the Christian message of love.[3]

The social model employed by Saint-Simon was adapted from the theories of the prominent eighteenth-century physiologist, Xavier Bichat. He had argued that all human beings possessed intellectual, emotional and motor capacities, but that only one of these was capable of development in each person. Society should therefore identify and develop the particular capacity of each individual, rather than attempting to develop all three faculties in everybody. This concept provided the justification for a new but still elitist social structure, and formed the basis for Saint-Simon's proposal that separate social functions should be performed by separate social classes. In Saint-Simon's view, the physiological model provided the only workable basis for a new social system. The ideal society would comprise a small elite group of scientists (Bichat's intellectuals) and a small number of artists, poets and religious leaders (those with strong emotional capacities), while the majority of people would be manual labourers. Conflict would disappear in such a society, since all people would be fulfilling their own potential.[4]

How women would fit into a society organised along these lines was not made clear, since Henri de Saint-Simon wrote very little about women. The issue was not singled out as one requiring special attention, or a distinct theoretical treatment. In his *Essay on Social Organisation* (1803), he stated that women would fill useful and productive roles in the new society, though they would be organised in separate industrial groups from men.[5] He may, there-fore, have envisaged different work roles for women and men, but this is not certain. Saint-Simon regarded women as intelligent beings, and believed that both men and women might be endowed with the exceptional talent of genius.[6] However, he did not specify whether male and female intelligence, or male and female genius, were identical in nature. We do not know, therefore, if he regarded men and women as essentially identical human beings, or as different and complementary types. Saint-Simon's legacy con-cerning appropriate social roles for women in the future was vague and ambiguous, but his emphasis on the juxtaposition of different natural capacities, and on the opposition between reason and emotion, was to provide a foundation for the ideas on women developed by his followers.

These ideas began to find expression in the newspaper *Le Pro-ducteur*, founded by a small group of supporters shortly before Saint-Simon's death in 1825. Olinde Rodrigues, a teacher at the Polytechnical School and one of Saint-Simon's earliest followers, and Prosper Enfantin, a young graduate of that institution, played a leading role in the paper's establishment. Other regular contribu-tors included Philippe Buchez and Saint-Amand Bazard, both formerly active in the revolutionary Carbonarist movement. They were joined by a group of young professional men, aged around thirty, including Léon Halévy, P.-M. Laurent and Adolphe

Blanqui.[7] *Le Producteur* was described as a 'philosophical journal of industry, science and the fine arts', and its contents reflected this wide-ranging programme. Its contributors examined agricultural and industrial improvements, reported on scientific and medical advances, and reviewed literature, art and music. Few articles discussed women in detail, but writers displayed a belief in women's moral role which forms an essential prelude to later Saint-Simonian views on women, and on the social significance of the feminine.

Women's specialisation in 'sentiment' and their destiny of motherhood were emphasised in *Le Producteur*. These qualities explained the altruism and responsiveness to the needs of others which women as a group were assumed to possess. Adolphe Garnier claimed, for instance, that women's maternal tenderness had wider implications: 'By their circumstances in society, by the duties which nature imposes on them, [women] are more accustomed than men to devotion and more disposed towards doing good.'[8] Female nature thus stood in opposition to selfish individualism, which by implication was the province of men. Women were cast in the role of healers of the social ills created by their male counterparts, though this female role was attributed to 'nature' rather than to social expectation or constraint.

As mothers, women were allocated primary responsibility for upholding moral standards in the family. *Le Producteur* suggested that they might employ the arts to assist them in this task :

> . . . the arts express the feelings of a society, and women are endowed *par excellence* with the faculty of feeling . . . [nor] are they unaware that the arts can lend powerful support to the moral influence which they are called to exercise on the family: that a certain statue, a certain painting might become for their subordinates, for their children or even their husband, a living and ongoing lesson which, given without pretension or rebuke, would produce the most moral effect.[9]

The association of morality with women and with the family, which was portrayed as the seat of moral values, juxtaposed both of these with the realm outside the family: the social realm inhabited by men. In that sphere morality was weak, as men were morally weakened by their lack of compassion. The identification of women with 'feeling', in the Saint-Simonian context, implicitly denied them rational capacity. Yet the definition was a positive one, stressing the special and valuable role of women as moral educators. Compassionate woman was out of place in an unfeeling and male-dominated society, but she also pointed the way to a new and more compassionate alternative. The recognition and valuation of feeling could best be represented by recognising and valuing the compassionate sex.

Neverthless, it appears that women's role was merely to implement the moral standards which were determined by the intellectuals, and the intellectuals were portrayed as male. According to *Le Producteur*, the arts only reflected and popularised the ideas and feelings which the *savants* had articulated.[10] This may well have served as a model for women as moral agents, and one which defined the limits to female influence within society. Emotion should remain subordinate to reason, and women's moral role should remain subject to male authority. Rethinking the value of 'female' qualities was not to be confused with rethinking the gender hierarchy in society. In fact, allocating greater value to traits defined as feminine could provide an alternative to that more radical undertaking.

Images of women as wives and mothers in *Le Producteur* indicate that women's responsibility for domestic labour was assumed. Whether they were regarded as filling the roles of 'industrials' in doing such work, however, is by no means certain. Saint-Simon had defined 'industry' very broadly as 'every kind of useful activity, theoretical as well as practical, intellectual as well as manual',[11] but discussions of industry in *Le Producteur* always dealt with activities which were literally 'industrial work'. Although work was eulogised as 'civilising', then, it was defined in terms which appear to have excluded the domestic and reproductive work of women, though not their artistic contributions:

[The new philosophy] has realised that in the institutions, the works and the actions of man, only those which are related to the sciences, the arts and industry have always contributed, directly and increasingly, to the development of civilisation; that, on the contrary, all those which do not properly belong to one or other of these three types of activity have only contributed indirectly, and consequently possess only a limited and temporary usefulness.[12]

This definition was clearly designed to validate Saint-Simonian theories about social organisation, by rewriting the historical record in terms compatible with those theories. It also maintained a male focus, which made women's work and their contribution to 'civilisation' invisible. Although the question of what 'properly belonged' to these categories remained open, women's roles in biological and social reproduction were apparently neither useful nor civilising. The activities of men, who claimed credit for the intellectual and social development of humanity, cast a shadow over the contribution of women in these fields, and the formula also excluded the essential but devalued work of women in ensuring its physical continuity. Moreover, despite the value attached elsewhere in *Le Producteur* to the moral role of women, the contribution of moral agents to the history of 'civilisation' was unexplored.

The difficulty in applying the analysis of work to women's experience stemmed from the fact that women's domestic and reproductive work was performed within the family, and the family was regarded as part of the realm of 'nature', rather than of 'society'. Bazard described the family as 'the most spontaneous, the most necessary, and up to a certain point the least variable of all orders of relations'.[13] Activities within the family were not analysed, since 'natural' phenomena were not subject to social control. Women's perceived responsibility for such activities placed them outside the area in which Saint-Simonian theory applied, and the relationship between the work performed in the family, and that performed in the world of industry, science and the arts, was not examined. The contrast between family and society also defined the arena for change, asserting the permanence and immutability of the domestic order. In 1825–6 the Saint-Simonians apparently had no intention of abolishing the family, and in this respect their plans implicity contrasted with the more radical designs of Fourier.

Given the characterisation of women, there was little discussion in *Le Producteur* of roles which women might fill outside the family. Only the arts were seen as a suitable field for women, since both women and the arts were characterised by the specialised development of sentiment and by their moral function. Provided a woman artist remained 'within the limits which her sex and the nature of her talent seem to prescribe',[14] *Le Producteur* announced, she might play a significant role. These limitations were never clearly outlined, though a distinction was drawn between narrative verse, which came naturally to the female poet, and lyrical poetry which was a male preserve. Unfortunately female artists insisted on blurring this distinction. After all, since sentiment was a 'female' specialisation, woman's nature would seem to fit her admirably for the artistic role, and it was male potential in the arts which needed justification and definition. Despite such contradictions the allocation of women to the arts confirmed both the nature of woman and the nature of the arts, as defined by the Saint-Simonians, and affirmed the social value of both. In the process it legitimated a view of the arts as 'irrational', and implicitly defined science as uninfluenced by emotion and thus 'objective'.

No writer suggested that any women possessed a rational specialisation fitting them for an intellectual role, or for the administrative functions of the elite industrials. Saint-Simon's recognition of the intellectual equality of Madame de Staël had slipped from view, or was rejected.[15] Le Producteur also contained an explicit rejection of the notion of political and social rights for women, condemning the feminist component of English Owenite socialism: 'These ideas are so contrary to the tendencies of human nature, that the degree of support they seem to enjoy at present is initially inexplicable'.[16] The Saint-Simonians not only reasserted the futility of democratic and egalitarian principles in a society organised by specialised function, such as they proposed, but discounted any reconsideration of the social subordination of women. The prospect that women might become men's partners in all areas of society, and their social and political equals, had apparently not been considered by 1826.

THE DISCOVERY OF WOMAN'S SPECIAL NATURE

When Le Producteur ceased publication in October 1826, the Saint-Simonian school comprised only a handful of men. Over the next two years the Saint-Simonians refined their ideas and made new converts through private discussions and a wide network of correspondence. The new adherents, like those who recruited them, usually had a professional background, and the Polytechnical School proved a fertile source of new recruits. Prosper Enfantin gradually became the dominant personality, and his personal charisma began to play an important part in determining the direction of the sect. Where differences of theory or practice emerged, the influence of Enfantin served to reduce both the number and the credibility of the dissidents, and to confirm his individual authority.[17]

The assumption that women epitomised 'sentiment' and were destined for social roles compatible with their nature had been evident in some articles in *Le Producteur*. This issue became a contentious one amongst the Saint-Simonians in the years that followed. Their correspondence for 1829 reveals a major disagreement between Prosper Enfantin, who defined women's nature as fundamentally different from that of men, and Philippe Buchez, who rejected the 'separate natures' model. This disagreement was not made public, and in Saint-Simonian works published between 1829 and 1831 Enfantin's concept of woman was uncontested. His claim that women were fundamentally different from men because of their special 'sentimental' nature remained the key element in Saint-Simonian theory on women until the end of 1831, and provided the rationale for Saint-Simonian proposals to open new social roles to women. Those roles were consistent with the belief in women's inspirational power, and their moral influence on men.

Enfantin insisted that male/female dualism was the fundamental feature of human experience:

> . . . before all distinctions of races, castes, slaves, workers, idlers, warriors, pacifists, there exists one to which God *must* have linked all the others, there is one which must be the initial source of all that is human, it is [the distinction] between the *two sexes*.[18]

This distinction was portrayed as a differentiation of attributes and talents, a specialisation for different functions. Only within the heterosexual couple could the 'social individual' exist: '*Man and woman*, that is the BEING whom God created; *man and woman*, that is the social INDIVIDUAL'.[19] The interdependence of the sexes was thus inescapable, and was essential to social organisation. As part of the couple woman would bring to society a range of attributes which were currently lacking, and which were essential for the transformation of society. Women would play new roles within society but those roles would be determined, not by their common humanity with men, but by their difference from them.

The essence of women's difference from men lay in their nature as 'sentimental' beings. Both men and women possessed the faculty of sentiment, according to Enfantin, but their sentimental capacities were different in strength and type and served to complement each other. Enfantin wrote:

Woman is the sympathetic being *a priori*, man is the sympathetic being *a posteriori*, together they form the complete individual, *active* or conceiving, *passive* or implementing; by one of the faculties of this dual being, the *end* is discovered, by the other the *means*; one conceives the *idea*, the other gives it *form*; one *descends* from God to humanity; the other *returns* to God through humanity; one is essentially *religious*, the other is essentially *political*; one lives in the *wider world*, the other in the *domestic world* . . .[20]

This characterisation of the sexes lacked any logical or empirical foundation. In fact, Enfantin's appeal to an *a priori* argument in defining woman as 'sympathetic' removed the need for supporting his case: it was an appeal to general principles and essential truths, and thus a claim that the essence of female nature was self-evident. This claim had merely polemical value, since it was made as part of a dispute about that 'nature'. It reflected the internal politics of the Saint-Simonian group, rather than any realities about women.

By defining women as 'sympathetic', Enfantin proclaimed that love was their dominant characteristic:

I am astounded that you have not detected the psychological principle on which my argument rests; if this principle is destroyed, it leaves me defenceless. This is it: man and woman, every human being loves and wishes to be loved, but the *dominant* factor in women is that they love; in men it is that they *wish to be loved*.[21]

This arbitrary distinction between the sexes restated Enfantin's own assumptions and beliefs. Women's love, and their qualities of altruism and devotion, indicated to him that women's destiny lay in inspiring and supporting men. They were 'new Eves' destined to civilise man and lead him to God:

It is from the hand of a woman that the *New Adam* regenerated by Saint-Simon will once again receive the fruit of the tree of knowledge, because it is by her that he will be *led* towards God . . . She will continue to fulfil this sweet *civilising* mission that she has exercised so skilfully, so tenderly over the centuries . . . Yes, my friend, it is in order that man might raise himself towards [God] that God has given man a companion; it is in order to sanctify *force* one day that he has linked it with *gentleness*; to destroy the forms of *egoism*, God has willed that man should experience the *need to be loved* by a creature more tender, more devoted than himself.[22]

According to Enfantin, therefore, women were designed for a moral and inspirational role, rather than for a political role. His theory thus reiterated a contemporary perception of women, and provided an alternative rationale for its preservation. It also defined the roles which women were to be allocated by the Saint-Simonians: those of supporting and nurturing individual men and society in general.

Enfantin's portrayal of the ideal pattern of relations between the sexes relied for its effect on a model of biological generation. Only man and woman together could create new life, so by analogy the union of male and female was essential for the creation of new ideas and for human progress. Enfantin defined the 'generative union' as that between head and heart, reason and sentiment.[23] He wrote to Buchez:

You say that great ideas are always produced by a *single* mind . . . you forget, my friend, that the conceivers, the inventors, the poets have always been in love; re-read the epistle of Ballanche to Madame Récamier: you will see there *partly*, I believe, what a man's *head* always seeks in a woman's *heart* . . . and wasn't Jesus himself the child of a *totally loving* being and of another *totally spiritual* being? Well Jesus is the great idea of God, his most magnificent revelation.[24]

Within this model the contributions of the sexes were not equal, though both were essential. Men drew the initial inspiration for their discoveries and inventions from the love of women, but creative power was defined as a male attribute.

The dualistic model outlined by Enfantin attempted to establish a unitary pattern of relations between the sexes. Significantly, the dualism was expressed as a male/female one, not a masculine/feminine one. Man and woman, not persons (of either sex) who expressed the diverse potentials of masculinity and femininity, were to constitute the social being. As well as implicitly disavowing the possibility or legitimacy of homosexual bonds, this formulation linked social roles clearly with biology. The anatomical basis of Enfantin's theory was even more explicit in his discussion of reproduction. In his view, women's biological specialisation for this function established it as their natural destiny:

> You say . . . that I always assign the same role to one sex or another in advance. Note firstly that *this role encompasses* all human groups; so I assign woman a role, as I say that it is always she who will bear children. I assign it to her because I find that her faculties are thus inclined. . . . [25]

While women were destined to be mothers because of their anatomy, Enfantin insisted that the male capacity for 'propagating the species' could not be interpreted as a sign that all men had this role. That would be tantamount to declaring that all men should be tailors or shoemakers, Enfantin declared, since they all possessed the necessary organs.[26] He also distinguished between potential roles and social duty for men, although this distinction did not appear to apply to women. Saint-Simonian theory did not differentiate, for instance, between women's function in bearing children and their responsibility for raising them.[27]

Enfantin even attempted to establish a connection between women's anatomy and their emotional and intellectual attributes:

> . . . these soft, rounded forms, this delicate skin, this mouth which seems able to express only peace and happiness; all this is combined before us in one being to reveal *physically* what we must expect from her *sentimentally* and *intellectually*. It is up to us to understand the idea which God has enshrined in these tender forms. They always seem to seek a strong support, and smooth out its roughness by enfolding it lovingly.[28]

A particular reading of the female body thus created an image not only of woman's difference from man, but of her dependence, vulnerability and weakness. Of course, real women did not necessarily fit this image. The very urgency with which the model was insisted upon hints at an anxiety that women were not dependent enough, not the embodiments of peace, harmony and happiness which could make them manageable and unthreatening to men. The characterisation nevertheless left the way free for Enfantin to claim strength and integrity as male attributes. The bifurcated image of the sexes provided a justification for distributing roles accordingly: man would decide and act; woman would create an aura of peace and love which influenced his activities. The heterosexual couple, ideally a union of different but complementary types, provided a model for a social union in which different groups pursued separate and complementary functions for a common end.

The harmony between male and female was assumed within this model, but the lines of power were clearly drawn by Enfantin:

> . . . will woman be more powerful than man? Yes, religiously; no, politically; yes, when it is a matter of recalling *the objective*; no, when it comes to devising and implementing *the means* to reach it; yes, as a sibyl *revealing* the future; no, when it comes to carrying out the social activity which must *bring it about*. . . . [29]

Woman was allocated the role of prophet and visionary, inspiring male action. Her power was of a nebulous kind, exercised from the pedestal, while the political and social power of man was explicitly reaffirmed. Woman was raised to new honours, made man's partner within society, but the remodelling of society stopped short of removing male authority.

Despite this fact, even Enfantin's opponent, Philippe Buchez, believed that the Saint-Simonian doctrine promised the liberation of women:

> There is no debate between us over whether women will be liberated completely by the doctrine and whether they will finally attain one day the same level as men in education and in social functions, whatever those may be . . . That future, in fact, derives directly from the same sentiments and the same historical considerations by which we announce the complete liberation of all the other members of the human family.[30]

However, Buchez rejected Enfantin's model of sexual dualism, and the concept of women's special 'sentimental' nature. According to Buchez, Saint-Simon's deathbed comment that man and woman together formed the social individual had meant simply that man and woman comprised the fundamental elements of an organised society, not that they possessed different and complementary capacities.

Buchez presented a rational argument against the concept of sexual dualism, countering the mystical approach of Enfantin. Enfantin had claimed that God must be an hermaphrodite, since creation exhibited male/female dualism,[31] and he used this circuitous argument to support his theory of human sexual differentiation. However, Buchez insisted that the concept of God as male and female was unprecedented, and that there was no philosophical or theological justification for the notion of distinct male and female attributes. Instead, Buchez argued that each person was created in the image of God, and hence was endowed with both rational and sentimental power.[32] Since Buchez denied any essential differences between men and women, he also rejected the idea of allocating social roles on the basis of sex:

> But, when it is a question of social functions . . . it is no longer necessary that the two sexes should work together simultaneously. In this respect, the person has no sex; we only consider aptitude, regardless of whether it is contained in a black or white, a male or female skin.[33]

In Buchez's view, the liberation of women required their individual freedom to develop their aptitudes, not the establishment of an ideal model of 'woman', and the allocation of all women to predetermined roles based on that model.

Whereas Enfantin described sexual identity as an essential attribute, then, for Buchez it was a superficial one. He therefore applied a concept of equal individual rights to all, regardless of sex. From one perspective this was a radical approach, for it provided a theoretical basis for women (and men) to move beyond sexually-defined social roles. However, Buchez did not ponder the implications of his concept of equality, which apparently meant allowing women to become like men. Nor did he provide an adequate explanation of how the eventual 'equality' of the sexes might be achieved. He regarded education as an important element in the process, and argued that the opportunity for a woman to assume the supreme social office (that is, the Saint-Simonian Papacy) in her own right would be a sign of the liberation of all women.[34] Buchez's assertion that women would one day attain equality with men was a logical deduction from his belief in social progress and in the essential similarity of men and women. It did not address the immediate problem of men's power over women.

The argument between Enfantin and Buchez was a struggle between potential leaders for supremacy within the Saint-Simonian movement. Buchez sought to defend both the legitimacy of his own interpretation of the Saint-Simonian doctrine, and the primacy of logic and rational debate. Enfantin's rather obscure formulation was designed to secure his own authority, rather than the position of women. His mystical, or perhaps mystifying, language asserted his pretensions to spiritual authority and served his own interests, rather than the interests of informed and open debate.

Enfantin's theory of women's 'sentimental' nature was accepted by most of the other Saint-Simonians, and this concept pervaded Saint-Simonian writings on women in the 1829–31 period. According to the Saint-Simonians, woman's persuasive grace offset man's cold logic; woman's delicacy balanced man's force; woman's love contrasted with man's wisdom. Women and men brought different strengths to the social organism, as eye and heart played a different role from head and arm in the individual organism.[35] Saint-Simonian writers reiterated that the couple was more complete than either man or woman alone, since only the couple represented the 'complete loving being':

> . . . the efforts, the ideas, the sentiments of WOMAN to whom God made a special gift of tenderness, of wisdom and grace . . . form with the love, knowledge and strength of MAN the harmonious complement of the social being, the complete and symbolic manifestation of the infinite Being.[36]

Man and woman together formed a complete human being who was simultaneously *'energetic* and *devoted, perceptive* and *prudent, dexterous* and *strong'*.[37]

Buchez remained isolated on the question of women, reinforcing his disagreements with the other Saint-Simonians over the group's hierarchical structure and religious theories. Since orthodoxy had become a major preoccupation of the Saint-Simonians, Buchez's unwillingness to accept the new teachings was a cause for concern. Olinde Rodrigues complained to Enfantin that Buchez was becoming an 'obstacle':

> . . . he found your work on women very good, but instead of meditating on it, seeking to discuss its principal idea immediately, he threw himself into opposition, and, for two sessions, we have made no progress . . . It is the same on the question of GOD, *love, intelligence and matter* etc. etc. He does not advance, and repeats the same objections endlessly.[38]

Buchez's unwillingness to surrender reasoned argument for 'meditation', and his refusal to compromise on important issues, soon led him to separate from the group.[39] By this time, however, the question of defining woman's nature and her place within society had clearly assumed great prominence. Buchez's departure from the Saint-Simonian movement symbolised the victory of the 'special nature' theory of woman, which was to determine the roles formulated for women in Saint-Simonian theory and practice.

5

The Saint-Simonians Define Women's Social Roles

In late 1829, as the debate over woman's nature continued in Saint-Simonian correspondence, the sect began its attempt to recruit a popular following. Private correspondence with potential recruits was supplemented by newspapers and pamphlets, while broadsheets in large print were aimed at less skilful readers.[1] Oral propaganda also became important in this period. Halls were rented in various parts of Paris, and the message was pitched differently to appeal to different audiences: workers, students, even Italian refugees from the 1830 revolutions. The Saint-Simonians' concern with the misfortunes of the workers, and their provision of free medical services in the workers' quarters of Paris, enabled them to attract hundreds to their ranks. 'Missionaries' visited many parts of France spreading the word, and a number of Saint-Simonian groups were established throughout the country.[2]

Saint-Simon's followers had increasingly emphasised the religious elements of the doctrine, and their system of organisation imitated that of the Catholic Church. The new religion had a hierarchy and an Apostolic College. Devotees moved into a house in the rue Monsigny, where they lived as a community. The movement had its priests and preachers, and its leaders, Bazard and Enfantin, assumed the title of Pope. Lectures were known as sermons, and confession of one's past life was encouraged. However, the male-dominated Catholic Church provided an unsatisfactory model for the society the Saint-Simonians sought to establish. Since woman's nature complemented that of man, they argued, women should be integrated into all areas of society alongside men. Their roles as wives and mothers should be transformed to give them social, rather than private, significance. In addition, women should assume new roles as scientists, artists and industrials, and even as members of the most elite category, the priest-

82

hood. The ideal of the domestic wife was discarded and women's liberty was proclaimed a social benefit.

However, women's future roles were often described so vaguely that the precise functions they would perform on a daily basis were unclear. This reflected the fact that it was not so much 'women' as 'woman' that the Saint-Simonians sought to integrate into society. The notion of the couple as 'the social individual' enabled them to explore the nature of the new society they sought to establish, and to convey the importance they attached to 'feminine' attributes and qualities in creating social harmony. Though this provided a theoretical opening for women to assume new roles, practical difficulties were soon apparent. The image of a newly 'feminised' society functioned as metaphor rather than model.

TRANSFORMING WOMEN'S DOMESTIC ROLES

In examining women's roles the Saint-Simonians turned their attention first of all to the family. While *Le Producteur* had focused on women's domestic role to the virtual exclusion of other possibilities, the Saint-Simonians now emphasised the inadequacies of the domestic life, and sought to give it new shape and meaning. Their critique of marriage drew a sharp contrast between the status of wives in contemporary society and in the idealised future. Arranged marriages, which remained the norm amongst the property-owning classes, were condemned as a form of legal prostitution. Woman herself was a piece of property, sold to the highest bidder: ' . . . they haggle over you, they sell you, they hand you over, they reject you; marriage is nothing but a speculation, a deal, a business arrangement, a bargain'.[3] Contemporary marriage thus epitomised the major shortcomings of social organisation in general. It was not based on respect for the dignity and rights of others, but was governed by the forces of the marketplace. It was therefore conflictual by nature since it was designed to benefit some over others. Personal gain triumphed over concern for the greater social good. In the Saint-Simonian view, human compassion was suppressed and the emotions were perverted in their society, as women were suppressed within marriage and excluded from social influence.

The new Saint-Simonian marriage system would establish mutual affection and compatibility as the basis for legal unions, making marriage a model and a foundation for the harmonised society they sought to create. They insisted that the new marriage would perfect the Christian model, giving it a renewed sanctity and inviolability.[4] This assumed that women's 'total liberation' was compatible with the continued prohibition of divorce: an assumption later abandoned by Enfantin. However, by linking Saint-Simonian marriage with Christian marriage they offered reassurance to the timid, and defined the limits to change rather narrowly.

The key factor making Saint-Simonian marriage superior to the Christian model was the equal relationship it supposedly established between husband and wife.[5] Yet Saint-Simonian support for the 'equality' of spouses depended upon a particular definition of this term. Marriage would be based on a strict division of attributes and roles, and the source of each partner's self-fulfilment would be quite different. The husband would derive fulfilment from his achievements within the hierarchy, but the wife would find her reward in '. . . the husband himself, whose existence and rank she completes. . . '.[6] Self-negation was equated with self-fulfilment, and assigned as women's destiny.

The inequality of the marital relationship was quite explicit in Laurent's portrait of the ideal marriage, in which his fictional wife argued:

> . . . when I expressed the desire that anything which supposed or supported servant/master relationships between man and woman might disappear, it was not to establish between them that equality which produces rivalry, independence and isolation, but rather to increase the intensity of their sympathy, and make the union of two beings in a single entity easier and more complete . . . we only ask to be relieved of our status as minors in order to attach ourselves more strongly to our guardians; we only wish to be servants no longer in order to identify ourselves completely with our husbands . . . we wish that people would cease reminding us of our separate and imperfect personality, by continually placing us, as inferiors and incompetents, beneath those in whom we should enjoy the fullness of social life. . . .[7]

Women would no longer be subordinate to their husbands, then, but nor would they be equals. Equality was divisive, and 'equal' wives would be rivals of their husbands, independent of their control and influence. Laurent could not envisage marital harmony between equal spouses, any more than could Rousseau whom he invoked.[8] Marriage required hierarchy, and gender hierarchy presupposed male supremacy. The immersion of the wife in the person of her husband reasserted his dominance, and her disappearance as an individual confirmed his presence and completed his identity.

The Saint-Simonian ideal of marriage thus remained ensconced in a hierarchical concept of sex roles rather than an egalitarian one. This enabled marriage to represent '*the* MODEL *and* NUCLEUS *of all other [forms of] association*', since association was based firmly on inequality and hierarchy.[9] In addition, Enfantin privately defended the need for authority in both the domestic and social spheres:

> Equality is a dogma particularly useful to those on the lower rungs of the social ladder . . . no-one is blind enough to claim that heads are not needed in the family, in the workshop, in the city and for the fatherland. The influence of this dogma observed in practice, that is, in the events occurring around us, is clear enough. Paternal authority is meaningless; by virtue of wishing to be equal, husband and wife cannot reach agreement; the obedience of the domestic servant is never based on affection; the worker is engaged in open warfare with his masters, the citizen with his administrators, the people with the government.[10]

Only the establishment of legitimate hierarchies in all areas of human society would produce social harmony.

Saint-Simonian writings on the relationship between husbands and wives were contradictory, therefore, combining the rhetoric of equality with a denial that equality was possible in human relationships. By emphasising women's inspirational contribution to marriage, Saint-Simonian theory ostensibly countered the doctrine of women's subordination. However, male theorists made the interdependence of the couple in the new marriage relationship consistent with the maintenance of male authority. Woman's acceptance of her assimilation to her husband became the basis for marital harmony, a condition for the elimination of her servitude, just as the acceptance of hierarchy and lawful authority was a prerequisite for social harmony in general. The Saint-Simonian theory of marriage thus reasserted male power in the domestic realm. Furthermore, since men's dominance within marriage was to be maintained by the consent of women themselves it was even more oppressive than the model it was designed to replace.

DEFINING NEW SOCIAL ROLES FOR WOMEN

Marriage would mark the commencement of full participation in Saint-Simonian society, since individuals would undertake their social responsibilities as part of a couple. Wives would share with their husbands a variety of tasks, and assume the role of 'social motherhood'. Their unique qualities would be placed at society's disposal through a sex-typed division of labour:

> We are not setting out to change the nature of woman or man, but to develop it; woman must play a social role, in other words society must be organised in such a way that the special virtues and qualities of women . . . can be practised in the wider circle of the *social family*. According to the particular grace bestowed on their sex, man and woman must co-operate in the universal task, the moral, intellectual and physical improvement of the greatest number.
>
> In the temple, in the scientific or industrial workshop, man without woman is henceforth incomplete.[11]

The new Saint-Simonian marriage thus had a social purpose, not a private or familial one. The family's interests would be harmonised with the demands and needs of society, not opposed to them.

The social orientation of Saint-Simonian marriage was demonstrated by a critique of the role of motherhood. Women's restriction to this role was seen as a consequence of *l'esprit de famille*. While private concerns predominated, Gustave d'Eichthal argued, man would remain a master and woman a servant, limited to the 'purely animal and servile functions' of childbearing, breastfeeding and domestic work.[12] He did not explain how or why the reproductive division of labour became a social hierarchy. Nor did he acknowledge the crucial importance of childbearing and rearing to the development of the social affections he sought to promote. He simply argued that the development of social affections would end the abasement of women.

Not only was maternity an 'animal function', motherly love was a selfish and individualistic affection, according to the Saint-

Simonians. In Enfantin's view, it was a hallmark of primitive society:

> Maternal love *alone* can only *entirely* fill the heart of a woman in a savage family, without a God, without morality, without friends, without brothers, but not in a human *society* . . . it is fine to be a wife, to be a mother, but above all it is necessary to be a woman, and to have a heart open to the joys and sorrows with which God surrounds us to raise us to himself.[13]

Whereas motherhood had been eulogised in *Le Producteur* as the epitome of altruism, it was now condemned as self-indulgent. In reality, few women could afford the style of life the Saint-Simonians attacked, devoted solely to the care of their families. However, the image of the 'social mother' suggested new scope for women's talents, and promised a new 'maternal' society where the weak and the helpless would find succour. Compassion and affection would transform the unforgiving and ruthless world portrayed by the Saint-Simonians, where 'womanly' and maternal virtues found expression only behind closed doors. The range of roles envisaged for women reflected the Saint-Simonians' definition of them as sentimental, intuitive and compassionate. In theory, the admission of 'woman' to the public sphere changed its configuration and highlighted the superior characteristics of the new order. However, the Saint-Simonians' insistence on a sex-typed division of tasks created theoretical contradictions and confusion, and left in doubt the place which women would occupy in real life.

The belief that women were innately 'sentimental' justified their presence, first of all, within the 'sentimental series',[14] that is, in the arts and the Saint-Simonian priesthood. The Saint-Simonians argued that the arts' ability to stimulate the emotions was currently cause for concern. Unbridled passion was dangerous, hence the poor reputation of actresses whose beauty gave them great emotional power over their audiences.[15] Nevertheless, women's participation would assist the moral transformation which the arts were destined to undergo. In Saint-Simonian society the arts would become a thoroughly moral force, assisting social leaders to instil the desired principles in their people.[16] The moral role of the arts in society thus parallelled the moral role of women, making the two particularly compatible. The woman artist would fill a semi-religious role in the new society, and would find her place in the temple:

> . . . that is where all the women will come to assemble around [the priestess], in the rows of a legitimate hierarchy; [women] who are worthy to support the religious and social movement by their noble ability to perceive the future of humanity, and by the power of enchantment given them by eloquence, poetry, and the other arts which are confined today to museums and theatres.[17]

Although the Saint-Simonians largely ignored the contribution women had so far made to the arts,[18] the archetypal artist was beautiful, religious, prophetic and emotional: in Saint-Simonian terms, the artist was 'female'. In ascribing to women a role within the artistic sphere, the Saint-Simonians reiterated their own assumptions about female nature, and portrayed a society in which the feelings were reinstated in value. Like women, the arts would be assigned an appropriate sphere and a legitimate means of influence in society. Rather than undermining values and morals they would reinforce them. The 'woman artist' of the future symbolised the enhancement of moral power, and its realisation within society.

Women's admission to the Saint-Simonian priesthood would serve a similar purpose, highlighting the transformation which patterns of government and authority would undergo in the new order. In considering this issue the Saint-Simonians were strongly influenced by contemporary events, for in 1830 Paris was once again torn by revolution. The Saint-Simonians acknowledged the legitimate grievances which provoked it, and some even took part in the uprising which overthrew Charles X.[19] Furthermore, they were well aware of the unrest which periodically besieged the workers' quarters in the centres of French industry, and which was consistently quelled at sabre-point. The Saint-Simonians argued that a new style of 'holy authority' was necessary to prevent such violent confrontation. The admission of women to the priesthood demonstrated their commitment to a social authority resting on persuasion and compassion, rather than on force and brutality.

Women's suitability for the priesthood was aided by the Saint-Simonians' redefinition of the institution envisaged by Saint-

Simon. In his theory, the priests were the intellectuals and scientists of society, and their superior intellectual gifts justified their social leadership. However, the Saint-Simonians elevated 'sentimental' qualities over intellectual qualities in the social hierarchy: 'It is from love, we have said, that the priest receives his mission . . . [sic] So we attribute the supreme direction of society to sentiment, to those men in whom this faculty is dominant . . .'.[20] The priesthood would therefore comprise those men who most resembled women, and women's special capacity for love made them clear candidates for priestly office as well. Their elevation to that task was also justified by the theory of separate natures. Together the priest and priestess formed the 'Holy COUPLE, divine symbol of the UNION of *wisdom* and *beauty*, [the] loving ANDROGYNE . . .'.[21]

The priestesses were superior women so the Saint-Simonians envisaged them excelling in the 'female' traits of beauty, sensitivity to others and intuition. In theory both male and female priests were dominated by sentiment, but males alone were attributed with a rational capacity as well. This distinction justified a division of labour in the Saint-Simonian priesthood:

> While her husband governs humanity in its entirety or one of its parts, depending on his level in the hierarchy, regulating its PROGRESS according to the *past* which he *knows*, as the companion of the priest, she measures this progress against the *future* which she *hopes for* . . . and the political regulation, the moral instruction which directs society, their joint product, belongs to *tradition* through the priest who is its faithful trustee, to *prophecy* through the priestess who is its intrument.[22]

The male priest played a role defined as that of government, one dependent on his rational capacity and understanding. The priestess incorporated within herself the progressive qualities of the future, and her priestly role was one of living prophecy, intuitive guidance of progress.

Women's role in 'government' was thus made to conform to prior definitions of female nature, but it also served to define the new mode of social authority. The Saint-Simonian priestly couples would have 'the heart of a father and the compassion of a mother'.[23] They would exert a new 'parental' mode of authority which would be accepted by those subject to it, and this would provide the basis for social harmony. The incorporation of a maternal presence into the priesthood thus made possible government by persuasion. In the future, the Saint-Simonians explained, to govern would mean to win over, not to constrain and enslave others. Women's compassion and conciliatory power would become particularly important:

> . . . today no-one can command by the use of violence, men no longer accept imposed authority; before obeying, they want to love and understand. So, who more than woman knows how to make herself obeyed by gentleness and persuasion? What word inspires tender respect and conviction more than hers does? Who more than she possesses that fine and delicate tact, which so clearly detects what is acceptable and what is repugnant? Therefore, woman can govern; because, in the future, to govern is to make oneself loved and understood.[24]

The Saint-Simonian definition of womanliness not only indicated women's potential for a role of authority, then, but made them models for the new mode of government. The depiction of the feminine was a depiction of the qualities of the new order, and highlighted its differences from the old 'masculine' order of violence and brute force. The vision of a 'feminised' priesthood thus foreshadowed an era of social harmony which was impossible within a male-dominated society.

The division between intuition and reason which the Saint-Simonians had emphasised when considering the priesthood became even more significant in their discussion of women scientists. Their theory of the couple required women's entry into this field on different terms from men, so the female scientist was defined not as rational but as intuitive. This was best expressed by Charles Lemonnier, who asserted that women's 'discerning and active enquiry . . . almost resembles divination. Woman springs toward discovery with a swift and almost instinctive movement'.[25] Although Enfantin had denied that the distinction between men and women was a clear dichotomy between reason and sentiment, the Saint-Simonians' definition of female intelligence effectively denied rationality to women.

The emphasis on female intuition had positive implications for women because it gave them a particular capacity for 'genius': a capacity usually denied by other theorists.[26] The Saint-Simonian view of intellect distinguished between 'conception' and 'verification', linking the former with insight, creativity and imagination, and the latter with methodical analysis.[27] Imaginative intelligence was defined as 'genius' and had priority over the more pedestrian functions of 'verification'. Initially, Saint-Simonian theory stressed the dual operation of conception and verification in the individual scientist. With their increasing emphasis on male/female complementarity, however, the dichotomy between these intellectual functions became a female/male dichotomy. Women were attributed with creativity and imaginative power, and men with observation and reason. The scientific couple formed a powerful force for the advancement of knowledge, indicating once again the superiority of new social forms over those of the past.

Genius was defined in terms of 'female' intellectual characteristics, yet most of the geniuses identified by the Saint-Simonians were men. Jesus, Saint-Simon, Newton and Chateaubriand were amongst the most important.[28] The only woman identified as a true genius was Madame de Staël. Her entitlement to the position was attributed to her pacifism, her religious sentiment and her implicit challenge, as a public figure, to the subjection of women.[29] In practice, then, the Saint-Simonians defined as geniuses not those who demonstrated particular intellectual characteristics, but those who foreshadowed the 'genius' of the Saint-Simonians. They singled out those who had advanced the causes they themselves espoused: religion, science or the emancipation of women.

While Madame de Staël's superiority was unchallenged, Charles Lemonnier maintained that there had been a number of other women of genius, whose work demonstrated the 'great power which can develop in women'. However, he dismissed these unnamed women as social misfits:

The women who have succeeded until now in piercing the gloomy vault of humiliation and subjection which weighed on their heads, in order to reach daylight and join the ranks of the famous, have been obliged to become *men*; and since the difference between men and women is too deeply engraved, they never managed to overcome it with impunity: while wishing to stop being women, they could not become men, they became monsters. . . .[30]

Lemonnier attempted to draw a contrast between the past, when there were no appropriate intellectual roles for women, and the future, when they would assume such roles. He did not explain in what ways women's past achievements were those which naturally belonged to men. After all, if genius was a 'female' quality the nature and incidence of 'male' genius was the phenomenon requiring explanation. However, his analysis emphasised the possibility of transgression for female intellectuals. While there would be no need for 'monsters' in the future, the warning against divergence from the female norm remained pertinent since gender difference maintained its importance.

Lemonnier asserted that women would fill a specifically 'female' role as scientists, and he distinguished their social and inspirational function from the abstract thought and problem-solving function of the male scientists:

> . . . precisely because woman, even she who is most suited to scientific elaboration, even she who most loves and admires works of this order, cannot isolate herself completely from the world, and live only by abstractions, as man does, her role in the intellectual couple is to recall man continually to a useful and social direction; to grasp and present to him the improvements whose importance and usefulness she perceives better than he: she will pose the problems, man will seek the solutions; she will introduce and prepare the work which man will carefully complete.[31]

Compassion and sensitivity thus became the hallmarks of female scientists, the emotional content of their 'intellectual' role contrasting with the rational role played by the male intellectuals. However, the incorporation of women into science highlighted the fact that the emotions were now considered relevant to that field. Female scientists, compassionate and altruistic, perceived and responded to community needs. 'Objectivity' would be tempered by consideration of the social implications of science.

Lemonnier's article was the only Saint-Simonian study of women as scientists and intellectuals, and it illustrated the ambiguity which characterised Saint-Simonian thinking on this issue.

He distinguished between the 'proper intellectuals, charged with perfecting and elaborating science', and the larger group who 'explain, popularise the discoveries of the former, and by instruction, make them common property'.[32] Although he had noted women's capacity for intellectual discovery, he argued that relatively few women would become 'proper' intellectuals. In Lemonnier's account, the majority of women scientists were suited only for the lower function of scientific teaching: ' . . . for woman's intelligence, swift and unfettered, active and impressionable, lends itself admirably to receiving and passing on truth.'[33] Since 'swift and unfettered thought' distinguished the creative power of the genius, Lemonnier showed some confusion in assigning women to the lower intellectual ranks on this basis, while men's talent for testing and verifying hypotheses did not justify their allocation to the role of discovery. However, in outlining the roles of men and women scientists, Lemonnier established a hierarchical structure which reaffirmed male dominance. Men were perceived as naturally suited to the role of true intellectuals, while women were ideally suited to reproducing the ideas and discoveries of men. In theory, then, the Saint-Simonians elevated intuitive intelligence over analytical reason. However, the assumption of gender hierarchy conflicted with this perspective, as Lemonnier's study indicated. Men were assigned to the superior tasks, even though this contradicted the theoretical formulation. A hierarchy was maintained between 'masculine' and 'feminine' forms of intelligence. The superiority of reason was validated by its masculine characterisation, while masculinity was reaffirmed by its identification with rational power.

According to Saint-Simonian theory, the majority of the population would take their places amongst the lower-ranked industrials in the society of the future. They stressed the value of such work, and although Saint-Simon himself had been vague about the role of women as industrials, his followers looked favourably on this prospect by 1830. However, women's role as industrials received little serious analysis from the Saint-Simonians. Despite the fact that working women were beginning to attend Saint-Simonian meetings and enrol in their ranks, they showed little awareness of the problems faced by such women, or of the issues which were posed by the theory of the industrial couple. Their limited discussion of women's participation in industry focused on the particular qualities which made women suitable for that role, but they failed to address the practical issues which it raised. Once again, the idea of the 'woman industrial' offered a sketch of a perfect future, rather than a guide to women's lifestyles.

The Saint-Simonians highlighted the 'progressive' traits of women as workers, thus pointing to the characteristics of industry in the future. Enfantin, intent on stressing the complementarity of male and female natures, emphasised women's intuitive recognition of what work needed doing, and contrasted this with the practical role of men in meeting that need.[34] Charles Lemonnier also attributed women's suitability for the industrial workplace to their 'progressive' traits, but he identified these as practical skills. This was an interesting argument, both because it contradicted the argument of Enfantin, and because he had previously assigned women to a subordinate rank in the sciences partly on the grounds of poor practical aptitude. Their practical talents were apparently of an inferior order, suited to the ranks of the industrials rather than the scientists. According to Lemonnier, the development of industry was particularly favourable to the participation of women. Industry was beginning to rely less on brute force, and to require the talents of dexterity, carefulness and skill which women possessed in abundance. This was borne out, he argued, by the role women were already playing in Paris and the industrial and commercial towns of the North as manual workers, book-keepers and workshop supervisors.[35]

His argument was partly correct. Women's participation in waged labour was increasing, and in towns such as Lille and Roubaix the gradual mechanisation of cotton-spinning created new jobs for women in the mills. The same was true in the silk industry of Lyon.[36] Lemonnier's analysis suggested, however, that women experienced an improvement in their working conditions by becoming wage-earners, but this is difficult to substantiate. In family-run workshops women were generally subordinate as workers. They were often poorly paid, and family members earned no wage as such. Nevertheless, the small scale of the workplace and its personal relationships prevented the grosser abuses of the factory or mill. Sexual harrassment and exploitation, the speed of the machinery and the dangers of injury added new problems for women wage-earners in those environments. Their suitability for the new industry might have been justified by their 'dexterity', but women's cheapness and relative docility were probably more important to employers. The fact that women's 'special talents' made them a poorly paid and disposable workforce, rather than a valued and well-rewarded one, was overlooked in Lemonnier's brief analysis.[37]

D'Eichthal's contrast between the new and old patterns of women's work also glamourised the emergent model in order to promote women's role as waged workers:

> Today as peaceful labour, which was formerly concentrated in the confines of the *family*, has gradually moved into the *whole social order* . . . woman must continue the role she played in primitive times; she must still preside over peaceful work with man; but when it has abandoned the *family*, she must no longer remain there; she must move with it into the heart of society. Let the *wife*, relieved of *the servitude of domestic chores* . . . enter, with her *husband*, the various paths which God has opened to the peaceful activity of humanity.[38]

This image of women in the workshop acknowledged the fact that women had always worked at income-producing tasks, even when they were not wage-earners. It also reflected the theory that all must fill a productive role in the new society and that they would do so as part of a couple, although it exaggerated the extent to which industry had 'abandoned' the family by this time. Nevertheless, d'Eichthal's account exemplified the inadequacy of Saint-Simonian theory on women's roles as workers. In encouraging women to move into industrial work d'Eichthal contrasted its productive character with the 'sterility' of domestic labour. Yet women had been relieved of domestic labour only by Saint-Simonian *fiat*, and an alternative system had not been investigated despite some experiments with communal living. Women's role as paid workers was also discussed in isolation from their role as wives and mothers. The Saint-Simonians criticised the 'non-productive' character of women's domestic work, but proposed no alternative pattern of childrearing and domestic labour. They thus ignored the potential conflict between women's participation in work outside the home, and their responsibility for children and for the moral guidance of the family.

D'Eichthal's emphasis on the peaceful character of the workplace denied the very real industrial conflict of the period, and the gender conflict which arose as women workers replaced men in some industries.[39] However, it foreshadowed the change which the Saint-Simonians associated with the new order, and especially with the increased participation of women in the industrial sphere. They believed that women would bring to industry the virtues of their special nature, and find there an outlet for their talents. References to the 'feminisation' of industry expressed the Saint-Simonian aspiration to transform the world of work, instilling not only the new skills and techniques of advanced industry, but the co-operative, harmonious and peaceful social relations appropriate to the new order.

Saint-Simonian theories on transforming the social roles of women reflected their belief in the progressive nature of history. The subordination of women and their confinement to domesticity belonged to the era of the reign of force. In the new era of association the subjection of women would cease and they would assume a broad range of social roles.[40] Nevertheless, the implications of re-shaping the social roles of women were not easily accepted, even in theory, and the extent to which their roles would alter in practical terms remained doubtful.[41] The hesitancy with which a change in women's roles was contemplated by the Saint-Simonians was exemplified by Barrault:

> . . . we only offer [woman] a place in the peaceful society of the future . . . Would we force her to sink beneath the weight of this immense collection of laws, by having her don legal robes . . .? Would we wish to call her either to the chaos of elected assemblies . . . or to the violent, bitter, sterile debates of the courtroom? Would we wish to impose power on her, when brutally or callously, politics forces the masses onto the battlefield . . .? Finally, would we desire for her the rewards of the arts and sciences, or the fruits of industry, when the field in which they must be reaped is a bloody battleground? God preserve us from ever having sought for her anything which might destroy her dignity or her gentleness! We declare that woman today is legitimately excluded from social office. But we ask, is this a condemnation of woman, or is it not rather an express condemnation of your society?[42]

Men's power to determine what the social roles of women should be was made explicit here. Woman herself remained outside the debate, confined to the third person. By denying any intention to 'impose' power on women, or 'force' them to assume new roles, Barrault obscured the real issue, which was men's exclusion of women from all these positions. He implied that women themselves did not aspire to any alteration in their assigned place and, in order to fend off criticism, delayed change until an indeterminate future. This position was a contradictory one. If the application of 'women's' values was to be the mechanism for transforming society, the exclusion of women from social influence until after that transformation had occurred was illogical and self-defeating. Woman appears, not as the agent of change or as its intended beneficiary, but as its symbol. The prospect of new and active roles for women was largely illusory, and this was to create tensions within the Saint-Simonian movement as women sought to grasp the opportunities which they believed the theory offered them.

FROM THEORY TO PRACTICE: WOMEN IN THE SAINT-SIMONIAN MOVEMENT, 1829–c.1834

Between 1829 and 1831 the presence of women became a notable feature of the Saint-Simonian movement, and they continued to play an active role until its slow disintegration in the mid 1830s. The women developed their own theoretical insights and practical applications of the Saint-Simonian doctrine. Not only were relations amongst the women sometimes strained by these developments, but disagreements arose with the men over the theory of the social roles of women, and consequently over the practical roles which women should fill within the movement. While many men found women's new social presence disconcerting, many women found the space they were allocated too restrictive, and sought to give a more practical form to Saint-Simonian adulation of the 'female' principle.

During 1829 women began attending the Saint-Simonians' weekly meetings, and formed their own discussion group and correspondence network.[43] Claire Bazard, the wife of one of the sect's leaders, was the central figure among the women, and she was joined by a number of the wives and sisters of prominent Saint-Simonian men. Women's participation increased during 1830, and by October nearly two hundred women were attending the Saint-Simonian meetings at the *Salle Taitbout* in Paris, although only about fifteen were taking instruction.[44] As the Saint-Simonian school began to attract working-class participants, women like Suzanne Voilquin and Adrienne Mallard were converted along with their husbands.[45] By August 1831, 220 workers had professed the Saint-Simonian faith, including about 100 women.[46]

Women's growing participation in the Saint-Simonian movement was no doubt due to a combination of factors, as male interest in including women in the group coincided with increasing female interest in Saint-Simonian teachings. The religious style adopted by the Saint-Simonian school may have been particularly attractive to women, whose education predisposed them to a religious outlook.[47] However, this aspect repelled devout Catholic women,[48] and also posed an obstacle to the conversion of radical women. 1830 and its aftermath drew women of Republican sympathies like Jeanne Deroin and Suzanne Voilquin towards an opposition movement, not towards a covert clerical party.[49] Nevertheless, the conversion experience could assume religious dimensions, offering a welcome focus of commitment to those who did not have a strong faith in Catholicism. Religion was deeply ingrained, for instance, in Suzanne Voilquin, raised by a devout mother and with a limited convent schooling.[50] Disillusionment with Catholicism left an opening which Saint-Simonianism could fill, and provided a set of ideas and a language through which the Saint-Simonian experience could be interpreted and expressed.

Some women were attracted towards the Saint-Simonian movement by its commitment to the cause of the workers,[51] and others also responded favourably to the Saint-Simonians' belief in ending the subordination of women. One aspiring member had learnt from the Saint-Simonians that 'the Eternal One who created me has not condemned me to absolute nothingness because he made me a woman',[52] while Jeanne Deroin was even more emphatic:

> The slavery of woman, the most odious, the most immoral of all abuses, is the one against which I have always protested most strongly; the one which inspired in me the greatest indignation. Consequently of all the principles of the doctrine the emancipa-

tion of woman is the one which has contributed most powerfully to my decision to adopt Saint-Simonism as soon as my reason is sufficiently enlightened.[53]

Women were admitted to the hierarchy of the new religion from March 1830, and by mid-1831 they were represented there at all levels. Some of them shared in the work being undertaken by the men, assisting with the instruction of others and helping to run the dining halls and other services provided for the workers.[54] The idea of public authority for women was so unusual at that time that the Saint-Simonians needed to offer a public explanation when Claire Bazard first officiated at a Saint-Simonian ceremony. The speaker pointed out that Madame Bazard had assumed her role not through special privilege, but on the grounds of her capacity, which provided the only criterion for rank in Saint-Simonian society. This was described as the beginning of a new era for women:

> Yes, my daughters, it is the initiation of your entire sex to social life, it is the admission of the mother and wife, not as *subject* but as ASSOCIATE, to the labours and dignity of the father and husband; it is the achievement by half the human race of the rank due to it in the hierarchy of a peaceful society; it is the promotion of women to the place which Providence reserved for them in endowing them with a more acute sensibility, a more delicate perceptiveness, a more gracious or more beautiful form; it is the reign of God that THIS WOMAN proclaims here loudly BY HER VERY PRESENCE.[55]

Her promotion also highlighted men's power, however, as they offered women 'initiation' and 'admission' to positions they controlled.

Women participated in the conversion efforts of the Saint-Simonians in the early 1830s. This was considered particularly appropriate work for women, who could touch hearts which male logic could not penetrate.[56] Claire Bazard was given the task of winning back the schismatic Philippe Buchez in 1830,[57] for instance, but her task was to make him receptive to the truth: to prepare him for the rational arguments which would come from men.[58] The ideal conversion team was a couple, who would be able to bring even difficult types to the new religion.[59] Nevertheless, women's increasing success in instructing and converting others was the subject of comment at a Saint-Simonian general meeting in mid-1831,[60] and their contributions to the propaganda effort continued throughout the early 1830s.

In attempting to convert other women, the Saint-Simonian women emphasised the benefits they were promised by the new religion. At first they generally reiterated the teachings put forward by the men, stressing their prospective roles as partners of men in the new society. Claire Bazard highlighted the leadership opportunity which the priesthood would offer to 'those women who, excluded by the condition of society from a more unusual life, exhaust their capacity for devotion within the family home without finding fulfilment'.[61] Palmyre Bazard emphasised that women would participate freely in industry, science and the arts in the ideal society, while still fulfilling their 'highest duties' as mothers.[62] How these roles would be reconciled she did not explain, any more than the male theorists had.

Some of the newer proletarian recruits attempted to give the Saint-Simonian doctrine a more immediate relevance for women. They sought not merely a glorious new world in the future, but a solution to their present problems. This approach was well illustrated by the newspaper, *The Women's Tribune*, founded by the seamstresses Marie-Reine Guindorf and Jeanne-Désirée Véret.[63] It appeared at irregular intervals between 1832 and 1834, providing the first sustained female voice on the Saint-Simonian doctrine, and expressing a primarily proletarian viewpoint. *The Women's Tribune* was open only to female contributors and was specifically intended to make known women's views on all issues.[64] This emphasis reflected Jeanne-Désirée's belief in the importance and legitimacy of a female doctrinal perspective:

> I would like to relieve the women who are capable of assisting in our work from the excessive Saint-Simonian preoccupation which prevents them having their own ideas . . . women must add to [the doctrine], and in order to do so it is essential that they look beyond it and that they summarise it themselves, and no longer according to what men have written, besides, what women have to say is as different as the natures of men and women [are different].[65]

Women's 'difference' became a source of legitimation, justifying divergence, disagreement and a more vigorous criticism of women's oppression.

The editors of *The Women's Tribune* aimed to encourage women to protest their subordination and assert their demands. One function of the *Tribune* was therefore 'consciousness-raising'. Writers outlined the injustices in the social position of women, countering male arguments against female liberty and exposing strategies used to silence women.[66] The *Tribune* condemned the gender hierarchy enshrined in the Civil Code, and the sexual oppression of women, whether as wives or prostitutes, which it fostered. Women's exclusion from education was discussed frequently, and self-help projects to compensate were promoted.[67] A detailed proposal for communal housing for single women – a response to their sexual and economic vulnerability – attempted to find an immediate solution to their problems.[68] The *Tribune* also defended political rights for women, and their rights as workers,[69] and urged the formation of a united women's lobby:

> Right now the men of all factions are forming associations to make their views prevail; we women must also spread our ideas, to make people understand that *our* EQUALITY *with man*, far from humbling them, as some seem to believe, will on the contrary be the measure of happiness for all . . . there are many [men] who deny that we can ever become their equals; we will only make them change their minds when we come before them with solid achievements, when we form a clearly united body, *all* with the *same aspiration*, the *same objective*. Women, understand this clearly, it is through association that we will achieve this goal. . . .[70]

There was, however, no single view even amongst the paper's editors. The *Tribune* actively welcomed the expression of diverse opinions, seeing debate as an essential prelude to policy-making.

The *Tribune* defined women's oppression as both sex-based and class-based. Proletarian women shared the legal, educational and political subjection, and the economic exploitation, of male workers. However they also suffered as women in a male-dominated society, hence their affinity with bourgeois women. Writers stressed the plight of proletarian women, but they also pointed out that women's oppression overlapped class boundaries. Women had common cause, they suggested, on issues such as marriage law reform and education, and in acquiring their fundamental rights as free beings.[71] The *Tribune* acknowledged that the privileges of bourgeois women were gained at the expense of their proletarian counterparts. But rather than viewing bourgeois women as beneficiaries of the property-based society, they noted that all women were its victims in varying ways. Even the comforts of bourgeois life could not compensate for enslavement, and the Saint-Simonian women set out to show that only a total transformation of society offered hope of freedom to all. The causes of women and of the workers were inherently connected: ' . . . let us not forget, our fate is bound up with that of the people, and our emancipation can only come about in conjunction with theirs . . .'.[72]

If women's rights depended on rights for workers, the converse was also true according to the *Tribune*: an improvement in the condition of workers was inconceivable without attention to the rights of women. Only the liberty of women could complete the task of social transformation underway:

> It is by liberating woman that you will liberate the worker, their interests are linked and the security of all classes depends on their freedom . . . We say to the politicians: God has not allowed you to overthrow unjust privileges only to stop half-way and turn to your benefit alone the weapons he gave you for the benefit of all. You will have much difficulty and little success if you continue to subordinate his will to your own, if you maintain the old idea that woman is only fit to bear children, clean a man's house and provide his pleasure; if you don't incorporate woman and the people into all branches of the social order, according to each one's capacity. . . .[73]

The *Tribune* gave favourable coverage to the theories of Fourier and Owen, and reported on the activities of Owenite feminists in England.[74] However, while writers acknowledged the efforts of some men on women's behalf, they insisted that women themselves should claim the credit for the work of liberation. Whatever male theorists had contributed, women's own desire to be free remained the most significant factor:

> Words of advice, counsel, opinions of amazing diversity reach us from every side. Each one on his own authority declares himself our liberator, and wishes to set us free after his own

fashion. Be that as it may, I am pursuing the goal which I have set for myself, without wavering to one side or the other. Let no one consider me under the influence of any system; whoever else desires our liberty, I wish it, that's what matters. I wanted it before knowing the Saint-Simonians, I wanted it before knowing M. Fourier. I desire it despite those who oppose it, and I am perhaps working towards it separately from many who seek it. But I am free. For long enough men have advised us, guided us, dominated us: it's up to us now to walk the path of progress without supervision. It's up to us to fashion our own liberty by ourselves . . . without the aid of our masters.[75]

The women of the *Tribune* attempted to assert their independence of thought by exchanging the title *Saint-Simoniennes* for that of 'new women', and signing articles only by their given names.[76] They also stressed the importance of having women work separately from men in order to allow them to gain confidence and experience.[77]

The Women's Tribune grew out of and built upon the Saint-Simonian experience, but it also challenged the men's theory and practice by exposing their shortcomings. Much of its criticism was directed at the broader society rather than at the Saint-Simonians, but the paper's existence, and often its tone, also called into question the harmonious gender relations posited in the Saint-Simonian emphasis on 'the couple'. Men's ambivalence about women's involvement in the Saint-Simonian movement had been evident before the appearance of *The Women's Tribune*. On several occasions men had criticised women's progression within the hierarchy since it did not conform to the male pattern, and female leadership and competition for promotion caused discontent amongst the more lowly-ranked men.[78]

Claire Bazard's elevation to the exclusive 'private council' evoked ill-feeling even within the College, as had several earlier male appointments, and attempts were made to have her surrender her administrative duties.[79] Despite her position of prominence, however, her power remained limited and she found it difficult to have her views taken seriously. The debate over the marriage of Jules Lechevalier to the actress Léontine Fay, when Enfantin and Bazard gave permission without even consulting her, demonstrated this powerlessness. Her protests, which were based on concern that all the Saint-Simonian women would be brought into disrepute by the admission of actresses into the movement, were overruled by them.[80]

Claire Bazard's installation as leader of the women had been based on the premise that she would reproduce amongst them the practices and ideas already developed by the men, but she admitted her failure to achieve this goal:

> Hierarchy is a meaningless word for us, it bears no fruit; our meetings take place in tumult and disorder, in such chaos that it would be impossible to tell the inferiors from the superior, for the mother cannot impose respect on the children, the children cannot submit to the Mother. We neither command nor obey, like slaves who recognise no rank amongst themselves.[81]

This 'chaos' had several causes. Firstly, it stemmed from the women's determination to debate issues, rather than accept passively what was imposed from above. They questioned the definition of legitimate authority, and insisted on the right of inferiors to scrutinise the conduct of their superiors.[82] Women's resistance to female authority also reflected ambition and competition for positions of prominence, particularly since many women believed that there were as yet no genuinely superior women. This opinion was voiced in Paris about Claire Bazard and Aglaé Saint-Hilaire, and was repeated later in Lyon when Clorinde Rogé attempted to install herself as leader there.[83] The view that women's talents were undeveloped and their capacities unknown may help to explain the more ready acceptance of the authority of Enfantin. However, as Claire Bazard suggested, male authority over women also had an air of legitimacy that female authority did not, in a male-dominated society: 'We only recognise dignity and power in the master, we only feel obedience and respect for the master, and the master for us is man'.[84] The reluctance of some women to accept the authority of others also resulted from class divisions. As Suzanne Voilquin later commented, her decision to remain outside the hierarchy had a social basis: ' . . . my heart could never utter the name of Mother in addressing one of these ladies'.[85] The politics of the women's group reminded the Saint-Simonians that their aspiration for class harmony was far from achieved. It also sat rather uneasily beside the appeals in *The Women's Tribune* for women to unite across class lines.

Women continually confronted men's misgivings about their separate activities. Enfantin had expressed some support for *The Women's Tribune*,[86] but he was less enthusiastic about Cécile Fournel's request that another periodical, the *Livre des Actes*, be produced by women. In private he expressed his doubts about the women's ability to run the paper successfully, although he admitted his willingness to be pleasantly surprised.[87] Men's acceptance of women's full participation in Saint-Simonian affairs was not readily obtained either. Suzanne Voilquin had to make a special request that women be present at all general meetings, participate in all ceremonies, and have a recognised role in 'all that is decided within the Saint-Simonian family'.[88] Her proposal for a family council consisting of both men and women, which would adjudicate on disputes and redress grievances within the Saint-Simonian family, indicated her dissatisfaction with women's lack of authority, especially in matters which concerned them directly. The men were generally wary of women's attempts to exert any influence within the movement:

> . . . our brothers, quite astonished by the revolution which has occurred in themselves . . . and the enormous step which they have allowed us to take, watch us, listen to us, I would almost say *fear us*. Since authority has always been arbitrary, despotic, they in turn do not yet understand what place we might occupy without infringing their rights: they see a tendency towards usurpation on our part, when we dare to manifest a *will*. In general men, even a *little* within the [Saint-Simonian] family, view women as governments view the people; they are *afraid* of us and do not yet *love* us. They speak of disorder. . . .[89]

The political metaphors of despotism and revolution, authority and disorder, illuminated sharply the gender conflict from which the Saint-Simonian movement was not immune. As Suzanne Voilquin commented, it was unlikely that, simply by becoming a Saint-Simonian, a man would have 'forgotten thirty years of life, appearing henceforth to the world as an angelic, completely regenerated being!'.[90]

Saint-Simonian theory sought to justify and explain the presence of women within the group by emphasising women's talents and special gifts. It also sought to deal with the practical issues which women's membership presented by exploring the actual and potential roles of Saint-Simonian women. However, the practical implications of women's emancipation proved a source of conflict and tension within the Saint-Simonian movement. The theory presented an image of an harmonious future characterised by co-operation between the sexes, and a clearly defined division of power and authority. In reality the distribution of power and authority was extremely contentious. Women's attempts to develop both the theory and practice of Saint-Simonianism according to their own insights challenged the neatness of the men's theoretical overview, and the male right to define the identity and the social roles of women. These contests were to continue after 1831 when the Saint-Simonian movement was further divided, and finally destroyed, by conflict over the moral question.

6

The 'New Moral Law' and Women's Sexual Roles

From December 1831, the distinction in Saint-Simonian theory between male and female natures took a new form. Enfantin's speculations had led him to distinguish between 'steadfast' and 'changeable' personality types, that is, between people who were inherently monogamous and others who were naturally promiscuous. Women were identified predominantly with the 'changeable' type and came to personify 'the flesh'. This characterisation of women was hardly new, but the Saint-Simonians' call for the 'rehabilitation of the flesh', that is, for a positive valuation of the passions, ran counter to the early nineteenth-century attempt to confine and restrain them. The 'disorderly' impact of sexuality, and its particular association with women ('the sex') had been used to justify the exclusion of women from public life from the late eighteenth century, so the redefinition of sexuality as a beneficial social force provided further justification for a public place for women.[1]

The emphasis on female sexuality added a new dimension to the roles women were assigned by the Saint-Simonians. Women would now employ beauty, attraction and desirability to influence men's actions. If women were identified with 'the body', the body was offered wider influence within society. Nevertheless, the dominant images of 'the sexual woman', whether faithful wife or independent lover, were not those of female autonomy and power but of service to men. Enfantin's 'new moral law' challenged the prevailing male-created prescriptions, but it substituted another prescriptive model which many Saint-Simonians rejected. A struggle ensued, crossing class and sex lines, to define 'the sexual woman' and her social position.

THE ORIGINS AND DEVELOPMENT OF THE 'NEW MORAL LAW'

Enfantin began to contemplate a 'new moral law' as early as 1829. At that time the Saint-Simonians were already committed to 'the rehabilitation of matter' through a vague pantheism which defined both spirit and matter as manifestations of God.[2] However, Enfantin's reading of Fourier, who sent the Saint-Simonian leader copies of his works in May 1829, apparently had a strong influence.[3] Enfantin began to link the 'rehabilitation of matter' with sexuality, and with the sanctification of woman's sexual role. He made this connection explicit in a letter to his mother in 1831:

> Until now flirtation, frivolity, changeability, beauty, grace, in general the so-called *exterior* qualities, have only ever given rise to trickery, deception, hypocrisy, licentiousness, adultery. [This] indicates that society has not known how to regulate, or satisfy, or utilise dispositions, human qualities, which consequently have become sources of disorder instead of being sources of joy and happiness, as they ought to be. For example, fickle, changeable, flighty people (and note that woman has these qualities more than man) were inferior according to the law of Christ. They often had to use their considerable power to demoralise rather than to moralise. That explains quite well the condemnation directed at *physical* pleasure and at woman . . . So I am wondering how *vivacious, flirtatious, seductive, attractive, fickle, ardent, passionate, exalted* people must be *directed, respected, employed* in the future so that their character may be, for themselves and for humanity, a source of joy and not of sorrow, of celebration and not of grief.[4]

After several months of heated discussion in the College, Enfantin outlined his new sexual theory before a Saint-Simonian general meeting in November 1831. He argued that the rehabilitation of the flesh legitimated the inclinations of people with a 'changeable' amorous disposition, who moved from one romance to another. A new moral law was required which recognised their virtues as well as those of 'faithful' personalities. Enfantin suggested that under this new law there should be three legitimate kinds of sexual relationships: 'intimate' relationships between people of the same personality type; 'convenient' relationships between opposite types; and 'religious' relationships which brought together a priest or priestess and one of the faithful.[5]

The theory was ambiguous on several counts. Firstly, the definition of the 'constant' personality type, characterised by faithfulness in love, was incompatible with 'convenient' relationships based on infidelity. The precise intention of the proposal also remained vague, since Enfantin maintained that the number and duration of 'convenient' encounters would be determined in the future by a woman, as would the form of the priests' loving relationships with the faithful.[6] Nevertheless, the theory of 'changeable' sexual appetites was clearly more than a system of divorce. It did not proclaim free love, but made that option a possibility.

Enfantin defended his theory as an attempt to find a moral law which was based on the 'holy equality' of men and women,[7] but it incorporated assumptions about the natural inequality of the sexes. The new morality did not assume equal tendencies towards changeability and faithfulness among men and women, but provided the same opportunity for 'changeable women' to follow their natural inclinations as 'faithful men' already possessed through indissoluble marriage. This premise was both arbitrary and illogical, implying that the majority of women would opt for sexual freedom while the majority of men would choose marriage, but it may have reflected the frustration with marriage which Enfantin tapped in women's 'confessions'.[8] The focus on sexuality also shifted the terms in which gender complementarity was understood by the Saint-Simonians. The sensory power and emotional intensity already ascribed to female nature were completed by the addition of sexual appetite, while male nature emerged as rational, measured and sexually restrained: a characterisation hardly consistent with the sexual histories of the Saint-Simonian men.[9] In Enfantin's theory, however, woman's confinement within the body was complete, and the proposed liberation of sexual power which became Saint-Simonian dogma was associated particularly with women:

> . . . the principal character of our apostolate is the REHABILITATION OF THE FLESH; in other words: in RELIGION, the establishment of a *cult*; in POLITICS, the organisation of *industry*; in MORALITY, the liberation of *woman*, and her ASSOCIATION in equality with *man*.[10]

The power of the flesh was pervasive, affecting not merely personal behaviour but the entire social order, and it represented the force of the female.

The theory of the new moral law created deep divisions within the Saint-Simonian movement and was ultimately responsible for its collapse as an organisation. It provided the opportunity for government prosecution on grounds of outrage to public morals. The closure of the Saint-Simonians' meetings, followed by the trial and imprisonment of Enfantin and other leaders in December 1832, reduced the sect to a rump of devoted adherents without a significant popular base. Ironically, perhaps, the government's actions confirmed Enfantin's claims about the social significance of sexuality. The Saint-Simonians had been holding several public meetings a week for two years before the law prohibiting such gatherings was finally enforced, and the challenge to Christian morality was the catalyst for action. The Saint-Simonians' 'new moral law', together with the 'liberty' already promised women, brought immediate repression.

SAINT-SIMONIAN RESPONSES TO THE 'NEW MORAL LAW'

Saint-Simonian responses to the 'new moral law' ranged from outrage to enthusiasm. The social significance of female sexuality was uncontested, and all agreed that the new social order depended upon appropriate definitions of its purpose and legitimate channels for its operation. However, opinion was divided on both these issues.

The Defence of Indissoluble Marriage

Some of the Saint-Simonians utterly rejected the new morality, and two of the sect's leaders, Bazard and Rodrigues, defected over the issue. The model of sexual relations which they promoted in opposition to Enfantin combined affectionate marriage with the idea of the shared functions of the couple.[11] Bazard reiterated the earlier Saint-Simonian claim that divorce would gradually disappear once relationships were based on affection, and he portrayed indissoluble marriage as the ideal model of sexual relations. For Bazard, human sexual history revealed a progression from an initial state of sexual confusion and promiscuity, to pairing, marriage, and finally love: ' . . . the love of two beings who, guided by a mysterious but certain revelation, find each other, choose each other from the crowd, in order to form, by an irrevocable agreement, a single being, a single life'.[12]

Where Enfantin viewed women as inherently passionate and 'changeable', Bazard defined them as innately chaste and destined to lead men towards monogamy. His reading of human nature contrasted man's capacity to 'abandon himself to any woman' with woman's 'need to make a choice, a selection based on personal qualities':

> What woman seeks today, what she expects, what is promised her by all the progress that has been made, is that man, whom she has ceaselessly called to the delights and duties of individual love, should finally accept this initiation, and thus aid her to free herself completely from primitive vulgarity, in order that an end may finally come to all this past confusion in which, to different degrees, brutality has constantly been the lot of one sex, and slavery and exploitation the lot of the other.[13]

For Bazard, woman was not a creature of carnal drives, but an innocent victim of male predation. Her moral role lay in subduing sexuality, now identified as male, and channelling it into the orderliness of domesticity. Woman's sexual inaccessibility was defined as a source of social progress since civilisation, like woman, was characterised by sexual restraint and the suppression of the appetites. The construction of woman as orderly and passionless, in contrast with the images conjured up by Enfantin's theory, was a powerful statement of a social ideal.

Bazard's concept of male/female relations reflected Enlightenment views of marriage, and the ideal of the moral role of the wife which gained increasing importance in post-Revolutionary France.[14] However, Bazard failed to analyse his ideal marital relationship in detail. The liberation of women was identified with the opportunity for all women to experience exclusive love. This claim suggested a recognition of the vulnerability of women in the current regime of money-based marriage, prostitution and spinsterhood, but it ignored questions about the means to achieve change, and about the sharing of domestic power.

Bazard's ideal model of sexual relations was shared by other Saint-Simonian men such as Olinde Rodrigues, Pierre Leroux,

Hippolyte Carnot and Jules Lechevalier.[15] It was also supported by many of the women, including a number of correspondents from the provinces who severed their relations with the Saint-Simonians as a result of the new moral law. These women defended indissoluble marriage because it served to 'lead man towards purity, not take woman away from it'.[16] The Catholic influence on their views was often explicit, but their hopes for an alternative focus of allegiance were shattered by the new sexual theories. Championing 'exclusive love' Elisabeth Celnart proclaimed:

> By sacrificing modesty, by giving full reign to the senses, any other doctrine belittles, degrades the intelligence of woman, and leads, step by step, to the monstrous assertion that, as an instrument of pleasure and reproduction, the companion of man lacks the spiritual faculty which distinguishes him from the beasts.[17]

She defended the ideal of female purity, but believed that this required a deliberate curbing of female sexuality, rather than being the natural female state. The reproductive imperative made woman seek sex, she argued, and unlike man, who had intellectual pursuits to distract him, she became a slave to pleasure.[18] Thus sexuality was once again located in woman. The suppression of passion was linked with the liberation of woman as a moral being, and with the moral development of humanity.

Cécile Fournel and Elisa Lemonnier, who were both active members of the sect, were also staunch defenders of indissoluble marriage, and their experiences demonstrate the dilemma which the new theory of sexual relations created for bourgeois women within the movement.[19] When the new morality was proclaimed at the end of 1831, both women rejected it and severed their ties with Enfantin. Since their husbands chose to remain with the Saint-Simonian group, both couples experienced a crisis in their relationship and separated temporarily.[20] The women's role as middle class wives imposed conflicting duties, since it required that they exert moral influence whilst remaining loyal to their husbands. This conflict caused them great distress, as Elisa Lemonnier revealed in a letter to her husband:

> . . . this union of which you speak, and which I hope for also, will it be achieved as you seem to believe by my adherence to the

ideas which you have adopted? I'm afraid you are mistaken. Yes, dear Charles, Elisa will be strong when she feels, when she loves the task which she is pursuing, but Elisa will never consent to do what her heart finds repugnant, what her intelligence rejects. . . O my dearly beloved, my good husband, your wife would be prepared for the greatest sacrifices, but for me the apostolate, as you people understand and practise it, is irreligious.[21]

The men were surprised by the strength of the women's resistance, and pressured them to accept the new moral law.[22] Initially, at least, Enfantin exerted a stronger moral influence over these men than their wives did. However, the women persisted in their defence of an alternative view whilst offering their husbands loving support. The self-abnegation of the wife's role was reinforced. In private Cécile Fournel lamented her broken marriage: 'Our love was indeed a love of the future . . . the most tender, the most total union that I have ever encountered . . .',[23] but private suffering was transformed into a public defence of the men's actions: ' . . . who can silence this world which showers abuse on them if not us? wouldn't this be a great lesson for [the world] to see us thus accepting abandonment, unhappiness, suffering of every kind . . .?'.[24]

Gradually both men rejected the new theories as social pressures, personal disillusionment, and the women's influence made their mark. Cécile Fournel and Elisa Lemonnier had assumed the role of 'friend and faithful companion' idealised by Bazard.[25] They were devoted wives, leading by example, drawing their husbands towards a 'superior' moral position. This Saint-Simonian stance imposed a heavy moral burden, however, and required women to sacrifice themselves to its demands.

The Defence of 'Progressive' Marriage

Enfantin's legitimation of sexual 'changeability' was attractive to some of the Saint-Simonians, though it gave rise to different interpretations. One view defined it as the right to establish and end intimate partnerships at will, but in an orderly way. Those who adopted this interpretation advocated 'regulated mobility', and envisaged women as wives in 'progressive' marriages. This model was a response to the prohibition on divorce as well as to the Saint-Simonians' new moral law. Women were its main defenders, and some of them also attempted to live up to the demands of their theory. Their role as the moral guardians of men was reaffirmed, but they attempted to redefine the moral role of the wife to make it compatible with the 'liberty' of women.

Suzanne Voilquin responded favourably to the new moral law from the outset.[26] She supported the cause of 'regulated mobility' in *The Women's Tribune*, arguing that indissoluble Christian marriage was no longer socially appropriate. The principle of changeability required provision for sexual 'variation'.[27] However, she favoured the transformation rather than the elimination of marriage, and sought to preserve the couple as the basic unit of society. Her commitment to this pattern of social organisation formed an important element in her rejection of free love:

> Without marriage, *with free love* . . . I believe that no society is possible, not only in the transitional period but even in the future . . . To establish such a system . . . woman would have to rule *alone*, to dominate *alone*, and I am far from claiming supremacy for my sex; I seek harmony, holy *equality*, relative equality in all the levels of the human hierarchy.[28]

She apparently saw no incongruity in attempting to graft a theory of sex equality onto one which was based on the notion of hierarchy.

Suzanne Voilquin also insisted upon the public regulation of sexual relations. This idea brought her into conflict with supporters of free love and underlay her criticism of the theories of James Lawrence, who apparently influenced many Saint-Simonians on the moral question.[29] Lawrence had argued that the discovery of paternity constituted the 'Fall' from the original state of grace, in which only the paternity of God was recognised. Given the uncertainty of fatherhood, he argued for the abolition of paternal rights and the establishment of a matrilineal system. Notions of legitimacy and illegitimacy would disappear, all pregnancies would be 'mysterious', 'miraculous' and 'immaculate', and all children would be recognised as the children of God. Furthermore, since marriage had stemmed from the recognition of human paternity, a matrilineal system would enable it to be eradicated, thus ending the proprietary rights of men over women and children.[30]

In Suzanne Voilquin's view, Lawrence's ideas offered women

'*moral liberty* . . . without regulation or limit', which could only lead to 'a crude and disgusting anarchy'.[31] Where Lawrence had called for a law of 'mystery', or the preservation of secrecy concerning sexual relations, she favoured a law of 'publicity', that is, a system for the control of sexual unions: 'I believe we would return to the state of savagery if all the important acts of life were not performed under the protection of GOD, before humanity and before the world . . .'.[32]

The call for a new system of 'progressive' marriage regulated by a new priesthood was also made by Madame Casaubon:[33]

> The names of the new contractors [of marriage] will be inscribed in the registers of civil status, and will bear the date of these voluntary and indefinite nuptials, the duration of which may be, according to the particular nature of each spouse, as fleeting as those slight atmospheric vapours, which a faint breeze deflects, speeds up or carries away; but which, for constant hearts, will be as steady and enduring as the ethereal vault of heaven.[34]

In Casaubon's view, women were dominated by sexual need, an accompaniment of the natural law of reproduction, but they were also the 'angel[s] of peace and love' in men's lives.[35] Sex and love were intertwined in her account, but sexuality was regarded as a positive force rather than a danger which required suppression, as Elisabeth Celnart had suggested. Both love and sexuality became means for inspiring and moralising men. Although Casaubon insisted on 'regulation', therefore, her theory was also consistent with considerable sexual freedom.

Suzanne Voilquin led the way in implementing the new 'progressive' form of marriage, interpreting her 'religious divorce' from Eugène Voilquin in 1833 as an example of a superior form of moral behaviour. She left two different accounts of this event, one published in *The Women's Tribune* in 1834, and another in her memoirs in 1865. Both underlined the moral leadership which women should exercise in such matters. Given their mutual acceptance of the new moral law, Suzanne's duty lay in freeing her husband once he fell in love with someone else.[36] By publishing her own experience she sought to demonstrate to women the new morality in action, and encourage others to free themselves from 'the need for *lies, moral adultery*, and *legal prostitution in marriage*'.[37]

The notion of the moral role of the wife shaped Suzanne Voilquin's interpretation of her divorce. She accepted responsibility for her husband's happiness and moral rectitude, and her task under the new morality was to ensure that he did not 'fall', did not become 'demoralised'. In her view, the divorce confirmed the individual and social morality of all three parties. Eugène Voilquin and Julie Parcy were saved from deception and adultery, while Suzanne ended the lie of a loveless marriage and progressed to a 'superior existence' devoted to the liberation of women.[38] She described her act as one of social love:

> I am free! I have laid down my rights on the altar of humanity! I have freed a man from a love which was not returned, *Voilquin* showed his *greatness*: yes, I say proudly, I have sent a man into the world, I have given him to *all*. . . .[39]

In reality, she had only 'given' Voilquin to his new partner, but his entry into society was likened to childbirth. In moral terms, Eugène Voilquin was represented as Suzanne's 'child', her 'creation', since she bestowed the 'gift' of moral life.[40]

In ceding her place in Voilquin's life to Julie Parcy, Suzanne also handed over responsibility for his morality. She surrendered her 'role as *guardian angel*' to another, who became his 'moral regulator'.[41] Both women were described as finding happiness in the process, but Eugène Voilquin's happiness was the determining factor in the way both women interpreted their actions.[42] Perhaps this provided a more socially acceptable justification for divorce than one centred on the needs of 'changeable' natures, or on female independence. However, the belief in women's moral influence was genuine, and the 'divorce' was an attempt to turn this theory into a positive and powerful role for women.

Caroline Carbonel's separation from her husband later in the 1830s was also justified on moral grounds. She was a seamstress, and a member of the proletarian 'family' in Paris. The date of her marriage to Carbonel, who was also a Saint-Simonian, is unknown, but she wrote to Enfantin in 1837 to explain that her decision to leave her husband was a matter of sexual honesty:

> People condemn me. By imposing my will on [my husband] I could, they say, continue in the world which would accept me

and my principles with him, although it rejects me on my own, and in that manner I could do much more good for women. But what could I say to the women of the world? Could I say to them 'be true', when my whole life was a web of lies? . . . My conscience tells me that if I have not told the whole truth, I should not debase the man whose name I bear by making him a laughing stock.[43]

Caroline Carbonel no longer loved her husband. She complained that he regarded her as his 'possession' and thus offended her womanly pride: an interesting comment on his poor grasp of Saint-Simonian principles. Not surprisingly, she felt that she had surpassed him in her understanding of the doctrine, so their marriage lacked a moral foundation.

For both Caroline Carbonel and Suzanne Voilquin, the decision to live according to the Saint-Simonian code of morality conflicted with the recognition that this would disadvantage and even harm them, unless other changes in women's social and material circumstances occurred. This point was emphasised in *The Women's Tribune*.[44] Although sexual freedom was regarded as an essential component of a new social order, women often stressed that it could not be considered in isolation from other changes. Marie-Reine explained:

I certainly feel that women must also demand their moral liberty; they are severely exploited in that respect; it causes them great unhappiness; but I do not think that this moral liberty can be established now . . . surely we must recognise that all freedoms must advance simultaneously; and, in order to be *morally* free, we must be *materially* free; for wouldn't our moral liberty be a sham if we were still forced to rely on men for our material needs?[45]

The accuracy of this assessment was demonstrated by the financial hardship experienced by both Suzanne Voilquin and Caroline Carbonel as separated wives. Suzanne began her life of 'freedom' by requesting a gift of one hundred francs from her departing husband.[46] The problems of supporting herself on female wages, and providing for the needs of an elderly father and an orphaned niece, continued throughout her life, and she was sometimes forced to accept assistance from friends.[47] Caroline Carbonel's financial position was even more precarious. In 1837 she earned twenty sous working a seventeen-hour day as a seamstress. On this money she was trying to support Judith Grégoire and her child, since Judith was too ill to work. Gifts from other Saint-Simonians were also essential for their survival.[48]

Those Saint-Simonian women who accepted 'progressive' marriage welcomed the notion of women's moral leadership and their duty to set moral standards, as did more conservative women like Cécile Fournel. However, women's moral role in marriage assumed a new form. They were no longer required to defend their marriages at all cost, but to end unsatisfactory relationships in order to form superior ones. The image of 'progressive' wives, tying and loosening the marriage bonds, encouraging and facilitating 'superior' unions, foreshadowed a more moral world from which deception and hypocrisy had disappeared. The appeal to 'morality' authorised women to pursue their liberty and take the initiative in 'regulating' relationships. However, it offered no protection against penury and isolation for 'progressive' wives in an unforgiving and unreformed society.

The Defence of Free Love

A few Saint-Simonians interpreted the new moral law as complete sexual freedom. They emphasised the importance of personal liberty for women, and saw sexual liberty as fundamental. In adopting this position they accepted a definition of women's nature which stressed the primacy of sexuality, and attempted to co-opt that definition in women's favour. Furthermore, women's liberty was once again juxtaposed with the task of providing the 'tender care' which satisfied all men's needs.

Claire Démar was the only Saint-Simonian who provided a theoretical defence of free love.[49] Little is known about her except that her real name was probably Emilie d'Eymard, and that she was about thirty years old at the time of her involvement in the Saint-Simonian movement.[50] She was a committed Republican, describing herself as 'a woman of the barricades',[51] and was not well liked by the other Saint-Simonian women. They regarded her as alarmingly radical while she found them timid and exasperating, although she maintained a friendly correspondence with Louise Crouzat at Lyon.[52]

Démar envisaged women as independent agents in sexual matters, as in life generally. She looked to a future when women were independent of men, classified according to their capacity and supporting themselves by their labour, as Saint-Simonian theory proclaimed. In a pamphlet entitled 'My Law for the Future', Démar explored the implications of women's independence for the future pattern of sexual relations, which she believed would be characterised by complete freedom. She called for:

> . . . a liberty without regulation or limits, a liberty as broad as possible, supported by secrecy, which I hold as the basis of the new moral law, even if it should lead us to the chaos which you find vulgar and disgusting.[53]

Démar's 'law' was a response to the moral stance promoted by Suzanne Voilquin through the pages of *The Women's Tribune*. In contrast to Voilquin's 'law of publicity', Démar called for a 'law of mystery', thus indicating her general support for the views of James Lawrence, whom she quoted.[54] She based her case on observation and experience, arguing that the public system of moral regulation through the marriage procedures, the registration of prostitutes, the rape and adultery trials was degrading for women. The intimate details of their personal lives were revealed to all. Under the 'law of mystery', Démar argued, no-one would know which of a woman's associates had her favour.[55] She did not address the issue of sexual assault.

Démar's case for the 'law of mystery' was also based on Saint-Simonian theory, and she accepted its implications more logically than many. Successful unions, she argued, required an extended trial period in which the couple could assess their compatibility, as the supporters of companionate marriage recognised. However, Démar insisted on 'the decisive proof': *The trial of matter by matter! the trial of the flesh by the flesh!!!*'.[56] Some 'trials' would fail, so the implications of this system were significant:

> When does the trial period finish? – when does the stage of marriage begin? – That is the question. – Or rather isn't marriage a continuous and prolonged series of trials which must sooner or later result, at least for changeable, inconstant natures, in cooling off, in separation.[57]

There were some similarities between Démar's ideas and Suzanne

Voilquin's support for progressive unions, although Démar assumed that the making and breaking of sexual alliances would pass unnoticed by all.

However, Démar argued that Enfantin's theory of two natures was illogical. In her opinion all people were unfaithful by nature, and she cited the pervasiveness of jealousy and illicit sexual attraction to develop a theory of free love: ' . . . association will rest one day on unlimited liberty, shrouded in mystery', and the system of sexual union would be based on 'more or less prolonged cohabitation'.[58] Furthermore, Démar did not reject the possibility that a woman:

> . . . might simultaneously give satisfaction to the love of several men; give a share of happiness and pleasure to all those who believe that they could only find happiness and pleasure beside her! through her![59]

Complete sexual freedom was a fundamental expression of women's liberty, in Démar's view, and the only appropriate sexual role for women in the future would be that of lovers, forming sexual liaisons as they chose.

Démar's system defined each person as fundamentally self-centred, seeking personal satisfaction rather than the social good. She stressed women's right to experience sexual pleasure, and praised Madame de Staël's definition of love as *'mutual egoism'*.[60] Women and men remained individuals for Démar, and this enabled her to envisage a radical alteration to the pattern of sexual relations. Despite her claim that the couple would be perfected under her system,[61] Démar's radicalism was achieved only by subverting a fundamental article of the Saint-Simonian faith.

Claire Démar's theories on the moral question were rejected by virtually all the other members of the Saint-Simonian group. She wrote to Enfantin early in 1833:

> Thursday evening I spent six hours in discussion at Voilquin's place. About fifty people were present, men and women. I was opposed on all sides. All the women renounced me, and almost as many men. *Only Mercier* understands the work which women must do. He defended me.[62]

After her death seven months later, when she and her lover

Perret-Desessarts implemented their suicide pact, the rejection continued in the Saint-Simonian press.[63] Démar's isolation within the Saint-Simonian group was probably due to several factors, of which her radicalism was only one.[64] However, her ostracism was significant in underlining the relative conservatism of the other Saint-Simonians on the issue of women's sexual role. There was no place for radicals like Claire Démar in the Saint-Simonian movement.

If those who advocated free love could expect little support amongst the Saint-Simonians, those who put this theory into practice became particularly vulnerable. The women who accepted the idea of free love distinguished themselves from the more moderate women by wearing a red ribbon, a symbol of their ardent passions.[65] They condemned the hypocrisy of men, who sought to 'restrain [women] within the bounds of Christian morality', formulated by men, while having neither the desire nor the strength to exercise that morality themselves.[66] Like the moderate women, they emphasised their desire for independence. They claimed the right 'to be what GOD has made us, loving women',[67] and defined woman's essence in sexual terms. Isabelle wrote in *The Women's Tribune*:

> . . . we wish to remain women, but women in the true sense of the word: in other words we will always remain, as far as possible, this being defined by grace, love and voluptuousness, this being born to charm and to please, this sweet, artful and persuasive creature; finally, we will be women and we will not be slaves! . . . Faithful to the laws of nature, we will love without pretence, and we will scoff at convention.[68]

The 'new morality' certainly revealed to some women their capacity for sexual responsiveness, or freed them to admit it.[69] Nevertheless, women who sympathised with this interpretation of the 'new moral law' often chose to delay exercising their sexual freedom until some indeterminate future.[70]

Some of the Saint-Simonian men were keen for women to adopt more liberal sexual attitudes. Although Enfantin had insisted that the maintenance of Christian moral standards was essential in the immediate term, he had nevertheless foreshadowed the implementation of the theory: 'we could find . . . that we do not have the virtues of a monk'.[71] A number of Saint-Simonians, including Enfantin, apparently made this discovery fairly rapidly. Some of the men urged women to experiment with the new morality,[72] thereby reinforcing the notion of women's sexual availability. As lovers under the new morality, women's role was little different from that of mistresses under the old morality. The fact that there was considerable sexual experimentation among the Saint-Simonians in the years following the announcement of the new moral law was confirmed by the alarm of the more conservative members. According to Aglaé Saint-Hilaire, it was 'raining babies' in the Saint-Simonian family in 1835.[73]

Women's acceptance of the role of lover is not explained only by their search for sexual freedom and pleasure. Not surprisingly, perhaps, few described their actions in terms of the total personal freedom which Démar had defended. Rather, women continued to view themselves as nurturing beings, and they realised this self-image in their roles as sexual partners of men. Pauline Roland, for instance, convinced of her ability to heal by 'the flesh', set out to 'save' Adolphe Guéroult, a young Saint-Simonian tormented by cynicism and doubt: 'My desire as a woman is to give myself mainly for the good that I can do for the man to whom I give myself . . .'.[74] Her sexual mission soon took her away from Guéroult, however, as she found in Jean-François Aicard another 'sceptical and desolate man' who also needed the care of a woman: 'Each day, I am more hopeful of saving him', she wrote.[75] Her relationship with Aicard was to last thirteen years.

Women's sense of their supportive place in men's lives may also help to explain their actions during the Saint-Simonian mission in Egypt. Enfantin and a number of male followers departed for the East in 1833 in search of the mythical 'Woman' who would complete their moral doctrine, and they soon called on the Saint-Simonian women to join them. Marie Talon had written of the roles women would play there:

> . . . they will have the right and power to enliven, to exalt those [men] whose glory they share, and to surround them with those joys, those pleasures, that tender care which makes them forget tiredness and hardship, and which will always be the attribute of women.[76]

As if in response to this statement the women did care for the men in Egypt, performing such 'female' tasks as doing their laundry and nursing them through the epidemic of plague.[77] Their 'tender care' of men also extended to the sexual sphere. The Saint-Simonians' letters and diaries reveal or suggest a network of sexual liaisons in Egypt, which highlighted the disparity between theory and practice on this issue for a number of individuals. Enfantin and Charles Lambert lived with Caroline Carbonel and Judith Grégoire. Judith had a daughter by Lambert, and the tone of Caroline Carbonel's later letters suggests that the relationship of both women with Enfantin was, at least, extremely affectionate.[78] Despite her theoretical opposition to the immediate implementation of sexual 'mobility', Suzanne Voilquin had an affair with Dr Delong, and possibly with Lambert as well, while she also addressed Enfantin as 'friend, lover, father'.[79] The fact that the new morality was being practised in Egypt was sufficiently obvious to cause Cécile Fournel to accuse Enfantin of a premeditated attempt to implement the new morality. She wrote to the Lemonniers:

> You are unaware, my friends, of the illusions which deluded us at the time of the departure for Egypt . . . [Henry] did not know that *Le Père* had especially in mind the trial of the theories which he hoped to attach to the industrial work, whatever it was, and it was only on the way to Lyon that he learnt of the projects concerning women . . . they wanted to implement a morality which I had always rejected, and they had decided on and speeded up their departure while concealing such plans.[80]

The implementation of sexual 'mobility' by the Saint-Simonians was not based primarily or deliberately on its potential for liberating women. While it is possible that some women may have sought to create for themselves a life of sexual independence by implementing the theory, other women who took lovers, such as Pauline Roland, had already recognised that sexual freedom was not necessarily liberating.[81] Women viewed their sexual relationships with men as an aspect of their nurturing and supportive function. By stressing the moralising power of women's sexual role, and its inspirational force, the 'new moral law' added another dimension to both men's and women's perceptions of the 'pleasures' and 'tender care' which women could provide for men, in the interests of social progress. The prospect of men's reciprocal 'tender care' of women, and their provision for women's physical, emotional and moral needs, did not feature in Saint-Simonian discussions of the sexual relationship.

'A MALE DESIRE': IMAGES OF WOMEN AS PROSTITUTES AND CONCUBINES

Some of the Saint-Simonian men envisaged a future when women might fill the roles of 'holy prostitutes', or concubines in a harem. In one sense these two roles are antithetical in that prostitutes are available to many men, while the concubine is generally reserved for a single man. But both roles allocate women to sexual service and define their social utility primarily in terms of sexual function. Although the Saint-Simonian men attempted to give these roles a positive moral value in accordance with the new morality, they revealed a fascination with models of sexual relations founded on female sexual servitude and the satisfaction of male desire.

Saint-Simonian analyses of prostitution combined a recognition of its social causes with a belief that it was due to the sexual drive of women. The neighbourhood in which the Saint-Simonian head-quarters were located made the issue of prostitution particularly visible to them.[82] They condemned the poverty and misery which forced young girls into prostitution, as well as the system of class relations which preserved the virtue of middle-class women by exploiting poor women.[83] However Enfantin also portrayed prostitution as the fate of passionate women in a society which did not recognise the moralising power of 'the flesh'. He argued that prostitutes were specially called by God, and should be allowed 'social and moral pleasures which fill their soul'. Under the new moral law Enfantin envisaged an 'army' of prostitutes whose 'beauty, strength, frivolity and ability' would be socially useful resources.[84] This concept was reminiscent of Fourier's proposal for an army of promiscuous women to encourage and reward the workers, although the precise uses to which Enfantin's 'beautiful army' would be put were not explained.

Some Saint-Simonian women also examined prostitution in the light of the new morality and its sanctification of the flesh. They argued that it resulted in part from the suppression of women's natural impulses, which consequently became deformed. With a moral law which was not restrictive, the inclinations which led to prostitution would acquire a moral sanction and a socially useful goal.[85] However, the analysis of prostitution in terms of relations between the sexes, rather than in terms of female nature, revealed a different perspective. The Saint-Simonian women emphasised the importance of male power in the maintenance of prostitution. Men privately took advantage of a system which they condemned publicly, and their perception of women as objects for male pleasure made seduction and abandonment a male game. Jeanne Deroin wrote:

> Accustomed to consider woman as a being created for his use, destined for his pleasure; man makes a sport of corrupting innocence and tarnishing Beauty, and his victims, cast with disdain from the arms of Society are swallowed up in those impure places whose existence dishonours humanity. . . .[86]

For Deroin, ending prostitution had less to do with acknowledging women's sexual desire than with transforming relations between the sexes. Similar views were also presented by women writing in *The Women's Tribune*.[87]

Gustave d'Eichthal also recognised that prostitution was a manifestation of male power over women. Speaking as counsel for Charles Duveyrier during his trial in 1832, d'Eichthal argued that all societies were male-dominated, and all enshrined prostitution in one form or another. He outlined the dual system frequently in operation. The absolute fidelity of some women was ensured by a range of punitive devices while the majority of women were required 'literally under pain of death . . . to submit wretchedly to the desires of the master': 'No doubt all that is brutal, repulsive, shameful, disgusting. But in the final analysis we must see it as it really is, the expression of a *male* desire, the expression of your desire, Gentlemen'.[88] D'Eichthal thus challenged the morality of the bourgeois judges who condemned the Saint-Simonians as immoral, but the idea that prostitution was an expression of male desire was not applied to Saint-Simonian visions of 'holy prostitutes'. Nor did d'Eichthal explain how men's desire for sexual access to a number of women fitted with the Saint-Simonian notion of superior male fidelity. By defining women as innately more loving and more 'changeable' than men, with an inclination towards 'holy prostitution', the Saint-Simonians transferred desire to women. They produced an image of women which satisfied the predominant male characteristic – the 'need to be loved' – and guaranteed male satisfaction. Issues of power were avoided rather than resolved.

Saint-Simonian writings on polygamy most vividly portray the manner in which, as objects of male theory, women also became objects of male sexual pleasure. Discussions of polygamy generally referred explicitly or implicitly to the Oriental harem. From 1833, when the Saint-Simonians undertook their 'mission' to Egypt, they had first-hand experience of a society which practised polygamy, although the men had no opportunity to study the harem at close quarters. Their portrayal of polygamy reflected the generalisations about the Orient which were becoming part of Western culture in the early nineteenth century, in the wake of exploration and colonisation.[89] Glorification of the harem as a model of sexual relations suggested a 'male desire', not merely for sexual gratification, but for reasserting men's centrality in women's lives, and their dominance over them. The complex relationship between male need and male power was explored through such discussions.

The idea of a polygamous pattern of sexual relations in the future was raised by Enfantin in 1833. He wrote to Cécile Fournel: 'I will not say that *polygamy* is no longer outrageous, because polygamy is certainly an ugly word; *galanterie* is better, though it is still bad enough'.[90] The attraction of polygamy for Enfantin was more explicit in a letter to Alexis Petit:

> Claire said one day, and even wrote to me, that I wanted to establish a *harem* for myself, and that she would have no part of it. She was wrong at least once in this twofold assertion. *Harem* is outdated, it is an ugly word of slavery, not much better than deer park . . . But beneath this ugly word there is an idea which could indeed be prophetic. We shall see.[91]

Enfantin thus suggested that, under a new guise, a harem might be acceptable. A new form of 'deer park' might offer private sport to the seigneur.

Whether Enfantin seriously entertained the idea of establishing a harem is uncertain. Before his departure for Egypt he had expressed the hope that 'the new family and the new morality could spring from that fertile ground', though he had not indicated what form he expected them to take.[92] However, Clorinde Rogé's reflections on her experiences in Egypt in the 1830s suggest that he was keen to imitate Egyptian sexual practices. She recalled him saying:

> ' . . . look around you, each woman is creating a role for herself, Madame Simon is making a pleasant home for her husband –

supposing that you were with me, would you not feel that you had a task, that of creating for me a court' and you hesitated a little, I completed your sentence ironically 'A court of love!' 'And why not?' you said.[93]

Even if Enfantin's idea of the harem remained at the level of fantasy, it ran counter to his proclaimed theory of human sexuality. Unlike Fourier, Enfantin did not consider the possibility of lesbianism, so the harem catered poorly for the sexual needs of 'changeable' women and 'steadfast' men, and in fact contradicted their requirements. However, it suggests that Enfantin remained attached to an image of women as instruments for male sexual enjoyment. He claimed to anticipate a new model of the harem which was not based on female servitude, but the concept was not compatible with the idea of women's sexual or social liberty.

Saint-Simonian writings on polygamy reflected the contemporary tendency to explain sexual difference in racial terms, and vice versa.[94] Gustave d'Eichthal and Ismayl Urbain claimed, for example, that the harem had particular benefits in Eastern countries for ending racial disharmony. Bringing together women of different races in the same 'family' was 'a powerful means of removing colour prejudice and establishing equality in the domestic and political family' in Africa.[95] Presumably they referred to 'equality' amongst these women and their offspring, rather than between the master and his concubines. They envisaged some modifications in the future, with a man able to have both a black and a white wife, thus furthering the cause of racial harmony.[96] They did not suggest that a woman might acquire husbands of different races, for the same noble purpose.

The defence of female oppression in racial terms was significant here. Black and white women became 'equal' by being equally subordinate to (white) men, but black people and women were also linked in other ways. D'Eichthal and Urbain defined the black race as 'female' and the white race as 'male'. Black people and women were attributed with the same personality traits, including an incapacity and a lack of desire for freedom. The 'vocation' of both was 'familial domesticity': a social structure which replaced slavery by 'protection'.[97] These writers did not suggest that polygamy could be instituted in Europe. It remained an exotic and appealing Eastern custom. However, their image of polygamy, as it was practised in some black societies, provided a vehicle for exploring gender (as well as race) relations. Despite d'Eichthal's earlier recognition of the oppressive character of the harem, he defended a model of sexual relations which justified the domination of (white) men.

A comparison of East and West also provided the means for Emile Barrault to outline an ideal lifestyle for women, and once again to defend the benefits of the harem. He argued that this 'sort of captivity' removed women from the conflicts of public life which 'deformed their genius': 'it forced them, by seclusion, to cultivate the peaceful inclinations and private virtues of their sex'.[98] The irony of advocating coercion to instil peaceful ideals apparently escaped him, as did the fact that 'virtues' which had to be force-fed were clearly not innate. There was also a total contradiction between this proposal and the Saint-Simonian theory that women's private roles should be transformed. His 'seclusion' of women provided no mechanism for transferring their virtues to society.

While Barrault admitted that the harem deprived women of their liberty, he constructed a romantic notion of the female role it institutionalised. D'Eichthal and Urbain had not viewed the polygamous system as suited to Western, Christian countries, and Enfantin's fantasies were largely private, but Barrault argued for the benefits of the harem in broader terms:

> No doubt the harem is only an elegant prison: but this mysterious section of the house, where the women and children live, this holy of holies in the domestic temple, this haven before which the step of every man halts . . . isn't this a protection of their dignity, as well as the refuge of private life? . . . If Oriental women need to share the liberty which European women enjoy, shouldn't European women in turn envy the mystery which shrouds Eastern women with obscurity, respect, grace, and which is also a [form of] liberty.[99]

Since Western women were not 'private' beings like their Oriental counterparts, they did not offer man the haven which Barrault found appealing. The shrouded and hidden figure of the Eastern woman was admired for the 'private life' which she represented, but she also had the mystique which aroused desire. Woman herself became the 'domestic temple', venerated and respected, a place of refuge and solace for man: a portrait of women's role consistent with Barrault's earlier defence of the domestic wife. His image of the harem emphasised man's need for womanly care and affection, as well as sexual service. Within the harem, however, the object of his desire was also more thoroughly under his control, and she was multiple.

Barrault's construction of the concubine as untainted by contact with the world ignored the oppressive pattern of sexual relations underlying the system. It contrasted markedly with the impressions of Suzanne Voilquin after a two-day stay in a harem in Egypt. She emphasised the male 'despotism' of polygamy, and the soul-destroying monotony of the harem for women. She also noted the sexual competition which characterised female relations in this system, since gaining favouritism with the master and bearing him sons offered the only insurance against abandonment.[100]

For Suzanne Voilquin, man's refuge was woman's prison. Women were immured in the harem for their sexual and reproductive functions, both exercised at the behest of man. The virtues of the concubine were the virtues of the slave. Barrault's discussion of female 'liberty' in this context was therefore particularly significant. 'Liberty' was one of the most fundamental demands of male politics throughout the nineteenth century, as well as being a constant demand by feminists. 'Liberty' had different meanings, as the class and gender conflict of the period attest.[101] However, no definition of liberty by and for men, and no feminist understanding of the goal, approximated Barrault's usage. According to Barrault, the possession of 'liberty' by women made them vulnerable and unfree; a preferable form of 'freedom' lay in imprisonment. Women's dignity lay in servitude rather than liberty: an understanding totally at odds with male expectations. As Suzanne Voilquin commented in her discussion of the harem, ' . . . in the absence of liberty there is no compensation for the emptiness of the soul, nor for the widowhood of the heart!'.[102] By linking sexual subordination with the denial of liberty, however, Barrault demonstrated that the sexual servitude of women ensured and required their social subordination. Conversely, since women were not destined for 'liberty' – the key characteristic of the political male – they were not destined to move beyond their 'elegant prison' of domesticity. In envisaging a model of sexual relations based on women's seclusion, therefore, Barrault also constructed a model of social relations which rested on female oppression.

The conflicting theories and practices of Saint-Simonian sexuality demonstrate the multiplicity of views of both men and women on this subject. However, the debate was not simply about which model of sexual relations was most appropriate. It was also about who should have the power to define sexual roles, and ultimately, to define women themselves, since they were generally portrayed as representing sexuality. 'Male desire' and 'male need' dominated the sexual systems which the men proposed. They ignored the tension between women's newly-promoted social 'equality' with men, and the primary role of serving men's physical, emotional and moral needs allocated to women by those theories. Women justified their sexual choices by linking their sexual and care-giving roles, attempting to reconcile the search for liberty with the overriding definition of themselves as nurturing beings. However, the difficulty of harmonising their role as care-givers with their search for 'liberty' was never successfully overcome.

7

The 'New Moral Law', the Family and Motherhood

The 'new moral law' required a re-examination of relationships within the family unit, and within the new 'social family' envisaged for the future. Opinions on the role of fatherhood were divided, but there was almost universal agreement on the importance of the maternal role. In this respect the Saint-Simonians shared the emergent cult of motherhood. The Saint-Simonian women embraced motherhood as a source of dignity and respect, asserting the importance of their reproductive function. In addition they claimed 'social maternity' as their own, and thus reasserted their right to social power and influence. However, since the Saint-Simonians represented their ideal society in 'maternal' terms, the men appropriated the 'maternal' as their social role. Moreover, the new moral law's association of women with 'the flesh' was consistent with the confinement of women to biological mothering. As men colonised the 'maternal' it became a new vehicle to assert their own social predominance. In this context the women's emphasis on motherhood, even its physical aspect, assumed a radical dimension.[1] The debate over maternity and over the new 'social family' not only had implications for the roles of biological parents, but also formed part of the struggle to define the ideal world, and the pattern of gender relations within it.

THE NUCLEAR FAMILY AND PATERNAL RIGHTS

Enfantin's views on family organisation under the new moral law were ambiguous. In public, he postponed consideration of the subject until the awaited 'Woman' had spoken,[2] but in private he advocated the abolition of the biological family, and supported 'the secret of fatherhood'.[3] Enfantin's behaviour was consistent with this commitment, since he refused to marry the mother of his son, Arthur, born in 1827.[4] Adèle Morlane clearly did not welcome 'the

131

secret of fatherhood'. She continually pleaded with Enfantin to regularise her position, and he eventually compromised by presenting Arthur to the Saint-Simonian family for 'adoption' in 1832: an adoption which had no legal status.[5] Rather than sympathising with the plight of Adèle Morlane, who was not a Saint-Simonian, Enfantin criticised her unwillingness to understand his mission. She was preoccupied with her own misfortunes, rather than with those 'of all the *women* of the whole world' whom he had come to save.[6] By defining his mission to liberate women in abstract terms, Enfantin evaded his moral responsibility to a particular individual. She had no recourse other than pleas while paternity suits remained illegal.

Enfantin's reluctance to accept the ties of fatherhood was shared by his friend Charles Lambert, another leading figure in the Saint-Simonian movement. Judith Grégoire was unable to identify Lambert publicly as the father of her daughter, Aline, apparently in deference to his wishes. He appears to have taken little interest in the child, despite the dire poverty in which she was raised.[7] Enfantin and some of his followers were keen to abolish the family unit, then, but had no solution for the problems of unwed mothers, even those of their own making, in the immmediate term. Enfantin's family policy proved remarkably similar to the existing one, which did not enforce paternal responsibility for children born out of wedlock. The very different implications of this policy for women and for men were glaringly displayed, since Saint-Simonian fathers continued to evade responsibility for children they did not wish to accept. For some men, paternal rights were far from sacred.

Other Saint-Simonian men resisted the abolition of the family, and defended the role of fatherhood. Enfantin claimed that Bazard had originally supported his views, and that only the objections of Olinde Rodrigues had persuaded them to preserve the family concept.[8] If that was so, Bazard had been swiftly reconverted to support for the family and remained one of its champions. He and Rodrigues placed questions of procreation and fatherhood at the centre of their critique of the new moral law, and defended the nuclear family as the ideal basis for social organisation:

> From birth, man wishes to be surrounded by those who really *love* him the most, so that, by their example, he can *learn to live* his life.

The *mother* always wishes to offer to the caresses of the *father* the child which God has produced from them, in order that the family might be *formed* through *them*, the ever *progressive* family which continually surrounds the growing child with the most *intelligent* and the most *active assistance*, in order to develop its faculties.[9]

Rodrigues clearly assumed that the biological family provided the best environment for childraising. Besides, both he and Bazard recognised that the 'powerful and imperishable sentiment of fatherhood' was particularly endangered by the new moral law. In Rodrigues' view, 'the child having hardly uttered its first cry would be snatched from the very sight of its newly-delivered mother, as well as from that of its father . . .'.[10] He rejected any notion of the 'secret of paternity',[11] and emphasised the paternal role. For Bazard and Rodrigues, the Christian family model needed major modification but not abolition. It should be replaced by 'the new marriage, the new family',[12] though there was little discussion of the types of changes which that would involve. Their brief references suggest that, while the legal subordination of women would cease and unions would be based on love, maternal and paternal roles would be largely unchanged.

THE IDEALISATION OF MOTHERHOOD

Motherhood was one of the most important issues debated by the Saint-Simonian women. They tended to assume an automatic link between sex and procreation, even though the small families of those whose reproductive histories are known suggest that they, like many of their compatriots, were practising some form of family limitation.[13] Contraception was not discussed, although Madame Casaubon made a veiled reference to the prevalence of abortion:

. . . I do not hesitate to assert that there is not a single home where similar outrages against God do not occur *behind closed doors*, and where the health of young women is not endangered by the violent medications which they take . . . Yes! moral men, doctors, traffic in the secrets which, safeguarding families by a false honour, inhumanly cut down their most vibrant plants![14]

Casaubon's personal adulation of motherhood was shared by most of the Saint-Simonian women. Some were already mothers at the time of their association with the Saint-Simonian movement. Other young women confronted the prospect of motherhood once they took lovers or husbands. For those like Suzanne Voilquin who were unable to bear children, such expectations intensified a sense of personal lack.

Given the way in which motherhood was lauded in their society, it is not surprising that many Saint-Simonian women also sang its praises: *'Motherhood!* It is our finest quality, it encompasses all other sentiments without exception, it is woman *in all her glory* . . .'.[15] Maternity was seen as an obligation imposed by nature, but it was one in which women expressed great pride, and they endowed it with religious significance. Suzanne Voilquin suggested that the maternal role would be the focus of worship in the future,[16] while Madame Casaubon envisaged mothers performing the most important religious ceremonies, which would celebrate regeneration. Departing from Saint-Simonian orthodoxy, she maintained that only 'The other sacerdotal functions will be performed by a couple, man and woman . . .'.[17]

Saint-Simonian women accepted the appeal to class harmony in the doctrine, and found within maternal love, 'generally recognised as the strongest and deepest of all sentiments', a specific focus for uniting women. It gave them a common desire to create a better world for their children, a desire unmatched in men.[18] The Saint-Simonian women also made the maternal role the basis for their claim to social rights. Employing unashamedly essentialist arguments, they asserted that their uniqueness as mothers, their difference from men, justified their claim to equality with men.[19] Suzanne Voilquin contrasted the certitude of the maternal link with the uncertainty of fatherhood: *'God* has entrusted to the mother *alone* the *certainty* of the family. In the breast of the young girl lies the *living link* which ceaselessly attaches succeeding generations to those which are ending . . .'.[20] Where Rodrigues had defined marriage as the generational link, Voilquin identified women's reproductive capacity as the source of continuity. In the new world, therefore, women would 'name their children', and the 'principle of motherhood' would become 'one of the fundamental laws of the State'.[21] The centrality of women's role to the reproduction of both individual and social life was highlighted by such arguments. Reproduction was not a private function but a social service; one unique to women and worthy of reward.

Suzanne Voilquin's emphasis on the 'principle of motherhood' ratified one of the key concepts of James Lawrence,[22] as well as challenging the Civil Code's negation of maternal rights. She attacked the 'despotism' enshrined in law and its unflattering assumptions about female incompetence, although she did accept the need for paternal protection for children in the interim.[23] Pauline Roland went further, insisting upon the concept of maternal independence in practice. Once she became pregnant by Adolphe Guéroult she reached an agreement with him that 'she alone was the whole family of this child. He will love it, but does not feel he has any rights over it'.[24] When her son was born he was given the family name Roland, as were her other children born later to Jean-François Aicard.

A forceful theoretical attack on the Civil Code was also launched by Madame Casaubon. She condemned the Code's provisions on the family as the usurpation of power over women and children, arguing that it contravened both Divine law and natural justice. Men appropriated children at birth, 'stamping them' with their name and making them their property, while those who were unclaimed by a man were branded illegitimate. The role of the mother in the reproductive process was discounted.[25] Like Suzanne Voilquin, she proposed a matrilineal system which recognised the sacredness of motherhood and its crucial role in society. It would give mothers primary control over their children:

WOMAN IS THE FAMILY.
The child must bear her name.
Certitude LIES *where no doubt exists*, and the fruit must
bear the name of the tree which gave it life, not that of the
gardener who grafted the bud.[26]

Casaubon thus challenged Napoleon's analogy, which likened male proprietary rights over women and children to the gardener's ownership of the tree and its fruits.[27] As her claims made clear, control over reproduction and over the symbolic representation of reproduction were crucial in the power struggle between the sexes. Analogies of despotism and usurpation, that is, illegitimate forms of political rule which were inconsistent with liberty and natural rights, provided a vehicle for women to challenge the legitimacy of male power over women. If images of transformed personal relations conveyed a vision of a transformed social order, the characteristics of rejected political models also provided a metaphor for rejected models of personal relations.

Since reproduction was a natural law, Casaubon maintained that the childbearing woman deserved acclaim and reward, not penalty. There should be none of the pressures on women which gave rise to abortion and infanticide in her society.[28] Casaubon also utilised Saint-Simonian theory to defend women's rights as mothers, applying its valuation of productive work to reproductive work. Women's reproductive labour gave them the right to control its products:

> . . . [woman] bears the children; she gives birth to them in suffering, and not without reason this act of her life has been called, in most languages, *the labour of childbirth*: we speak of a *woman in labour*.[29]

Paternal rights were indefensible according to this line of argument, since men's contribution to reproduction was minimal in comparison with that of women. Furthermore, women's valuable work as mothers entitled them to commensurate material rewards. She welcomed the Saint-Simonians' plans to abolish inheritance, but argued further that half of the communally-held land should be vested in women. Revenue from this land would provide a 'mothers' tribute' in payment for women's reproductive services to society.[30] This would be the basis for a 'new social contract' between men and women, and she attempted to ground it in the realities of political economy.[31] In Casaubon's plan, men would manage the women's land as well as their own, and this act of homage would be repaid by women's love.

Casaubon defined the private family as oppressive for all and sought its abolition.[32] Women would then be freed from dependence on individual men, while men would be freed from responsibility for supporting individual women and children. The private patriarchal family would be replaced by a system in which couples would form loving, if often ephemeral, relationships and in which all women would be mothers to all children.[33] However, the specific process of childraising which she envisaged remained obscure. She apparently assumed that women's maternal role would extend, first of all, to their 'primitive' family, but that maternal feelings would embrace all children, ensuring the adoption of orphans.[34] There was no suggestion of collectivised childraising.

Suzanne Voilquin also argued that women needed to become more 'social' in their attitude to their children, recognising that those children belonged first and foremost to the 'great family of humanity'.[35] Like Casaubon, she envisaged an end to women's material dependence on men through the guaranteed ownership of property by women, which would enable them to care for children and the aged with more security.[36] Childcare was defined as a female responsibility, but she did not specify whether some women or all women would share this task, or whether it would be a private or socialised service. However, Suzanne's experience of childlessness added weight to her idealisation of the private maternal role. She claimed in her memoirs that the hope of motherhood had been her sole motive for marrying, but she was infected by her husband's venereal disease, resulting in three miscarriages in five years.[37] Her only living child, born to Alfred Delong in Egypt in 1836, died at the age of two weeks.[38] Suzanne found some consolation in raising an orphaned niece, 'a gift from God to compensate for my unfortunate pregnancies',[39] but throughout her life she longed for a child of her own, and devoted herself to supporting mothers and their babies. She trained as a midwife and founded the 'Maternal Society for the Support of Unmarried Mothers', which used monthly contributions from its members to finance its services:

> To be entitled to our care and our financial assistance one only needs to be destitute and in an illegal situation, the poorest and most abandoned have the greatest right to our care and our aid. In this case I perform the delivery for nothing.[40]

But the service was only available to those women who intended to keep their illegitimate children, as Caroline Carbonel explained:

> Suzanne performs free deliveries; but . . . assistance is not given to the poor girl who does not have the strength to reveal her fault to the world by keeping her child . . . Ah! Suzanne, Suzanne, where is your compassion? When Sophie, Judith, myself and several other women objected, she replied that she had no sympathy for women who were heartless. . . .[41]

Caroline's close friendship with Judith Grégoire gave her an insight into the problems faced by unwed mothers, and sympathy for those who found the prospect of single parenthood too daunting.[42] Suzanne's adamant stance, on the other hand, probably reflected her realisation that infants abandoned by their mothers had very poor prospects for survival in her society. Her own childlessness also led her to emphasise the special bond between the biological mother and her child. Despite her enjoyment of adoptive motherhood, and the Saint-Simonians' theoretical encouragement of 'social motherhood', she did not advocate breaking the biological tie. Nor did she argue that women with the 'capacity' for the maternal role, such as herself, should find fulfilment in raising the children of the 'great human family'.

The theories of both Casaubon and Suzanne Voilquin contained a fundamental ambiguity in extending women's social rights and responsibilities while at the same time giving added emphasis to their maternal role. Voilquin regarded motherhood as 'one of the obligations imposed by nature',[43] but she was also committed to the 'liberty' of women. She anticipated their participation in medicine, law, public administration, education and religion. Women's place was everywhere:

> . . . I envisage woman . . . as *daughter*, *wife* and *mother* in the family, *citizen* in the state, *elect* of God in the temple, and fragment of the infinite in the *world*! I seek a position for *her* everywhere, a *recognised* but *regulated* position, large enough, spacious enough so that she will be comfortable there, sufficiently beautiful and honoured so that she will be happy there.[44]

Casaubon held a similar view. She called for all civil and political rights for women, and demanded their participation in government and religious office. She also advocated equal educational opportunities for women, and argued that they should be able to develop their industrial, artistic or scientific talents freely.[45]

How women would fill these diverse roles and still exercise the main, if not sole, responsibility for childraising was not explored. Like Bazard and the supporters of the nuclear family model, Voilquin and Casaubon failed to examine the difficulties implicit in combining women's care of children with their full and equal involvement in social life. However, women's exclusive allocation to childrearing was a bourgeois ideal unavailable to poor mothers, who generally combined childcare with paid work and community involvement. Women like Voilquin were thoroughly familiar with such patterns. Their emphasis on motherhood echoed the bourgeois pattern, then, but drew on other definitions of the maternal role as well. Besides, given the lack of any clear alternative, women's reluctance to abandon a role which was highly praised (if not well rewarded) was understandable.

Only Claire Démar questioned the compatibility between women's allocation to childrearing and their full social participation:

[In the future] woman will only owe her existence, her social position, to her capacity and her work.

Well for that it is essential that woman performs a task, fulfils a function; – and how can she, if she is always condemned to spend a more or less lengthy period of her life in the tasks which the education of one or several children demand? Either the function will be neglected, poorly performed, or the child poorly raised, deprived of the care which its weakness, its long period of growth require.[46]

Where many of the Saint-Simonian women supported matrilineality, then, Claire Démar extended the abolition of the 'law of blood' to motherhood as well as fatherhood. In her view, women's physical ability to bear children did not justify allocating them all to the social function of childrearing. The precise pattern of social organisation she envisaged remained unclear, but she advocated the conversion of childraising into a professional career. The private family would disappear, and the new social individual would be raised by the social family:

. . . from the breast of the *natural mother* take the newborn infant to the arms of the *social mother*, the professional *nurse*, and the child will be better raised; for it will be raised by one who has the capacity to rear, to develop, to understand children. . . .[47]

Once again Démar opposed the dominant Saint-Simonian view. She challenged the assumption that mothering was instinctive and universal in women, and demanded an end to obligatory motherhood in the name of liberty. Démar regarded the maternal and social roles as antithetical, while other Saint-Simonian women sought to use maternity as the basis for their claim to social rights. They stressed the beneficent impact of women as 'maternal' beings on the society as a whole. Suzanne Voilquin summarised this perspective:

> To you men [belong] *production*, the great tasks of subjugation, the conquest of the earth, of the material world. To us [belong] *population*, the transformation of humanity, to us falls the task of forming the heart, the sentiments of man, to us falls the moral education of the world. . . .[48]

In this analysis man was allocated responsibility for the material realm, woman for the moral and social sphere. Masculine power and domination were offset by the moderating and humanising influence of the feminine. Without the educative and moralising contribution of women, the world would be dominated by the rule of the strongest. This maternal image justified a wide-ranging social role for women, and conveyed the type of social transformation which the Saint-Simonian women sought to undertake.

THE ROLE OF THE PRIESTHOOD: REPRODUCING THE SOCIAL FAMILY

Enfantin and his male followers constructed a theory of social reproduction which ignored but assumed the biological prerequisites for this process. The social mode of reproduction was portrayed as superior, since it ensured the survival of the social family rather than the biological family. Although the theory of social reproduction made provision for the inclusion of women as mother/ priestesses of the new social family, the rudimentary form of that family which was put into practice by the Saint-Simonians relegated women to a secondary place. The social family emerged as the special province of men, and social 'maternity' as their function. The masculinisation of 'social maternity' justified a superordinate position for the new 'maternal' male.

The 'Parenthood' of the Saint-Simonian Priests

In developing the new moral law Enfantin focused on the social family he sought to establish – the 'family chosen by love' – and on the 'parenthood' to be exercised in that family by the priests and priestesses. His vision of a new form of social family was based on an idiosyncratic model of religious and political development. He contrasted the patriarchal priesthood of the Old Testament period, when the family was united solely by the bonds of the flesh, with Christianity's fraternal priesthood, which governed a family united by spiritual ties. In the Saint-Simonian era, Enfantin argued, a parental priesthood would govern a family united by both carnal and spiritual bonds. Family members would love each other not through instinct or duty but through choice, 'a *choice* of LOVE made by the COUPLE and accepted by the *children*'.[49] The new priesthood would be a new parenthood, a 'more clearsighted fatherhood, a more competent motherhood'.[50]

The Saint-Simonians emphasised that the priests would possess both physical and spiritual superiority under the new moral law. Their assigned virtues included both 'fidelity' and 'changeability'. This ensured that 'changeable' types would be attracted towards the priests for their 'carnal' qualities of beauty, aimiability and passion, while 'faithful' people would respond to the priests' spiritual gifts, and to the enduring love of each priest for his or her partner.[51] While faithful to each other, the priests would exercise their talent of 'changeability' by regularising the love of others. This required intervention in the sexual lives of the faithful, and they would use the knowledge provided in the confessional and their own physical and spiritual attractiveness to eliminate intellectual and sexual disorder.[52] The celibate relationship of the sacerdotal couple promoted in earlier Saint-Simonian theory[53] was thus redefined as a passionate relationship under the new moral law:

> The Saint-Simonian priest and priestess who are the most tender in love, who know all the joys of *restraint* and of *abandonment*, of modesty and of the most ardent embraces, this couple, the most LOVING of couples, the WISEST and the most AMOROUS, the most reserved and the most *passionate*, this couple has lessons of *tenderness* to give rather than lessons of *algebra*.[54]

Furthermore, Enfantin apparently believed that there would be a place for 'carnal' relationships between the priests and their 'children', and declined to indicate the precise limit to the priests' sexual role.[55] He also refused to rule out a community sexual role for the priestess who would be his own wife:

. . . I can imagine *certain circumstances* in which I would consider that only my wife would be able to give happiness, health, life to one of my sons in *Saint-Simon*, to call him back to the social sympathies ready to desert him, to revive him in her loving arms at the time when some enormous sorrow required a powerful distraction, at the time when his broken, withered heart was bleeding with disgust at life.[56]

Charles Duveyrier, too, was reluctant to specify the sexual role of the priests with the faithful, but his suggestive interpretation earned him a prison sentence for immorality. He speculated on the implications of having a priesthood who exercised both 'fidelity' and 'changeability', and who enjoyed both 'intellectual' and 'sensual' pleasures:

If this were the case, we would see what has never been seen on earth before. We would see men and women united by a love without precedent and without name, since it would know neither diminution nor jealousy; men and women who would give themselves to several without ever ceasing to belong to each other, and whose love would be, on the contrary, like a divine banquet, growing in magnificence according to the number and selection of the guests. . . .[57]

Duveyrier's account left little doubt about his support for this imaginary system, which he regarded as a powerful means of achieving social harmony.

The sexual function of the new priesthood was well demonstrated by the role envisaged for the Saint-Simonian priestess. The men defined this role by establishing a number of parallels with the imagined role of the medieval lady. Both were portrayed as 'faithful' and 'changeable' in their loving relationships. Their 'changeability' was presented as a source of social harmony, and as a means of inspiring others towards virtue, rather than as a source of social disorder. Both were assigned a major role in the moral regulation of society, providing a new moral force which replaced the superseded Christian priests. Both also exercised their regulatory role through physical as well as spiritual qualities. However, while the medieval lady had been a platonic lover, the priestess would have a sexual role as well.[58] The Saint-Simonians' stress on the priests' sexual relationships with the faithful was intended to contrast with the celibacy of the Catholic priests, and their inability (according to the Saint-Simonians) to regulate the affairs of 'the flesh'. However, it redefined the parental role which they were also assigned and, in their hierarchical model of interpersonal relations, opened unexamined possibilities for sexual exploitation.

The Saint-Simonian Concept of the 'Mother-Priestess'

The conflict surrounding the new moral law gave added import-ance to the awaited 'Woman' who would rule society in partner-ship with the 'Pontiff-King'. The prospect of her arrival served as a device for defusing anger and anxiety over the 'immorality' im-plicit in the theory, and also enabled Enfantin to claim that the theory itself was only a tentative one. No definitive formulation of the new moral law could be made until 'the Woman' had spoken:

> . . . if the law which I, a man, formulated, had been accepted by men, that law made without a woman would have been im-posed on women, who would thus have remained in subordina-tion and slavery: but, as I had foreseen, my law was rejected by men, and the woman is awaited who must find with man the definitive law under which man and woman will unite and live in *holy equality*.[59]

The mythical 'Woman' would modify and purify the moral theory of Enfantin, setting out the limits to the 'carnal' relations between the priests and the faithful and solving the related question of paternity.[60] She would also be the 'Woman Messiah', making known to the world 'the voice of God the MOTHER'.[61] Women would be rescued by her coming from prostitution and adultery, and the masses would be freed from poverty and slavery.[62] By attributing such extraordinary power to this figure, the Saint-Simonians admitted their inability to solve these social problems in the foreseeable future. However, although the theory ostensibly placed great power in the hands of this 'Woman', the men at-tempted to define her identity and her role, and thus to limit her influence. Enfantin claimed that 'you cannot call the woman by a DENIAL, by a NEGATION, you can only call her by *affirming*, by saying what you desire for her, how you envisage, how you anticipate the future for her'.[63] His acceptance of a candidate would be the only real proof that she was the awaited 'Mother'.[64]

She would thus have no power over men that they did not choose to give her. They remained ambivalent about the prospect of female authority, being attracted by the possibilities it raised but fearing the loss of power that it implied.

The Saint-Simonian women had less to lose from the coming of the 'Woman', and much more to gain. Some of them did expect from this 'Woman' a maternal figure who would rule society in partnership with Enfantin, and thereby raise the status of women in general:

> The New Mary, the woman we await is called to complete the work of God; but in partnership with man, not as a submissive slave. She too will save the world and crush the serpent's head; but the redeemer who must do so with her will not say to her with an authoritative air: Woman, what is there in common between you and me? He calls her to his side to share authority, to bring her face of light, of grace, of modesty and wisdom to the work which he has so nobly begun and which he is completing with such courage. . . .[65]

However, others saw in the call to the 'Woman' an opportunity for women themselves to impress their virtues upon society and demonstrate their social value. They declared that the world would be transformed, not by an individual woman, but by 'the *feminine* sex, *Mother, Lover, Wife, Friend* of the *masculine* sex'.[66] Suzanne Voilquin told the Saint-Simonian sympathisers at Bordeaux:

> . . . I have only ever seen a symbol in Barrault's call. In my opinion, every woman must demonstrate that she is free of masculine influence, by feelings and actions of her own free will . . . these women will come together by force of events, in order to form a council where each will bring her stone to the moral edifice of the future. It is this sentiment, *thoroughly feminine*, which will create what the saint-simonians [*sic*] call the Mother![67]

Suzanne thus defined the expected 'Woman' as the collective female spirit, expressed through an assembly of real women. She incorporated the myth of the 'Mother' into her ongoing attempts to give women a voice within the Saint-Simonian movement and within society.

The Saint-Simonians established parallels between the role of the awaited 'Woman' and that of Jesus Christ. Barrault became her 'prophet', identifying the signs of her imminent arrival, and both he and Enfantin claimed to be her 'precursor'.[68] She was likened to the Suffering Christ, and her followers, the Saint-Simonians, to Christian martyrs.[69] However, the expectation of the Saving Woman also served to underline the inadequacy of the Christian Messiah, and the superiority of the new vision of a Saving Couple. As Colin argued, 'Jesus *alone* was not the *true* Messiah', for 'the MESSIAH is not a *man*, but a MAN *AND* a WOMAN'. Only as man and woman would the Messiah be the 'temporal and spiritual Messiah, the flesh and spirit Messiah . . .'.[70] Woman's association with the flesh was reaffirmed, and through the notion of the Saving Couple Saint-Simonian salvation was extended to embrace both body and soul.

The role of the Saint-Simonian 'Woman' was essentially a moral one. Her task was not simply to announce the new moral law, but to set in train the moral renewal of society. She would be a 'Woman Napoleon', ending moral disorder as he had ended political disorder.[71] The 'Woman's moral role was emphasised through the maternal guise in which she was portrayed. The concept of the 'Woman' as 'Mother of Humanity'[72] reflected a belief in the universal character of maternal qualities, which both men and women expected the 'Woman' to embody.[73] She would bring to the Saint-Simonians and to the whole world the love, tenderness and moral power which were associated with mothers: 'the severity of the FATHER will be tempered by all the *grace* and all the *tenderness* of the MOTHER . . . the great day of RECONCILIATION and of UNIVERSAL LOVE is arriving, the MOTHER approaches!'.[74] Like the Christian Madonna, she became the hope of all:

The Madonna! in the image of the Madonna it is *woman* to whom the people pray with such fervour; it is *woman* that the sailor invokes in the storm; she also cures the ills of the body and the sorrows of the soul. The poor man finds her by his pallet, and the sinner confides himself to her in his final hour. *Woman* is the refuge of man in his afflictions. But GOD will renew all things, and his *word of love* will be heard by man from an unknown mouth . . . The MOTHER is coming, the MOTHER of all women and men. At her voice each heart burns with a new charity, each arm is raised to put an end to all misery. At her word the earth, shaking off its mourning clothes, is covered in wealth, adorns itself with many riches, sets out an eternal banquet to which all women and men are invited, at which all women and men have their place.[75]

The image of the 'Mother' drew upon the notions of love and security associated with the maternal figure, and already invoked by Catholics in the devotion to the Madonna.[76] It added to this image a concept of the renewing and revitalising power of maternal love in the material as well as the spiritual sphere. The new 'maternal' world would be a world transformed; a world of plenty, in which equality, unity and happiness prevailed.

The Saint-Simonian concept of the Mother/Priestess, like that of priestesses generally, drew much of its meaning from idealised images of women. It stressed the moral and loving qualities of women, but it also emphasised women's biological functions as mothers. The image of childbirth conveyed the life-giving qualities of social maternity in a direct way: the Saint-Simonian 'Mother', for instance, would 'give birth to, suckle and educate all men and women'.[77] However, reference to the process of childbirth also justified an emphasis on the biological character of women's roles as mothers:

> . . . the bond of the SACERDOTAL FAMILY is not broken between the generations. It continues strong in the tenderness of the MOTHER. By willing that the new generation should be carried, nourished, and developed in the breast of WOMAN, and at the time of its entry into the world, should be bound by the living cord which attaches it to the flanks from which it emerges, God has portrayed wonderfully the bond which he wishes to establish between the generations through the affection of MOTHER-HOOD.[78]

The ties binding women with society were not necessarily limited to physical motherhood, but the physical process suggested the innate and fundamental character of maternal ties and, by implication, the absence of such compelling ties in the experience of men.

In fact, the discussion of 'social parenthood' by the Saint-Simonian men drew a significant contrast between the role of the priestesses as 'social mothers' and that of the priests as 'social fathers'. Emile Barrault's vision of the priestess demonstrated this clearly, for he portrayed her as the biological mother of the 'social' family through her *saintes mésalliances*. Barrault argued that the 'mysterious' pregnancies of the priestess would serve an important purpose in breaking down social divisions. She would bring together 'the royal race and the common race', the 'sons of the *gods* and the sons of *men*' in a maternal genealogy. The priest would surrender his prerogatives within the private family and take pride in his role as father of the universal family, since he would be unable to identify his own biological children.[79] The conflict between public and private interests, between family and society, would finally be eradicated.

For Barrault, the priestess became the biological mother of the 'social' family. While this role was construed as a form of 'social maternity', it contrasted significantly with the experience he envisaged for the male priests. They would move beyond biological fatherhood, and their paternal relationship to all would be confirmed. The concept of the social family therefore provided a theoretical opportunity for men to transcend a limited biological role and fulfil a higher destiny as social beings. By contrast, women remained confined to the biological realm, since their reproductive function was essential if men were to experience 'social paternity'. Moreover, the biological relationship provided a model of the maternal role which stressed innate ties, rather than the capacity for transcendence of those ties which was assumed for men.

The Male Mode of Reproduction

Reproductive analogies provided a powerful way for the Saint-Simonian men to express their understanding of the creative social mission in which they were involved. Since those analogies were drawn from human experiences in which sexual difference was crucial, they inevitably conveyed messages about power relations between the sexes in the process. While women remained essential agents for the reproduction of the social family (as well as the biological family) in Barrault's model, the Saint-Simonian men also attempted to construct models in which they carried on the process of social reproduction themselves, unaided by women. They developed the concept of social reproduction as a male mode of reproduction: the intellectual 'procreation' of some men by other men, who assumed not only the powers of 'fertilising' and 'begetting', but those of 'pregnancy', 'labour' and 'childbirth' as well.[80] Women were excluded from the exercise of social reproduction in these models, retaining implicitly the biological function assigned to them by Barrault: that of ensuring a supply of candidates for admission, through male intellectual 'childbirth', into the social family.

The Saint-Simonian men defined themselves as the begetters of sons, and the progeny of the supreme father, Enfantin, was the most numerous. In their apostolic life, the Saint-Simonian males described themselves as spreading the 'fertile seed' which sprang to life in receptive hearts, denoting the beginnings of the new world:

> WE are the ones who are *beginning* the new world: . . . we will BEGET [others] will DEVELOP; our life as APOSTLES is the act of GENERATION itself . . . *Glory* to US THE BEGETTERS, the REVEALERS of the new world![81]

They would 'beget' this new world through their actions, as they 'embraced' the earth, 'fertilising' it by their labour. The Orient provided the immediate focus of the Saint-Simonians' industrial pursuits in 1833, and their task was to make it productive. Sexual metaphors blended with racial images conveyed messages of power and domination, as the Saint-Simonian men described their mission in the East. Enfantin likened the countries of the Orient, perceived as rich but untapped resources, to '. . . rich virgins who call for the visit of their husbands, as in the Canticle of Canticles; *their hearts leapt* when Fournel and Lambert touched upon the port of Alexandria'.[82] Building the Suez Canal became a symbol for the Saint-Simonians of their potency, as they sought to transform the 'virginal' East into a productive partner of the 'male' West:

> Suez
> Is the centre of our life of work,
> There we will perform the act
> Which the world awaits
> To confess that we are
> Male.[83]

This explicit sexual imagery, with its references to sexual arousal and intercourse, linked male potency with the dominance of the masculine over the feminine, and the power of the West over the East. These ideas were conveyed simultaneously by casting the Orient as female, and stressing her submission to her protector/ invader. Furthermore, the articulation of the Saint-Simonian mission in such male terms left no role for the Saint-Simonian women in the industrial project.

Not only did the men describe their task of producing the new world in terms of male reproductive function, however, they also employed images of gestation and childbirth. The Saint-Simonian men would not only be the 'fathers' of the new world, therefore, but its 'mothers' too. They thus challenged the Saint-Simonian women's attempts to ground social maternity, and thus women's social power, in their reproductive mission. By reversing and transforming male and female roles in the metaphorical process of social reproduction, the men construed that process as one in which women's role was peripheral and men's central. Men found a way to transcend the limitations of male biology, and assert their own social primacy.

The Saint-Simonian men claimed to possess new life within themselves, enabling them to produce new children for the doctrine. Saint-Simon himself had begun this life-giving process. As the initial revealer of the new but incomplete doctrine, he had been 'pregnant with the future of humanity', 'carrying within himself the destinies of the world'.[84] In a reversal of images Rodrigues, the direct successor of Saint-Simon, described himself as having been metaphorically impregnated by him:

> . . . this man, pierced to the very core by the living flame of Saint-Simon, felt a new life penetrate within him, and recognised in Saint-Simon a new father, from that day he gave birth to the association of the new universal family. . . .[85]

This was a dramatic attempt to give authenticity to the doctrine which Rodrigues was promoting, as he entered into combat with Enfantin over the new moral law.

Enfantin also positioned himself in a maternal, life-giving role, passing on his '*flesh* and *blood*' to his sons and nourishing them with 'the milk of [his] soul'.[86] The extent to which this intellectual childbirth drew its meaning from the physical process it imitated was underlined by Enfantin in recounting a visit to the birthplace of his son, Arthur Enfantin: 'It is for you especially Massol that I recall this memory, because today I must give birth to you; you must become a complete man, and end your life of indecision'.[87] Enfantin had simply been present at the birth of his biological son, but his intellectual 'son' would owe his spiritual life directly to his male 'mother'.[88]

The Saint-Simonians likened the inauguration of their faith, in individuals and in society, to the birth process. The difficulties and problems of their intellectual parturition were also described in reproductive terms:

> Remember that a new life only emerges through pain, suffering and anguish. It has taken all the disorder, all the revolutions which have wracked humanity for three centuries, to prepare the delivery of the Saint-Simonian revelation.[89]

A reproductive image also prevailed in Enfantin's appointment of Delaporte as the man responsible for difficult conversions: 'You will be a valuable man when it becomes religiously necessary, in order to give light and life, to perform a painful operation; let us hope that these difficult deliveries will be rare'.[90] Despite the intervention of the 'obstetrician' in the intellectual birth process, however, losses occurred. The analogy of death in childbirth was applied, first of all, to the premature death of the young Eugène Rodrigues, who had succumbed to the 'sorrows of a sublime childbirth' as the doctrine initially came into being.[91] It was also used to explain the departure of the dissidents as the new moral law was being created: they had 'given their remaining energy to the first movements of the new life', and had now been replaced by 'the newborn . . . sons that they had produced themselves'.[92]

This use of the reproductive analogy demonstrated the extent to which the Saint-Simonian experience was perceived by a number of the men as a male concern. While the women's theories had allocated to the men the business of 'production', reserving the task of 'population' to the women, some of the men attempted to construct a model in which both 'production' and 'population' were under male control. Furthermore, in the male Saint-Simonian system of social reproduction the pattern of continuity between the male generations acquired a certainty not experienced by men in the process of biological reproduction.[93] By supporting 'the secret of fatherhood' they sought to discount the significance of biological continuity, implicitly recognising its uncertainty for men. They de-emphasised biological reproduction in favour of a concept of intellectual reproduction, which elevated the process of continuity to the intellectual plane:

> It is through the *realisation* of our FAITH with all its enthusiasm and all its holiness, that we feel within us the new LIFE, the LIFE OF PROGRESS, which LINKS us to the *past* and to the *future*; the LIFE OF LOVE which ATTACHES us in the PRESENT to *past* generations and to those to which we are *giving birth*; the LIFE without limits, indefinite, divine, which encompasses simultaneously all the memories of our PAST LIFE and all the hopes of our FUTURE LIFE.[94]

In this system Saint-Simonian life was predominantly a life of fathers and sons, related by the ties of intellectual procreation which replaced the biological bond.[95]

The retreat to Ménilmontant in 1832 symbolised the establishment of this all-male family. In their celibate retreat, the Saint-Simonian men set about creating a 'new man' characterised by gravity and severity, and a new male lifestyle of order, obedience, leadership and work. Enfantin laid aside his claim to be 'the MOTHER who rocks her children and puts them to sleep gently with her kisses', and stressed instead his role as 'the FATHER of men'.[96] A male society of brotherhood and fatherhood was established, from which women were excluded.[97]

The establishment of the social family of men at Ménilmontant was achieved at the cost of weakening the biological family and breaking its ties. The separation of married couples by the formation of the celibate male family demonstrated this fact. In addition, the 'adoption' of Enfantin's biological son by his social 'fathers' proclaimed the superiority of the social family over its biological counterpart. While the apostles assumed joint responsibility for the future of Arthur Enfantin, their wives and children were left to their own devices, as Cécile Fournel revealed:

> . . . we will have to work *materially* for several of us whose husbands have donned the Apostle's habit are penniless, and to those of us with the most energy falls the happy task of providing the livelihood of others, and of their children. . . .[98]

The situation of the Saint-Simonian women and children belied Enfantin's claim that the adoption of Arthur symbolised the strengthening of family sentiment,[99] unless that claim was intended to refer to the new social family he sought to establish.

Women's exclusion from the adoption ceremony except as observers, and in particular the absence of the child's mother, reinforced the gulf between the two modes of reproduction. The biological family remained the realm of women, and from it new social beings emerged at the time appointed for their entry into the social family. The social family remained the domain of men, and women remained spectators to the processes of male social life. Like the theoretical construction of the new social parenthood, the Ménilmontant episode demonstrated the extent to which a distinction between the roles of the sexes was maintained by the Saint-Simonian men. Women were perceived as tied to biological functions, while men interpreted their own destiny as that of transcending biological functions to fulfil their roles as social beings.

After five months of retreat, the Saint-Simonian men began to leave Ménilmontant in November 1832, many resuming secular dress and occupations.[100] This dispersal was attributed to the failure of the 'Woman Messiah' to appear. The Saint-Simonians pointed out somewhat belatedly that 'while the new man lacked the revelation of the new woman, the formation of the *model* of the Saint-Simonian society was necessarily postponed'.[101] They therefore went in search of the 'Mother', and this search became the Saint-Simonians' prime concern during the early months of 1833. Groups of Saint-Simonians began to search for her in various quarters of the globe. Emile Barrault led a group calling themselves the *Companions of the Woman* to the Orient; Rigaud left this group to seek the 'Mother' in India and the Himalayas; Duguet set sail for South America; Louise Crouzat and Claire Démar planned to look for her in North America if they could find the money; other Saint-Simonians travelled to Africa and throughout Europe.[102] Their search was unsuccessful, however, and by 1834 the expected arrival of the 'Mother' was being delayed to an indefinite future. Charles Duguet argued that the time of her appearance could not be predicted with any certainty. Claire Démar did not expect to see the 'Mother' in her lifetime, although Cazeaux predicted that she would arrive during the nineteenth century.[103]

Enfantin began to divert his followers' attention from the search for the 'Woman', encouraging them to subordinate the 'moral idea' to the industrial programme. He chided the *Companions of the Woman* for the 'abnormal, exclusive, stupendous development' which this aspect of their apostolic life had taken, although he had formerly given his encouragement to Barrault's plans.[104] He also argued that they should focus less on 'the Woman' and more on women: 'Forget the MOTHER for a moment . . . think of *women*, of *industry*, of the *cult*, of GOD, the *creator*, the *producer*, the *generator*, the *doer*'.[105] The true appeal to the 'Mother' was redefined as one of labour: she would respond to a peaceful army of workers pursuing the Saint-Simonians' industrial goals.[106]

However, the Saint-Simonians' emphasis on the mythical 'Woman' led to a decline in the position of women within the group. They had been dismissed from the hierarchy when the new moral law was announced in November 1831, on the grounds that only the 'Mother' could rank her daughters. An empty armchair remained as a symbol of the future role of the 'Woman' in the leadership of the movement.[107] The myth of the 'Mother' thus served a diversionary function for many Saint-Simonians. It focused their attention on an imaginary woman, from a distant and exotic society, who would be liberated by the homage of the Saint-Simonian men. The needs of women in their own society were inadequately addressed, and the solution to their problems postponed to a vaguely-defined future. The focus on the coming of the 'Mother' thus highlighted the idealisation of woman in Saint-Simonian theory. 'Woman' became a mythical figure endowed with superhuman powers: an image which contrasted with the very limited power of real women within the Saint-Simonian movement, and in French society generally. Significantly, the power attributed to this 'Woman' stemmed from her female, and especially her maternal qualities. The Saint-Simonian 'Woman' represented the 'eternal feminine'; her coming denoted the social renewal of a 'feminised' world. However, the construction of the mythical 'Mother' as the social mother *par excellence* depended upon denying the potential for 'social motherhood' in real women, since otherwise the 'Woman' would have been redundant. While the absence of the mythical 'Mother' allowed men to claim the resulting void as their domain, the women sought to establish their capacity for social maternity on the basis of their biological predisposition to mother. Definitions of biological roles and their social meanings were contested and conflictual, and formed a crucial point of struggle between men and women within the Saint-Simonian movement.

8
Flora Tristan and the Moral Superiority of Women

The concept of women's special nature shared by Fourier and the Saint-Simonians was developed to its logical conclusion in the social theory of Flora Tristan. Her view of human nature stressed not merely women's difference from men but their essential superiority. This gave rise to her vision of an ideal society which would realise the values and virtues particularly associated with 'the feminine', that is, love, altruism and moral integrity. In Tristan's theory, however, the special character of 'the feminine' was defended not only by reference to 'natural' differences between the sexes but also to Divine law. The characteristics she assigned to women were also those she attributed to God's female nature, so a radical theology provided the ultimate justification for her view of gender relations. Since women's innate qualities contained the foundations for a new and better world, the liberation of women was crucial to social change. Furthermore, those qualities indicated the nature of the desired social transformation, so the new society was designated 'the reign of women'.[1] Feminist and socialist aspirations were brought together within this concept.

Tristan was well acquainted with both Fourierist and Saint-Simonian theories, and was friendly with a number of people involved in those movements. She read Fourier's works, and when she first became involved in the social movement in Paris in 1835 it was to Fourier that she turned for an ally. She tried to arrange a meeting with him to discuss his theories and to seek his support for her own projects, which at that stage focused on the special needs of women.[2] Her relations with Fourier's followers remained friendly throughout the 1830s and 1840s, despite significant points of disagreement on ideology and tactics.[3] Tristan's friends also included Saint-Simonians like Elisa and Charles Lemonnier, Pauline Roland and Eugénie Niboyet (who became a follower of Fourier).[4] Tristan may have attended Saint-Simonian meetings in Paris during their hey-day and she certainly read *Le Globe*, but she was highly suspicious of the authoritarianism of Enfantin.[5]

However, Tristan's commitment to social change was not a product of her exposure to Fourierist or Saint-Simonian activism, but grew from her own life experiences.[6] The death of her aristocratic Peruvian father when she was four years old reduced the family to poverty. They moved to the country, returning to Paris in 1818 when Tristan was nearly 15. She found work colouring designs in the engraving workshop owned by André Chazal, but she and her mother lived in straitened circumstances, and they sometimes accepted gifts of candles and firewood from her employer. Tristan married Chazal in 1821, but after a stormy relationship left him in 1825 when she was pregnant with her third child. Marital strife continued over custody of the children, which was solely a father's right under the Napoleonic Code. Tristan's difficulties in supporting herself and her children were complicated by the need to move frequently in order to elude Chazal. She surrendered her surviving son in 1832, but her daughter, who was born after the separation, was the subject of repeated quarrels and litigation. This continued until 1838, when Chazal was gaoled for shooting his estranged wife. Thus Tristan's early experience of poverty, and her hardships as an unhappily married woman and separated wife, provided fertile soil in which both socialist and feminist commitments could grow. Wider experience of the world, which demonstrated that her own hardships were far from unique, would transform a self-interested young woman seeking redress of her own grievances into a feminist and a socialist.

Tristan worked briefly in Paris after leaving her husband, and in 1826 travelled in England and Europe with two English women who had employed her as a ladies' companion. Little is known of her life between 1826 and 1832. After re-establishing contact with her father's family she travelled to Peru in 1833–4 at her uncle's expense. Tristan's claim to a share of her father's estate was not successful, but the allowance of 2500 francs which she received over the next four years relieved her struggle to earn a living. By the time this allowance was discontinued, in response to Tristan's criticism of Peruvian society in *Les Pérégrinations d'une Paria*, Tristan had served her apprenticeship as a journalist. She was able to support herself by her writings for the remainder of her life.

Tristan's first published work appeared in 1835. It was a short pamphlet dealing with the problems of women travellers, and suggesting the establishment of an organisation to assist them.[7] She produced a number of newspaper articles between 1836 and 1838,[8] when her first book appeared. This account of her voyage to Peru expressed her belief that women were universally oppressed. It also revealed her interest in other social issues, examining the conditions necessary for establishing a just society.[9] This theme was expanded further in Tristan's only novel, *Méphis*, which also appeared in 1838. It advocated the liberation of both women and the *prolétaires*, and defined the two objectives as interrelated.[10] The book's popular romantic style, and its well-timed appearance soon after the attempt on her life by Chazal, ensured its financial success.

The commitment to socialism first expressed in *Méphis* was intensified by Tristan's voyage to England in 1839, when she set out to study the condition of the working class in the country at the forefront of industrialisation. *Promenades dans Londres*, which she published on her return, was intended to warn French workers of the situation they faced as industrialisation accelerated. The dedication to the workers in the 1844 third edition made this clear.[11] The work also reaffirmed Tristan's feminist commitment by investigating the position of English women, and the social implications of their subordination.

Tristan subsequently formulated her plan for *The Workers' Union* (1843) through which she hoped that French workers, and eventually workers everywhere, might achieve their own liberation. This concept marked a significant departure from the class collaborationist approaches of Fourier and the Saint-Simonians, although Tristan did urge co-operation and believed class conflict was avoidable. Her focus on the special interests of working people, and the prospects and problems of organising them, reflected the increasing significance of the urban workers as a force in French political life in the 1830s and 1840s. The resistance of artisans to their proletarianisation, and the protests of workers in new industries against their exploitation, resulted in strikes and even armed uprisings. In addition, attempts were increasingly made to organise workers, and to strengthen craft-based solidarity.[12] *The Workers' Union* reflected this climate of opinion but attempted to surpass its craft-centredness. All workers should be drawn into the union,

Tristan argued. She also stressed the interdependence of sex and class oppression, and hence the need for a bifocal approach to social transformation. Her efforts to impress such strategies on French workers were cut short, however, by her premature death in 1844. During a tour of France to study the conditions of workers' lives and promote the workers' union, she died of a stroke at Bordeaux, aged 41.

FEMALE SUPERIORITY AND THE MORAL EVOLUTION OF SOCIETY

Tristan believed in female superiority, contrasting women's un-rivalled moral qualities with male physical prowess. She argued that men's social dominance would inevitably give way as society progressed, and the higher human capacities, in which women excelled, assumed greater importance. This contrast between the masculine past and the feminine future was drawn very clearly in her novel, *Méphis*, when she had the hero produce two paintings to represent the course of human history. The first was entitled 'THE PAST: *clerical power and brute force are crushed*', and showed a bishop blessing a soldier's sword. This contrasted with an image of woman as the 'guide of humanity':

> A woman in the foreground was my main character; – she was slowly climbing a rocky path which gradually wound upwards and continued on to merge with the horizon. – It was the idealised woman as I envisaged her, drawing humanity towards perfection by her attractive power. This woman . . . personified her sex, as source of life and driving force of progress. . . .[13]

In the painting, this 'Woman' was followed by those eminent thinkers who had recognised 'the moral role which Providence has allocated to [woman] to counterbalance the muscular strength of man', and then by an assortment of ordinary people, 'to indicate that, in all races, man's destiny was to be *guided by woman*'. The painting bore the caption: 'THE FUTURE: *intellectual power replaces brute force.*'[14] Women were collectively assigned responsibility for social progress, and the ideal society would see the flowering of the moral and intellectual qualities in which they excelled.

Tristan's evolutionary model of human development reflected

the increasing popularity of biological models of social organisation in the nineteenth century. The body's transition from infancy
to maturity provided a prototype for humanity's progression over
time through defined 'stages'.[15] Both Fourier and the Saint-
Simonians had defended their projects of social reform by reference to evolutionary models of social development, and had linked
social progress with improvements in the position of women.
Tristan's evolutionary perspective was especially pertinent to her
theories on women, which she defended by reference to a survey
of the march of progress.

The proof of society's progression towards higher states lay, for
Tristan, in the differences between 'civilisation' and 'savagery',
evident in the contemporary world and through the historical
record:

> If we compared the misfortunes to which the savage races fall
> prey with those which still trouble the peoples who are most
> civilised, the enjoyments of the former with those of the latter,
> we would be amazed by the enormous gap which separates
> these two extremities of human achievement. But it is not
> necessary to compare two states of sociability so removed from
> each other in order to establish progress. Gradual progress from
> century to century is easily verified by historical documents
> which reveal to us the social condition of peoples in earlier
> periods. To deny it, one must not wish to see, and only the
> atheist, trying to be consistent, is interested in adopting that
> position.[16]

According to Tristan, human progress gradually made possible a
better understanding of the Divine laws governing social and
moral life, revealing the Providential design which was insupport-
able for the atheist. The culmination of the process, she argued,
would lie in the establishment of an altruistic society.[17]

Tristan's depiction of different cultural and racial groups reflected her concept of a Divinely-directed social evolution. Although she had previously travelled within Europe, her voyage to
South America in 1833–4 provided a dramatic experience of culture
shock as she encountered distinctly different societies for the first
time. Her encounter with other racial groups enabled her to explore the notion of progress in some detail. This was critical to her
own social project, since it allowed her to justify change, and to

identify the causes of society's crisis. In addition, Tristan's overview established that: ' . . . in all social periods, love is, for woman, the pivotal passion of all her thoughts, and the motive for all her actions'.[18] By establishing women's innate capacity to love, their inherent altruism, Tristan 'proved' the natural superiority of women in all societies: a necessary prelude to assigning them the major role in society's advance.

Lowest on Tristan's evolutionary scale were the negroes, whom she encountered in the Cape Verde Islands, off the West Coast of Africa, during her voyage to Peru. Tristan's immediate reaction to them was repulsion. She was offended by the 'negro odour',[19] and imputed to them a range of character traits which she believed were reflected in their expressions. As an amateur physiognomist Tristan paid considerable attention to physical appearance and costume when describing people, because these indicated to her their level of cultural and moral development. Clothing was an extension of the body, and the body was a mirror of the soul.[20] Her impressions of the negroes reflected these views: the men were perceived as tough and ferocious, the women were insolent and stupid, and the children were 'horribly ugly, completely naked, thin [and] puny; one might have mistaken them for little monkeys'.[21] The men were categorised in physical terms, the women in terms of character. Negro men exhibited the 'brute force', the capacity for violence, which was the basis of male power. The negro women's traits indicated that the moral qualities which would provide the basis for women's predominance, intelligence and love, remained underdeveloped.

Tristan did not regard the negroes as sub-human, but as a less highly developed race. Their infantile social condition was compounded by their enslavement to others, which Tristan observed both at Cape Verde and in Peru. The debate over slavery was then raging in Europe, and Tristan joined it by denouncing slavery as a 'monstrous outrage against humanity'. It denied its victims their right to freedom, and to basic human dignity and respect. The slaves' dishonesty and baseness (which Tristan accepted) were the consequences of an even more immoral act: the theft of their liberty.[22] Despite the fact that this immoral act had been committed by Europeans, Tristan defined Europeans as morally more advanced than the negroes. However, like other feminists of the period, she would make slavery an analogy for the position of European women in relation to their white 'masters'.[23]

The negro slave in Peru who allowed her infant to die by refusing to feed it represented for Tristan a silent protest against oppression, as well as revealing the potential of the negroes for moral advancement. Observing the resignation of this imprisoned mother, Tristan wrote:

> Under this black skin, there lie great and proud souls; moving suddenly from natural independence to slavery, there are some indomitable negroes who endure torture and death without submitting to the yoke.[24]

The fact that a woman made this protest was particularly significant. Her recognition of the importance of liberty signified her superiority, as woman and mother, over those around her, and illustrated Tristan's belief that female moral strength was an innate gift, even in its purely instinctive form. The superior spiritual qualities that Tristan distinguished in this woman transformed her appearance, and alone of all the negroes she was perceived by Tristan as strikingly beautiful.[25]

The Peruvian Indians represented a higher stage of moral and social evolution than the negroes, and they displayed more clearly the natural superiority of women. The *ravanas*, the female camp followers of the Peruvian army, outstripped the men both physically and in strength of character. They were strong and robust, violent when opposed, showing great stamina and endurance. Tristan's view of 'primitive' women as physically superior to men contrasted with that of the Saint-Simonians, who had attributed women's historical subordination to their physical weakness and reproductive role.[26] It also blurred the contrast between male and female modes of superiority. However, at this immature stage of social development women's superiority assumed an underdeveloped form. Dominance in such societies was based on physical rather than moral strength, even when wielded by women. Besides, since the moral was inscribed within the physical, according to Tristan, the contrast between energetic women and languid men made a point about their respective moral conditions.

This point was reinforced by Tristan's insistence upon the bravery of the *ravanas*, which indicated female superiority of a higher order. The survival of the army depended upon the courage of its female supply force:

When one remembers that while leading this difficult and perilous life they still have their maternal duties to fulfil, one is amazed that any of them can endure it. It is significant that, while the Indian prefers to *kill* himself rather than *become a soldier,* indian [*sic*] women embrace this life voluntarily, withstanding its fatigues, and facing its dangers with a courage of which the men of their race are incapable. I do not believe that one can summon a more striking proof of the superiority of woman, in the infancy of societies. . . .[27]

Women's courage was a moral quality and a sign of their incipient moral superiority to Indian men. In addition, Indian women demonstrated the natural altruism associated with motherhood. The 'maternal' ability to sympathise with and attend to the needs of others was a quality which Tristan made a hallmark of moral strength, and a prerequisite for social progress.

Although the *ravanas* surpassed the men of their own race, however, they remained morally primitive by Tristan's standards. This was revealed again by their appearance, for they were 'horribly ugly' and semi-naked. More significantly, they lacked self-discipline and gave full vent to their passions although, according to Tristan, they showed more control than the men.[28] Altruism had not yet become their dominant characteristic, therefore, and the ability to subordinate personal concerns to social interests had not yet been achieved in this society.

Spanish Peruvian women, closer to the European standard, were placed higher on the scale of civilisation. They provided Tristan with further evidence of the natural superiority of women, and again this superiority was portrayed as both physical and moral. The women were bigger and more strongly built than the men, more healthy and robust. They were also more energetic, as though 'they consumed, by themselves, the small proportion of energy left to the happy population by this warm and soporific climate'.[29] This physical portrait of Peruvian women suggested a vitality which was denied to men, and which made them superior. The traditional costume, which allowed women to disguise themselves completely, also contributed significantly to their freedom of lifestyle and their ability to influence men, even in political matters.[30] But their superiority also extended beyond the physical plane:

. . . the women of Lima govern the men, because they are markedly superior to them in intelligence and in moral strength. The phase of civilisation in which this race is situated is still well removed from the one we have reached in Europe. In Peru, there is no institution for the education of either sex; intelligence only develops there by its own natural strength: thus the pre-eminence of the women of Lima over the other sex, no matter how inferior, in moral terms, these women may be to European women, must be attributed to the superior intelligence with which God has endowed them.[31]

The innate gifts which distinguished women's destiny were revealed in these women, and again were identified as natural and God-given attributes.

Despite the superiority of Peruvian women to Peruvian men, however, Tristan argued once again that their potential remained hampered by the stage of development of their society. It was still 'reduced to sensual pleasures',[32] and although women's potential could be glimpsed, they sought only hedonistic satisfaction. They were pleasure-loving, materialistic, dominating men by their powers of seduction.[33] Tristan insisted that physical qualities such as beauty and charm could not ensure the predominance which women were destined to exercise. They had to develop the intellectual and moral qualities which were the true basis of their superiority:

> . . . if beauty makes an impression upon the senses, the duration of its reign is prolonged by the inspirations of the soul, moral strength, the talents of the spirit. God has endowed woman with a more loving, a more devoted heart than man; and if it is through love and devotion that we honour the Creator, and there is no doubt of that, woman has an indisputable superiority over man; but she must develop her intelligence and especially achieve self-discipline to maintain this superiority.[34]

Tristan's stress on self-discipline demonstrated her belief that 'social progress' required the gradual harnessing of the lower human passions, and the development of the higher spiritual faculties of intelligence and love. Unlike Fourier and many of the Saint-Simonians, Tristan did not eulogise 'the flesh' and assign it a moral purpose. Sensuality and seduction were inferior applications of female potential in her view, and the model of womanhood that she espoused stressed women's superior ability to rise above the passions of the flesh. Peruvian women lagged behind European women because they had not completely surpassed a domination based on the senses.

Peruvian women's moral potential was evident in their 'loving and devoted hearts', but according to Tristan their lives lacked a higher moral purpose. They did not value altruism, and had not acquired 'the talents, the virtues which have as their objects the happiness, the improvement of others . . .'.[35] They had not come to realise that they were destined for a spiritual mission: 'to be the guide, the inspiring genius of man, to perfect his morality . . .'.[36] The formula for female perfection, and consequently for social perfection, was contained within this idea.

Tristan's survey of the 'march of civilisation' in the non-European world confirmed and ratified some of her fundamental assumptions. Firstly, it revealed her thoroughly Eurocentric perspective, although her racism was patronising and benevolent rather than strident and hostile. The opposition posited between each racial group and an essentially European ideal confirmed her belief in European superiority. However, the qualities assigned to non-Europeans were not seen as innate and irredeemable flaws justifying their exploitation and abuse by Europeans, but as signs of their social and moral immaturity. That immaturity would be overcome with time since progress was the Divine plan for the world.

Tristan's racial survey also conveyed her ideas about sexual difference. The progression from savagery to civilisation was portrayed as a progression from the dominance of physical needs and physical power, to that of moral preoccupations and moral power. Social progress therefore entailed a development from a 'masculine' to a 'feminine' society. This view conformed in some ways with Saint-Simonian visions of social change. However, they had also utilised notions about the 'femininity' of the less advanced black races and the 'masculinity' of the dominant white races, contrasting the biological imprisonment of the 'feminine' with the capacity for transcendence of the 'masculine'. For Tristan, masculinity was not associated with strength of reason, or at least not with the 'enlightened' reason which might have given men a claim to social superiority.[37] It was associated with 'brute force' or with physical and moral inertia. By contrast, women's capacity for moral development indicated their superiority, and linked moral progress with the progress of women.

RELIGIOUS RADICALISM AND THE DEFENCE OF FEMALE SUPERIORITY

Tristan's appeal to a Divinely-directed process of social evolution was one indication of her deep faith. She was imbued with a sense of the presence of God, and had confidence in the operation of Divine Providence in the world and the events of her own life. Her familiarity with Catholic doctrine and rites suggests that she had received at least basic instruction in the faith, although she was never a practising Catholic as an adult. She married without a religious ceremony, criticised the Church in all her writings, and held extremely unconventional beliefs. These evolved in parallel with her social radicalism, and had a significant impact on her concept of social change. In her view, faith only had meaning when it was lived out in service to others. The proof of faith lay in 'the love of God in humanity', and this concept provided the formula for the establishment of an altruistic and harmonious society. Moreover, Tristan revered God as 'Father and Mother' of humanity. She identified a 'female' aspect of the Godhead, and assigned to God as Mother the intelligence and love which she believed were the characteristics of femininity. This portrait of God provided a theological basis for her theory of the innate superiority of women, and their allocation to the task of achieving the moral and social salvation of humanity. Women's influence would create a 'feminised' society based on justice and altruism. Socialism would be a female achievement, and would create a 'feminine' world.

Tristan's combination of religious fervour, doctrinal innovation and strong anticlericalism was not unique in early nineteenth-century France. This period saw the proliferation of unorthodox and unconventional sects promoting occultism, illuminism, theosophy, freemasonry and diabolism.[38] By providing an alternative focus of faith these sects offered an implicit critique of Catholicism, but for some religious radicals the critique was explicit and deliberate. Attacks on established religion formed one aspect of the critique of contemporary society, for the Catholic Church was the bastion of the established order, guardian of its biblical and theological defences. Tristan's religious beliefs demonstrate the interrelationship between her religious and social radicalism, and between her feminist and socialist commitments.

There were two main sources of radical religious influence on Flora Tristan, the first being provided by the Saint-Simonian school. She shared Saint-Simon's energetic criticism of Christianity, especially for its failure to implement its founder's commitment to the poor.[39] As we have seen, Tristan was friendly with a number of people involved in the movement under Enfantin's leadership, and read its publications. The Saint-Simonians' increasingly religious orientation, and especially their insistence on the female attributes of 'God, Father and Mother', found echoes in Tristan's own thinking.

Her association with Simon Ganneau and Alphonse-Louis Constant provided the second radical influence on her religious ideas. Ganneau was an impoverished artist whose main contribution to radical theology was a concept of Divine androgyny. Constant spent several years training for the priesthood, interrupted by periodic lapses into heresy, and finally drifted into occultism.[40] Ganneau and Tristan first met in 1838 or 1839 and she immediately felt an affinity for his ideas.[41] They remained friends until 1844, when he contributed to her appeal for funds to publish *The Workers' Union*.[42] Tristan's friendship with Constant began in 1837. They corresponded, travelled together on occasions, and were believed by some to have been lovers.[43] Tristan's influence intensified Constant's feminist and socialist inclinations, and she clearly felt some measure of agreement with his ideas.[44] She placed epigraphs from his works in her writings, and left to Constant the task of editing her notes for *The Emancipation of Woman*, which he published after her death.[45]

The religious radicals all regarded themselves as prophets, individuals specially chosen by God to reveal his message.[46] They used the Scriptures to justify the movement towards socialism, and reinterpreted the Divine message in the light of their own personal revelation. Belief in Divine Androgyny was one of their key doctrines.[47] This view presupposed the existence of different male and female attributes within the Godhead, and justified an emphasis on the hitherto neglected 'female' attributes of God the Mother. The Saint-Simonians envisaged God as 'Father and Mother', while Simon Ganneau renamed God *Evadah* to emphasise the androgyny of the Supreme Being.[48] Tristan's commitment to this idea was exemplified by her admiration for Ganneau's position, and by her adoption of the plural forms for *Dieux* and *adieux*.[49] The significance of these forms was emphasised by the stamp which she used as a letterhead. It comprised a triangle bearing the words *Père*, *Mère* and *Embryon* on its sides, with *Dieux* in the centre. This stamp began to appear on her letters in 1839.[50]

Tristan's only reference to the composition of her Trinity was brief. She defined God as 'father and mother of the universe, their only son, whom they form from their own substance in their eternal ecstasy'.[51] Constant later explained her concept of God, as he understood it. It combined the notions of active and passive generation, he declared, with the *Embryon* or universe as the continually proceeding product of that generation. 'Intelligence and love' comprised the active element and were defined as female. 'Strength', defined as male, was the passive element. However, in the process of generation these states were also reversed, strength becoming active to fertilise the female element, which then produced the Divine 'fruit', the universe. Constant continued:

> The principle recurs in its effects, and God is manifested in humanity; the creative principle, intelligent love becomes woman: strength is represented by man; so man is only the Promethean arrow, and it is woman who has received the sacred fire from heaven to give him life.[52]

Perhaps a theologian might have taken issue with Tristan's attempt to rank the Divine attributes and distinguish the creative qualities from others. However, as Constant realised, Tristan's concept of God had significant implications for her social theory, since her interpretation of the Divine natures justified her model of female/male relations at the human level. Tristan assigned a higher value to the female principle. God's female nature manifested itself in the human soul, while God's male nature found expression only in the human body. Male essence was associated with physical strength, and female essence with intelligence and love. By tying masculinity to the body and associating the feminine capacity for emotion with the soul, Tristan modified the Saint-Simonian formula which defined women as 'the flesh' and interpreted their emotional strength as a function of their biology. She also countered Fourier's belief in the cosmic superiority of the masculine element. Not only was the female principle the creative and life-giving principle, according to Tristan, it was also the moral principle, since the soul was the seat of moral behaviour. The theory provided a theological basis for the superiority of women, who embodied the feminine, and thus justified their allocation to social leadership. It authorised the roles she assigned to women in the movement towards social perfection, and the role she assumed herself.

As well as identifying a Female principle within the Godhead, radical theologians frequently magnified the role reserved for a woman within salvation history. One version of the Saving Woman presented her as a new female Messiah, whose role would complete that filled earlier by Christ. As we have seen, the Saint-Simonians looked to the coming of a 'Woman' who would complement their earthly father, Enfantin, and complete the revelation of true morality. Tristan's concept of her own Messianic role revealed a similar faith.[53] A second version, as in Ganneau's theory, portrayed this woman as a redefined version of Mary. She was raised to the status of co-redeemer with Christ, becoming the female form of the incarnate God. This theme, an heretical reflection of the flowering of Mariology in nineteenth-century France, was developed more fully by Constant who virtually deified Mary. In *La Mère de Dieu* (1844) he envisaged a forthcoming apocalypse in which Mary would complete the redemptive process. She would end women's oppression by men, and establish a society ruled by 'the eternal laws of a mother's heart'.[54] Tristan claimed some participation in the authorship of this work, and was anxious to promote it.[55]

Both versions of the Saving Woman stressed that human perfection would only be achieved by the intervention of a female figure, the incarnate form of God's female nature. This Woman would define the path to progress, and progress would rely on the 'female' qualities of altruism and love. The prospect of a new 'maternal' society signalled that empathy, compassion and a tender concern for the weak and needy would become integral principles of social life, in contrast with the ruthless struggle and the dominance of the strongest which characterised the 'reign of force'. The radicals prepared for and worked towards the new world by celebrating 'female' qualities, and by advocating female participation in social life in the new society. Radical theology thus provided a justification for Tristan's emphasis on the special, and innately superior, qualities of women, and their potential for achieving the moral transformation of society.

EUROPEAN WOMEN'S OPPRESSION AND ITS MORAL CONSEQUENCES

Tristan's belief in the superiority of women lent a special intensity to her critique of the position of women in European society. She insisted on the 'much greater moral strength and intelligence' of English women compared with 'their masters', and the 'stunning brilliance' of English women's writings on moral issues.[56] She also argued that French women possessed greater moral sensitivity than men. They felt a particular need to improve society and facilitate progress,[57] thus demonstrating the altruistic outlook only emergent in non-European women. Tristan's observation of French working-class women prompted a similar verdict. By nature, she claimed, they were 'sweet, good, sensitive, generous' although constant ill-treatment and hardship made them brutal and indifferent.[58] Their ability to endure greater physical and moral suffering than the men, and their greater self-control, indicated to Tristan their greater moral strength, and she resolved to compare the intellectual differences between the sexes during her tour of France.[59]

However, Tristan's writings on European women generally focused less on their superiority to other women, than on their current subordination to men. She regarded French culture as more advanced than the others she had experienced, but observed that all women remained in a disadvantaged position in European society. Women were 'a class of pariahs', she wrote, whose oppression remained legal everywhere:

Slavery is abolished, they say, in civilised Europe. Certainly, slave markets are no longer held in the town square; but in the most advanced countries, there is not one where numerous classes of individuals don't endure legal oppression. The peasants in Russia, the jews in Rome, sailors in England, women everywhere. . . .[60]

Tristan's emphasis on the oppression of European women added an element of ambiguity to her account of society's moral evolution. She argued that 'moral power' had the potential to overcome 'brute force' and would eventually do so. In that case women's progressive moral development, and the moral evolution of society overall, should have given rise to an increasingly powerful position for women in society. Instead European women, morally the most advanced to date, appeared as more oppressed than women in some of the less advanced societies. The process of moral evolution had reached a stalemate, and Tristan argued that only ending the oppression of women would allow society to progress further.[61]

Tristan identified the structure and organisation of the family as the cornerstone of women's oppression. In this respect her views resembled those of Fourier and the Saint-Simonians, who had written extensively on the subordination of women in the family. She quoted Fourier in likening women's position in marriage to slavery, and adopted his formula equating the degree of civilisation of any society with the liberty of its women.[62] Tristan also shared her contemporaries' criticism of the indissolubility of marriage, arguing that the prohibition of divorce failed to recognise the changing nature of human affections.[63] Women's lack of legal rights in marriage, and their inability to extricate themselves from unsatisfactory partnerships, made marriage an oppressive institution. Tristan documented this oppression in England, Peru and France. Wherever she travelled women were totally subject to their husbands in law, although in Lima, for instance, they managed to avoid the full impact of such laws.[64] Women were deprived of their liberty, subject to a double standard of morality, and to a regime of domestic despotism. The French working-class wife was 'the very humble servant' of her family, in Tristan's view, and was regarded by her husband as his property.[65] The English middle-class wife was no better off:

> The English husband is the personification of the *lord and master* of feudal times; he believes, quite sincerely, that he has the right to demand from his wife the passive obedience of the slave, submission and respect. He locks her in his house, not because he is loving and jealous of her like the Turk, but because he regards her as *his property*, like a piece of *furniture*, which must

only serve his use and which he must always find at his
fingertips.[66]

The English wife was forced to 'live the life of a plant', she argued,
and was reduced to being little more than a baby-making machine.[67]

According to Tristan's analysis, the juxtaposition of despotism
and servitude which marriage enshrined provided the model for
male/female relations in all areas of society. Women were deprived
of civil and political rights, and had no legal existence except
through their male relatives.[68] The servile status of proletarian
women was also evident in the workplace, where they experienced
both economic and sexual exploitation.[69] Prostitution provided the
ultimate demonstration of women's subjection to men, in Tristan's
view. She outlined its economic causes, noting women's lack of
recognised work skills and their inability to support themselves on
the wages considered appropriate for women.[70] However, she also
viewed prostitution as a moral problem, the ultimate form of moral
degradation:

> . . . I will never understand the prostitute! Surrendering her-
> self! Smothering both her will and her feelings; delivering her
> body to brutality and suffering, and her soul to contempt! The
> prostitute is an impenetrable mystery to me . . . (*sic*) I regard
> prostitution as a frightful madness, or else it is so sublime that
> my *humanity* cannot comprehend it. Defying death is nothing;
> but what a death faces the prostitute! She is betrothed to sorrow,
> dedicated to humiliation! Ceaselessly repeated physical tortures,
> constant moral death! And *disgust with herself!!!*[71]

Unlike the Saint-Simonians and Fourier, Tristan clearly did not
regard women's sexual frustration as a factor contributing to prostitution. The prostitute was a victim of her own moral weakness,
and thus a sign of the brutality of her society. The prostitute's body
became a symbol of moral death, a 'worst case scenario' of the fate
of woman in such a society. Prostitution was an unavoidable
feature of a social order which was based on force, which denied
women personal rights and economic independence, and which
accepted a double standard of morality.[72]

Tristan argued that, in oppressing women, society failed to
recognise their crucial moral role. It therefore refused to accord

them an education to prepare them for that role. Middle-class girls were raised like concubines, to please or to serve men.[73] Proletarian girls helped at home while their brothers went to school, and were then sent out to work.[74] Tristan protested at the neglect of general and professional education for girls, since such preparation was essential for personal independence. She regarded girls' lack of true moral development as even more serious. In her opinion, the growth of morality required the development of intelligence and love: the faculties of the soul. However, the intellectual development of girls was ignored, and their loving faculties were destroyed by their upbringing. The education of middle-class girls 'hardened their hearts' and 'numbed their souls'.[75] The lack of education of French proletarian girls had a similar effect, for their loving and generous natures were deformed, producing brutal, unkind and hard women.[76]

Tristan's argument against the oppression of women stressed not merely its injustice to women, but its moral impact on women and on society. Rather than being 'moralising agents for the men over whom they have influence from birth until death',[77] women were insufficiently capable of making either a material or moral contribution to society. Oppression destroyed women's morality, in Tristan's view, because moral integrity depended upon personal liberty. Without that liberty women, like the slaves of South America, were incapable of making real moral choices:

> Virtue or vice supposes the freedom to do good or evil; but what morality is a woman capable of when she has no control over her own life, when she has nothing of her own, and when, throughout her life, she has become used to eluding arbitrary rules by her cunning, evading constraint by her charm? . . . As long as she is subject to the yoke of man or of prejudice, receives no professional education, is deprived of her civil rights, no moral law can exist for her![78]

The oppression of women was thus a fundamental moral flaw in society, according to Tristan, and its elimination was an urgent necessity.

Tristan therefore based her call for women's rights on moral imperatives, linking women's freedom with the progress of society overall. The appeal to women's specific differences from men enabled her to make this argument forcefully. Her survey of different cultures had emphasised the superior intelligence, and moral and emotional sensitivity, of women. In this context, the denial of rights to women demonstrated clearly the moral inadequacies of society: the rule of brute force – the rule of men – prevailed, and moral force, represented by women, was suppressed. Liberty for women was essential for moral progress.

In addition, Tristan presented an argument for women's rights which relied on natural law, and hence on women's shared humanity with men: women in European society were deprived of their 'sacred and inalienable rights' to liberty and equality.[79] This reference to the Revolution's 'Declaration of the Rights of Man and the Citizen', which had made fundamental human freedoms a birthright for the generic collective 'men', asserted women's inclusion within that collectivity. The social impact of the fundamental freedoms was then emphasised to enhance the claim for their recognition in women: since individuals require personal freedom in order to behave morally, a moral society was one which guaranteed the liberty of all its citizens. The denial of human rights to women thus negated their possibility for all, Tristan declared, and indicated that society functioned according to the dictates of tyranny. The contrast between despotism and liberty urged the application to gender relations of the principles which the Revolution had enshrined as the basis for a legitimate social order and for social justice. Tristan cited Mary Wollstonecraft's *Vindication of the Rights of Woman* in support of her case:

> Mary Wollstonecraft demands women's liberty as a *right*, in the name of the principle on which societies establish what is just and what is unjust; she demands it because without liberty no moral obligation of any kind can exist, because without equality between the sexes morality lacks foundation, ceases to be valid.[80]

Only the principle of justice could ensure individual rights and hence true social morality.

The question of society's treatment of women was a fundamental moral issue, according to Flora Tristan, second only to the question of humanity's relationship with God.[81] Women were portrayed as the human representation of God's Female essence, which needed to be made manifest in society. Furthermore, since the hallmarks of female nature, intelligence and love, were the qualities which established human superiority over the remainder of the animal kingdom, there was a clear implication in her theory that women were more highly developed humans than men. Like Fourier and the Saint-Simonians, then, she regarded women's oppression not merely as an undesirable facet of contemporary society, to be eliminated in some improved model, but as a symptom and cause of deeper social malaise and disorder. The moral evolution of society towards perfection required and foreshadowed the emergence of a radically different society in which women were no longer oppressed.

9

Flora Tristan, Socialism and the 'Reign of Women'

Flora Tristan's belief in the moral superiority of women, and her commitment to the moral perfection of human life as well as its material transformation, largely explain her espousal of a feminist socialism. Her concept of socialism emphasised moral factors which, in her view, were inseparable from questions of economic and social organisation. This perspective ensured a significant role for women in the movement towards socialism and in the socialist future. The morally perfect society whose establishment Tristan regarded as inevitable would therefore be characterised by the 'reign of women'.

A 'FEMALE' MODE OF SOCIALISM

In Tristan's view, any body of knowledge which sought to give a valid explanation of human experience had to be a 'human' science, that is, one centred on and responsive to people's needs as physical and spiritual beings. She regarded true understanding as a spiritual state, not an act of reason. It resulted from the combined effect of faith and love on the intelligence. Faith was essential, because it bestowed 'knowledge' of God, the source of all other knowledge.[1] Love was also necessary, because it ensured an empathetic view of the world. It was a powerful force enlightening the mind and inspiring action, and even without learning it could produce a true understanding of the 'social question'.[2] A purely rationalist response to social issues, on the other hand, lacked the human sensitivity necessary for true understanding. This view explained Tristan's criticism of the artillery officers she observed at Saint-Etienne, whom she regarded as 'men of mathematics':

I regard them as dangerous men, for every person whose heart, whose compassion, whose inner feelings are atrophied and withered, is a person who is dangerous to society. – So! the science of mathematics affects the heart, the compassion and the inner feelings of man as fire affects a corn field, it burns it down to the roots.[3]

In Tristan's writings, 'mathematical' became a term of reproach, indicating a lack of compassion and hence of true intelligence.[4]

Tristan applied her critique of rationalism to economics and political science,[5] and also to socialism itself. While many of her socialist contemporaries sought to defend their theories as thoroughly scientific, therefore, Tristan defined passion, faith and humanitarian concern as firmer bases for socialism. Only this form of socialism could avoid elitism, she argued, by avoiding a distinction between those who possessed a sound understanding of a body of knowledge, and those who did not. Besides, passionate conviction, not dispassionate analysis, made people work for change.[6] This was not an argument against theory, but a claim that theory required an emotional component if it was to respond adequately to the human condition.

Since Tristan defined heartless rationalism in opposition to empathy and sensitivity, she implicitly contrasted male and female forms of knowledge. She did admit that some men were capable of developing the sensitivity necessary to become good socialists. The worker Touron was one of these:

> I greatly admire this worker Touron. He is what I call a phenomenon! A man who cannot read, who has had no education, who cannot express himself and who despite all these obstacles has extraordinary powers of comprehension! And the cause of this fine intelligence? This man is tender-hearted, he has feelings and he is aware of his dignity: reaching out to his brothers. He loves! that is the secret. He understands all because he loves![7]

While women were inherently capable of 'true intelligence', then, men needed to develop the 'female' attributes of love and empathy in order to achieve it. Men had to become feminised. This theory provided an important justification for enhancing the role of women, making them natural leaders in the movement towards socialism.

Tristan regarded socialism as the perfect moral law. It was destined to supersede Christianity, though preserving the elements of truth which that doctrine contained. Describing the role of her prototype socialist in the novel *Méphis*, Tristan had explained:

> . . . in the writings of this child of the people lies the résumé of the ages, the explanation of all symbols; in them the Gospel is clear as heavenly dew; the thought of Christ emerges from its veils in its entirety. In short, it is a new law; a law of love and union destined to end all conflict between men. . . .[8]

Socialism was the logical outcome of the Christian exhortation: 'Do not do to others what you would not like to have done to yourself'.[9] By offering the means to both material and spiritual salvation for the workers, socialism fulfilled the Christian command of mutual love. It was a 'new religion', but one which would bring about immediate improvements in people's lives through the moral principles on which it rested.[10]

The ultimate objective of social progress, and thus the hallmark of the new religion of socialism, lay in achieving 'union', the fusion of 'thoughts, sentiments and moral being' which would characterise the perfect society.[11] This objective inspired Tristan's plan for the organisation of the working class. Tristan believed that all socialist leaders shared some insights into the ideal pattern of social organisation. However, she also maintained that one theory would ultimately emerge providing a complete guide to social reform, a divinely-inspired package deal for social perfection. Clarity, simplicity and comprehensiveness would be the hallmarks of its Divine origins for, as she argued with the Fourierists, Providence would not have decreed a plan for humanity which was too complex to be understood, or impossible to implement. Tristan's own proposal for the 'universal union of working men and women', which she developed during the early months of 1843, appeared to her to have all these qualities, and she did not doubt its divine inspiration.[12] Her principal objective was 'TO ESTABLISH THE WORKING CLASS',[13] and she saw her workers' union as the immediate means for achieving the 'common happiness' which was society's goal.[14] As a united group the workers would control a large body of capital, acquired by small individual contributions, and they could use this capital to educate the young and care for the old in 'worker palaces'. By becoming united, the workers would acquire the power to gain recognition of the most fundamental human right, the right to live. In practical terms, this required recognition of the right to work and the right to education.[15]

In Tristan's view, the workers' union would be the means to self-liberation for the working class, and she stressed the material advantages it would provide. It would enable the workers, by their united action, to break out of the cycle of misery and ignorance in which they were caught: 'Alone, you are weak and sink beneath the weight of miseries of all kinds! So! end your isolation: unite! *Union is strength.* You have numbers on your side, and that is a lot.'[16] Together they could educate their children, provide for their old age, and experiment, within their palaces, with projects for the organisation of work. In this manner, the workers' union and the system of palaces could provide 'a *bridge* between civilisation which is dying out, and the harmonic social order foreseen by some superior minds'.[17]

While Tristan always stressed the importance of material gains for the workers, and rejected the idea that misery should be endured on earth in exchange for heavenly rewards, her workers' union was far more than a construction project. She regarded her book, *The Workers' Union*, as the blueprint for the implementation of socialism. Just as the Gospel had preceded the establishment of the Church and provided the law which governed it, so her work set out the principles on which socialism would be constructed.[18] It was the 'new gospel for the worker . . . which teaches him his rights'.[19] Where the Christian gospel had preached '*brotherhood in God, union in God*', she proclaimed '*brotherhood in humanity, union in humanity*',[20] that is, the translation of the Christian principle into reality within human experience.

God's dealings with humanity had therefore brought about a progressive perfection of moral principles, according to Tristan, and a movement towards their implementation. The Christian precept of love had stated the fundamental principle of perfect social relations, which would only be realised under socialism. Tristan's 'workers' union' provided the means to achieve the socialist objectives, and thus made possible a transition to the 'harmonic social order'. In doing so it marked her out as the Messianic Woman, the bearer of the definitive revelation of the Divine purpose, and hence the agent of human salvation. Furthermore, Tristan's definition of socialism as a perfected moral system provided a justification for assigning a major role to women under socialism. As the moral evolution of society continued, women's moral superiority would allow them to assume the dominant role indicated by their divinely-bestowed capacities.

FLORA TRISTAN AS 'WOMAN GUIDE' AND FEMALE MESSIAH

Tristan's theory of a 'female' mode of socialism – one which emphasised love and empathy, and gave weight to the 'female' moral sphere – influenced the role she assumed herself in the process of social transformation. It also reinforced her religious beliefs, which provided a theological justification for a messianic self-image. Tristan was convinced of her own special insight into the causes of social ills and the requirements for reform, and like Fourier and Saint-Simon, she regarded herself as one of a number of special providential agents sent by God to direct the course of progress. However, Tristan increasingly regarded her part in the Divine plan as a special one, shaped largely by her womanhood. She developed the image of herself as the 'Woman Guide', in the Saint-Simonian tradition. Their search for 'the Mother' had symbolised their belief that God's revelation would be complete only when the *Dieu-Mère* had spoken. The 'Woman' whom they sought would reveal a new moral law. She would liberate women and the workers, unify all opposing elements, and initiate the reign of peace and love.

In 1838 Tristan had explored the theme of the 'woman guide' in her novel *Méphis*. The hero had described woman as 'guide of humanity', 'drawing humanity towards perfection by her attractive power',[21] and the novel concluded with the imminent arrival of the new order. The hero's daughter, Mary, described as 'the new daughter of Eve', was charged with implementing the new regime. She would bring about a transformation of social relations, undoing the 'Fall' and completing redemption.[22] Several incidents suggest that Tristan envisaged herself as this 'Woman Guide' in real life. Her encounter with the English socialist Robert Owen in 1837, for instance, can be interpreted in this Saint-Simonian way. At a meeting he conducted in Paris during his visit, Owen was criticised (probably by a Saint-Simonian) for not having a female leader beside him: 'At that very moment a woman stood up, held out her hand and said, "I am here". Then Mr Owen bowed to her . . . That woman was Mme Flora Tristan.'[23] Tristan may well have viewed herself as the necessary complement to Owen, since she regarded Owenism as too materialistic.[24] The male possessed the law of material progress; she, the female, revealed its moral component.

Her encounters with former Saint-Simonians during her tour of France revealed even more clearly the extent to which she identified herself as the 'Woman Guide'. Tristan experienced an immediate rapport with them because they interpreted her work from a Saint-Simonian perspective, seeing her as the long-awaited 'Woman'. This, according to her, was the only element of their former faith which they maintained:

> . . . only one thing remains, the rehabilitation of woman, the superiority of woman, the coming of the woman – my presence, the presence of a woman coming to talk to the proletarians, is for [them] the coming of the woman. . . .[25]

The beliefs which she shared with the Saint-Simonians enabled Tristan to engage in a discourse with them which she could share with few others, discussing '"the gods" and not "free will"'. Tristan asserted that she alone could understand the meanings expressed by the 'madmen':

> [Pérelle] is a madman to everyone else. – That has been the verdict in every age on those who surpass their times and live in the future – Jesus was regarded as insane by his contemporaries and those who came after him have made him a God.[26]

The Saint-Simonians Pérelle and Lallemant might be considered mad, she concluded, but 'in the future they will be judged superior men having been the first to recognise the coming of the woman'.[27]

While Tristan saw herself as the fulfilment of the Saint-Simonian prophecy, the degree of similarity between her beliefs and theirs was exaggerated in her eyes. They did believe that the 'Woman' would save the world since she would reveal a new moral law, but her powers were seen as complementary to those of 'the Father', Enfantin. He maintained a certain advantage, since it was he who 'called' the Woman, went in search of her, and would have validated an individual's claim to be that person. The 'Woman' idealised by the Saint-Simonian men was above all an imaginary woman. She was an absent woman, an idea of 'Woman', who had no human form. She was unlike the real women who surrounded them in the Saint-Simonian movement but whom they found lacking as representatives of 'the feminine'. For many of the Saint-Simonian women the 'Woman' was the collective female spirit, embodied in them all and therefore without a specific female representative. Tristan's concept of herself as the 'Woman Guide of Humanity' confounded both these images. Her 'Woman' was independent of male sponsorship, with an authority stemming from her own integrity and Divine inspiration. She was an exceptional representative of her own sex, destined for a role as social leader. She was not the 'complement' of a man, but was superior by virtue of her sex and thus could achieve what men could not. Tristan interpreted her own success in preaching to the workers in this way:

> . . . here are men who no longer have faith in men, whether deputies, intellectuals, priests or kings . . . so guided by commonsense these men have said to themselves: here is a woman who comes to us to serve us, God has sent her . . . So without having planned it, here am I as the Woman-Guide, just as I had also quite sensibly imagined myself . . . Man thinks that the word of life is dangerous – and that's the difference, woman is forced to spread this word of life. – Woman is life and man is limitation [*la borne*] – That is why woman is superior to man.[28]

Tristan confirmed her messianic self-image by the emphasis she placed on a chance meeting with another self-appointed Messiah, Chabrier, during her visit to a London lunatic asylum in 1839. Chabrier entrusted his mission to her:

> . . . God has sent you into this place of desolation, not to save me, for I must perish here, but to save the idea which I have come to bring to the world! . . . *I am the representative of your God, the Messiah foretold by Jesus Christ.* I have come to complete the work which he has assigned me; I have come to end all forms of servitude, to free woman from the slavery of man, the poor from that of the rich and the soul from the slavery of sin.[29]

He bestowed on Tristan the 'sign of redemption', a small straw cross, saying: 'Take this cross, wear it on your chest and go into the world to proclaim *the new law*'. The 'reign of God' would soon replace the 'reign of the devil', he announced.[30] Significantly, Tristan did not regard Chabrier as a madman, for in her view this type of 'madness' demonstrated only superiority. She likened his discourse of love and righteous indignation to that employed by Jesus, Saint-Simon and Fourier, who had also been regarded as mad. Tristan claimed to understand perfectly the ideas which inspired Chabrier, and rather than seeing herself as his successor, she defined him as her precursor, as 'a new St. John'.[31]

The main point of reference for Tristan as a messianic figure was Christ. Like Christ, Tristan brought the message of salvation, the 'new Gospel', thus completing earlier revelations.[32] The essence of her role as the new Messiah, however, lay in undertaking the work of redemption. This required suffering and martyrdom for Tristan, as it had for Christ. She would be crucified by those she had come to save, who were 'hard-hearted' and deaf to her message. Like Christ, she suffered 'for all and through all', taking upon herself the sufferings of humanity. Her 'crucifixion' would re-enact the crucifixion of Christ, and her sacrifice would achieve the collective redemption of the people.[33]

Tristan also envisaged her messianic role as a creative one. Like Christ, she both suffered to save humanity and brought them Divine life. She described this creative function as one of spiritual maternity, that is, as a process of giving life to others by creating the idea of God in their souls. Through Divine intervention, the 'words of life' which she had passed on to them became incarnate in their souls:

> With what maternal love have I poured out upon them my care and my sollicitude! When I saw that one of them was ready to receive life, my strength increased a hundredfold to make him great, beautiful and magnificent. Oh! however strenuous this childbirth may have been, it brought heartfelt joy! Giving spiritual life to a brother! but that is being God creating in the universe! Oh! it is the supreme joy![34]

Each new soul she 'created' was a cause for celebration, and Tristan found herself more attached to her spiritual children than to those of her own flesh and blood. She claimed to love Eléonore Blanc more than her daughter Aline, for instance, and with a superior kind of love.[35] Tristan's concept of her maternal function was not limited to the individual plane. She envisaged her task as giving 'moral and intellectual and physical life to thousands of individuals, in short to humanity'.[36] Ultimately, she would give birth to a new world:

> The jewish [sic] people were dead and debased, and Jesus raised them up. – The Christian people are dead and debased today and Flora Tristan, the first strong woman, will raise them up. Oh! I feel a new world within me and I will give this new world to the old world which is crumbling and dying.[37]

The image of childbirth provided a powerful analogy for Tristan's creative role, as it had for the Saint-Simonians, and gave weight to her insistence that social transformation would be a female achievement.

In perceiving herself as the messianic Woman, therefore, Tristan saw herself both as guide and redeemer, drawing on the Saint-Simonian tradition but also revealing her affinity with Ganneau and Constant. The role of 'Saving Mother' which she assumed was reminiscent (for instance) of that attributed by Ganneau to Mary who, as 'Great Mother of Humanity', both died for and regenerated the human race.[38] By casting herself in such a role, Tristan showed that her messianic vision surpassed that of her contemporaries. Rather than raising the status of Mary and locating her within the Trinity as others did,[39] Tristan envisaged herself in partnership with God, replacing Mary and succeeding Jesus as agent of human salvation.

TOWARDS THE 'REIGN OF WOMEN': THE ROLES OF WOMEN UNDER SOCIALISM

If Flora Tristan was a special Messianic figure in human history, all women shared her role as guide of humanity in lesser ways by virtue of their innate moral gifts. The image of women as 'guides of humanity' was brought to life in practical ways in *The Workers' Union*, where Tristan portrayed women both as ideal wives and mothers, and as social activists. Firstly, Tristan anticipated an improved family model as society progressed, and assigned to women responsibility for this task. She stressed the influence women exerted on men at every stage of life. However, only with education would women be able to maximise that influence, and fulfil their moralising role as they were destined to do.[40] The family would then be transformed. Women would raise their children lovingly and intelligently, instilling moral standards and overseeing their education. They would be the *confidantes* of their families, a source of advice, comfort and guidance. As the centres of family life, women would exert a moral attraction, drawing husband and children to the happiness of the family circle, and counteracting the pernicious influence of the *cabaret* and the streets.[41]

Women's moral influence as wives and mothers would also have ramifications beyond the home. Since 'love and inner contentment triple, quadruple man's strength', domestic harmony would increase man's productive capacity.[42] Furthermore, Tristan's ideal women would also be members of the paid workforce. She argued that individuals contributed to society through their labour, and universal labour was an essential element of her plan to eliminate poverty. Riches would increase indefinitely 'when women (half of the human race) are summoned to bring their share of intelligence, strength and capacity into social life'.[43] Similar arguments had been employed by Fourier and the Saint-Simonians to justify a role for women beyond domestic responsibilities, a role many working class women already anticipated by their participation in paid labour.

Tristan's emphasis on paid work for women reflected the importance she attributed to their economic independence. It was also consistent with the family model defended by many artisanal workers in this period. Both men and women artisans believed that childraising and care of the household were primarily female responsibilities, though women's roles as wage-earners were also widely acknowledged.[44] Tristan's ideal woman, combining family responsibilities with paid work, was a perfected image of her proletarian contemporaries. With adequate education and properly remunerated work women would be: '. . . workers skilled in their trade, good mothers capable of raising and guiding their children . . . and moralising agents for the men over whom they have influence from birth until death.'[45] Through their influence on men they would build a society based on the values they embodied.

This model of the ideal proletarian family had a strategic purpose, since it was calculated to woo the artisanal men who formed Tristan's main audience. The prospect of having a well-organised and comfortable domestic life had a strong appeal to them, as

Tristan realised, and the distinction between male and female responsibilities was central to their definition of themselves as skilled male workers.[46] Her discussion of the delights of domesticity was addressed specifically to men, aimed at making them understand the importance of women's inclusion within social transformation. It appealed repeatedly to their self-interest, as Tristan sought to defuse any fears about her feminist demands:

> It is not in the name of *women's superiority* (though I will certainly be accused of it) that I tell you to demand rights for women; no indeed. First of all, before discussing *her superiority, her social identity must be recognized*. I rest my case on a firmer foundation . . . your own self-interest as men. . . .[47]

Significantly, Tristan did not deny her belief in women's superiority, and continued to defend this claim during her tour of France.[48]

The model of family harmony may also have served a more allegorical purpose, by projecting a vision of social relations which contrasted with current practices. Tristan was severely critical of contemporary working-class family life, regarding it as generally loveless and brutalised by circumstance.[49] She also condemned the bourgeois family model for its introspection and self-indulgence, and was particularly critical of its encouragement of full-time motherhood.[50] The idealised proletarian family which Tristan described provided an appealing alternative, offering her audience a vision of emotional fulfilment and harmony which transcended the grim realities of poverty, and the emotional sterility of the bourgeois marriage market. Rather than attempting to describe a future social reality, however, it delineated the qualities and values which would characterise perfected social relationships: tenderness, compassion and love.[51]

Despite the moral significance with which Tristan invested the idealised working-class family, she envisaged the ultimate disappearance of the family structure:

> If children were placed in public institutions from two years of age, the need for the household would be less obvious; with the education she would have received, woman would be able to support herself by working as man does, and this state of affairs would bring us towards the phalansterian system.[52]

Tristan never delineated the pattern of social organisation which would ultimately emerge under socialism, since she regarded speculation about the details of future social forms as pointless.[53] However, she criticised socialist theories which stressed retention of the private family, and applauded those which anticipated a radical change in the pattern of social organisation, even its family base. Although she expressed reservations about Fourier's overall system, therefore, she looked favourably on his proposals for communal childraising, and condemned Cabet's advocacy of a male-dominated family system.[54] Her preference for communal childraising was based on the claim that such a system was better suited to developing the moral qualities of children, and preparing them for social responsibility, than the self-interested private family. Besides, her own experience as a single parent had perhaps confirmed that women's participation in society on equal terms with men was impossible while they took sole charge of childraising. Under the communal system women would apparently raise their children until at least the age of two, but Tristan did not discuss how such a system would operate or what the role of fathers would be.[55] Perhaps her focus on immediate objectives, or her fear of alienating her working-class readers, deterred her from enlarging on her vision, or perhaps she simply failed to resolve the questions which this issue posed.

Significantly, neither the model of the perfected family, nor that of communal childraising, relied on female domesticity for its moral impact. The moral role of woman was not only compatible with her broader involvement in the community, but demanded that she apply her maternal gifts within the broader social family. The workers' union would make possible the extension of women's moral role from the domestic to the social sphere by extending the participation of women in economic and social life. They would bring their intelligence and love to bear in all areas of society, and the new social order, permeated by women's influence and values, would constitute the 'reign of women'.

This belief underlay Tristan's call for a second, more overtly political role for women in the movement towards socialism. She stressed the importance of women's involvement in the so-called public sphere, as activists in the struggle for social change. Firstly, she suggested that all women could play a role in establishing the 'universal union of working men and women'. Rich and powerful women could contribute their money and protection; educated women could instruct the people; proletarian women could become members and encourage others to join. They could become, collectively, the defenders of the Union.[56] Because of their 'holy devotion', she believed that 'in the current state of affairs, [women could] serve the cause more effectively than men',[57] and she anticipated their ready support:

> Women, whose souls, hearts, spirits, senses are endowed with such sensitivity that . . . you have a tear for every sorrow, – a cry for every groan of anguish, – a sublime enthusiasm for every generous action, – a self-sacrifice for every suffering, – a consoling word for every affliction:- women, who are consumed by the need to love, to act, to live; who *seek everywhere* for an outlet for this burning and ceaseless activity of the soul which inspires you and consumes you, torments you, kills you; women, – will you remain silent and *hidden* forever, while the *largest* and *most useful* class, your brothers and sisters the proletarians, those who work, suffer, weep and groan, come and implore you to help them overcome misery and ignorance.[58]

Women had not merely the inclination for good works, according to Tristan, but a physiological and spiritual need to devote themselves to others. They needed a mission if they were to experience fulfilment. Tristan believed that the propagation of the workers' union corresponded perfectly to that need, even among the bourgeois women to whom the above call was addressed.

While Tristan recognised the different material situations of women, she nevertheless focused on their shared identity as women, and the qualities which they could bring to the social struggle: a stance sometimes adopted by the Saint-Simonian women. This view suggested that all women experienced a common oppression amongst themselves, and with male workers:

> Women, the WORKERS' UNION has cast its glance your way. – It has understood that it could not have more devoted, more intelligent, more powerful allies. Women, the WORKERS' UNION deserves your gratitude. It is the *first* to have recognised women's rights in *principle*. Today your cause and its cause have become one and the same. Women of the wealthy class, . . . you are oppressed by laws, by prejudice; UNITE YOURSELVES with the oppressed and by means of this legitimate and holy alliance, we

will be able to fight legally, loyally, against the laws and prejudices which oppress us.[59]

The Union's defence of women's rights 'in principle' placed women on an equal footing with workers, since the Workers' Union was first and foremost an expression of the principle of workers' rights. The interests of rich women were identified with those of the poor, but in focusing on the sexual oppression of wealthy women, Tristan's analysis glossed over the ambiguities of their position and the extent to which they had a vested interest in preserving the social order. Similarly, in suggesting that working men co-operate with rich women to achieve both class and sex freedom, she anticipated a positive male response to her argument that the preservation of the existing sexual order prevented the liberation of the workers. Their unwillingness, in many cases, to accept this idea was soon evident.

The leadership roles assigned to women reflected Tristan's conviction that moral reform was an essential accompaniment of socio-economic transformation. Women's moral superiority, reflected in their altruism and compassion, marked them out for roles as agents of a moral revolution. Using a religious analogy, Tristan described them as *prédicatrices*, preachers of the new religion of socialism.[60] However, women's status as moral leaders did not imply that their role was apolitical. On the contrary, Tristan stressed that women should be militants fighting for their own rights and those of all oppressed people. Her own success amongst the workers became a sign for Tristan of the potential of women in general to fill a guiding role. She wrote at Lyon:

> It was really a touching a scene, all these foremen, married, heads of families, intelligent and educated men 30 or 40 years old, coming to listen to a woman, to thank her for her sympathy, to describe in turn their misfortunes, their sorrows . . . Oh! yes what is happening here is a subject and a development worthy of notice. It reveals in germ a new order . . . What I am doing at this moment, and the results I am achieving say more for the superiority of woman than anything that could be written or said on the question.[61]

Tristan promoted the concept of women's rightful leadership in attempting to establish Eléonore Blanc as her successor, holding her up to the workers of Lyon as the first of 'the women capable of continuing the great work' which Tristan herself had initiated.[62] She also emphasised women's potential as leaders within the social struggle in a speech to those workers:

> I briefly said a few well-chosen words about what could be expected from women, from their love, devotion, intelligence, activity, if they were called into the social movement. I pointed out to them that we had reached the reign of women, – that the reign of war, of brute force, had been that of [men] and that now women could achieve more than men because they had more love, and today love alone must rule.[63]

Love would characterise the perfected society, so women, who excelled in this trait, were both the ideal agents of change and the models for change. The 'reign of women' not only suggested that women would exercise new forms of social power in the emergent society, therefore, but highlighted the peaceful and altruistic character of that society.

The concept of women as moral guides of men may suggest to us a largely passive role for women, elevated to the pedestal and worshipped at the domestic altar. However, Tristan's attempt to promote an active role for women amongst the working class, by speaking to meetings of women, enrolling them in her union and looking for women to represent her once she moved on, reveals that her vision was not so restricted. She was aware that educational deprivation and social norms limited the role which many women might play in the immediate future. This explained her insistence that the committees of the workers' union reserve a proportion of their places for women, and that workers encourage their womenfolk to join.[64] Tristan encouraged women to become involved in 'political, social and humanitarian affairs', pointing out that 'politics reache[s] right to the hearth': in other words, the personal is political.[65] Tristan's 'women guides' were not envisaged as domestic ornaments but as social activists.

In general, the workers' reaction to the idea of a leadership role for women, or even to the notion of equal rights, was not encouraging. Tristan could define women as superior, but translating that definition into reality was another matter altogether. The workers' newspaper, *L'Atelier*, mocked her proposals:

> . . . Madame Flora, you know, desires the emancipation of woman, of woman who is currently a slave, as you are all aware, a slave under civil law, and especially under religious law. You are aware, also, that we have no women priests, no women deputies, no women military captains; but all that will happen with the union and in time.[66]

Even some workers supportive of her calls for improving the condition of women insisted on a clear distinction between the public and private spheres, and women's natural predestination for the latter. One wrote to Tristan:

> I protest against the public exercise of her authority. Woman's life is household life, domestic life, the life of the interior. Not that I claim that she should serve her master as a slave . . . there would be no subjugation for woman in having man represent her at least tacitly, in civil life.[67]

Women were frequently hostile to her ideas also.[68] The notion of moral power for women within the home may have been acceptable, but the broader understanding of women's 'power', as Tristan sought to promote it, remained an alien concept to many. Tristan never investigated the implications of this hostility for her theory, and in particular for the natural liaison which she had affirmed between the liberation of women and that of the working class.

Tristan's anticipation of the 'reign of women' stemmed from her esteem for the qualities which she defined as female. She stressed women's love, sensibility and moral influence on men. In her view, these traits made female nature markedly superior to male nature, which was characterised simply by brute force. For Tristan, separate natures did not mean separate spheres. Rather, women's innate superiority justified their leadership in society and in the home, both of which they were destined to transform. Since moral transformation was a prerequisite for altering social conditions, women's moral superiority made their participation in all areas of society essential.

Women's special role in society was symbolised by their maternal function. They gave physical life, participating in the act of creation. Their life-giving powers would assume broader dimensions in the new order, however, as the full scope of their maternal powers was revealed. They would bestow spiritual life, pouring out upon men the divine light which they possessed and leading them out of darkness towards their destined state of perfection.[69] Woman herself would become perfected in this process. Her intellectual power would be realised, and her capacity for love would find its fulfilment in the 'love of God in humanity'. Tristan described this new woman as *la femme forte*, regarding herself as the first of the lineage.[70]

In a general sense, then, all women were assigned the guiding role which Tristan had assumed for herself in a very particular way. Their influence would ensure an end to violence and oppression, and the establishment of social harmony. The era of 'brute force' would give way to that of 'intellectual power'. The baser 'male' drives would be suppressed, and the intellectual and affective qualities exhibited more strongly by women would gain dominance. Since these 'female' qualities were those of the higher human faculties, the move towards female dominance represented the perfection of human potential. Conversely, the perfection of humanity lay in its feminisation.

Conclusion

Charles Fourier, the Saint-Simonians and Flora Tristan all emphasised the separate natures and distinct social roles of women and
men. Sexual differentiation was central to their ideal patterns of
social relations, and to their attempts to define the principles and
values which should govern the new society. They all agreed upon
the 'sentimental' superiority of female nature but there was no
consensus on the way in which this should be interpreted, so the
concept of separate natures did not create a unitary model of
female potential. Rather, the belief that women's biology determined their special nature gave rise to a range of views on
women's 'natural' traits, and in particular, to a range of opinions
on the relative importance of sexuality and maternity for women.
Fourier emphasised female sexuality, defining women as 'the sex'.
In his view, women's powerful libido was a hallmark of their
biological type as sensory beings. By contrast, Tristan's image of
women's nature focused on its maternal character, and placed little
emphasis on its sexual aspects. She did not regard sexuality as a
'female' characteristic, and her belief in women's capacity to overcome their 'baser' drives contrasted sharply with Fourier's sceptic-
ism about female sexual self-control. Saint-Simonian opinion
encompassed the views of both Fourier and Tristan, and a range of
intermediary positions. Some Saint-Simonians emphasised women's
highly-developed sexual responsiveness; others interpreted women's
sensitivity primarily in terms of nurturing qualities; still others
combined these images and produced the concept of women's
'maternal' sexuality.

Fourier's emphasis on the sexual aspect of femininity was reflected
in the priority he assigned to women's sensual and sexual roles in
Harmony, and his denial of the value of the maternal role. The
Saint-Simonians, on the other hand, promoted a range of both
maternal and sexual roles for women. They affirmed the social
importance of childrearing, defining maternity as the focus of
women's lives and the justification for their participation in all
areas of society. The Saint-Simonians' stress on the maternal
character of women also influenced their views on women's sexual
roles. They insisted, like Fourier, that women exerted moral influ-

ence as sexual partners of men, but defined this influence in 'maternal' terms: women's 'tender care' of men encompassed the provision of sexual fulfilment, moral guidance and emotional support.

Tristan also emphasised the maternal roles of women but sought to promote their responsibilities as social 'mothers', since she regarded this role as more significant than biological maternity. However, like the Saint-Simonians, she did not specify whether biological and social maternity were alternative or complementary roles for women. Tristan's view of women's ideal sexual role is also unclear, since she wrote little on the subject. Her belief that couples were predestined for each other resembled the dominant Saint-Simonian view, rather than the ideas of Fourier. However, Tristan's concept of affectionate marriage contrasted with her speculation about the possible elimination of the family. This ambiguity was never resolved in her writings.

Drawing on their definitions of female nature Fourier, the Saint-Simonians and Flora Tristan stressed women's potential to be the arbiters of social virtue and the moral leaders of society. But women's 'moral power' remained a vague concept. Preoccupation with this aspect blurred the issue of women's right or capacity to exercise other forms of social power. Since leadership would be determined by natural talent in the future, Fourier and the Saint-Simonians separated the leadership spheres of men and women whose talents were believed to be different. Fourier expected female leadership predominantly in the moral and amorous spheres rather than in the industrial sphere. This expectation was particularly significant given Fourier's gradual deferral of amorous reforms in favour of economic reforms: as the inauguration of the 'new amorous world' receded, women's promised leadership opportunities receded also. Nevertheless, Fourier insisted upon the economic independence of women, who would accumulate and control wealth in their own right. His system thus allowed scope for women to achieve economic self-determination, although he rated women's earning power lower than that of men.

In Saint-Simonian society women's power would always be exercised in partnership with men, and the female role was defined as 'inspiration' rather than action. This formula made female authority an ambiguous concept, and Saint-Simonian difficulties in accepting women's authority were demonstrated by events within the school. The concept of the couple also made the question of female economic independence irrelevant, and obscured the issue of power relations between the sexes. Nevertheless, a number of Saint-Simonian women stressed the need for economic self-sufficiency for women, despite the conflict of this idea with Saint-Simonian orthodoxy.

According to Flora Tristan, women's right to leadership in society was due to their status as the superior sex. She aspired towards a society under the moral leadership of women, but attempted to give this concept a practical shape by playing an active leadership role herself and encouraging other women to do the same. Her proposal to give women an equal voice within the committees of the workers' union was a clear attempt to offer women a decision-making role on equal terms with men, since Tristan did not limit women to 'inspiring' their male colleagues. She also made women's economic independence from men a key requirement for their liberation, but gave few details about the roles they should fill in the workforce.

The problems these theorists faced in defining women's power highlight the conflict between hierarchical and egalitarian principles in their social theories. Both Fourier and the Saint-Simonians rejected egalitarianism, yet sought to establish relations between the sexes on a non-hierarchical basis. By contrast, Tristan supported egalitarianism but defended the superiority of women. The notion of sexual complementarity ostensibly resolved these contradictions. Rights and opportunities comparable to those of men were sought for women in such areas as education and work, but the distinctive character of women's experiences was also emphasised. The concept of sexual complementarity thus gave rise to calls for 'equality in difference', but the preservation of women's difference took precedence over, and frequently negated, the notion of their equality with men.

The discussion of power for women also highlights the gulf between ideas and implementation for Fourier, the Saint-Simonians and Tristan. Women were attributed with the moral leadership of society, but this proved impossible to achieve. Fourier envisaged successful power-sharing between the sexes in his imaginary world, but this idea made little impact on his contemporaries. Saint-Simonian attempts to translate the theory of women's moral leadership into practical leadership roles for women were unsuccessful, and were finally abandoned. The notion of female power became part of a vision of the future expressed in the wait for 'The Woman', and an end to social domination by men was deferred. Flora Tristan also faced problems in having her provisions for female leadership accepted. Resistance to her proposals, and her own early death, prevented the development of her plan. Her 'reign of women' remained an aspiration, like many of the ideas of Fourier and the Saint-Simonians.

These theorists shared the widespread early nineteenth-century interest in identifying the pattern of social relations which was compatible with, and ordained by, an assumed universal order. The study of sexual difference served as a tool in this process. The sexual order was regarded as an expression of the natural order, so by determining the 'natural' relationship between the sexes a model for social organisation could be established. The socialists linked the failings of the old social system with the oppressive character of its sexual relations, and anticipated an alternative social system modelled on a new pattern of relations between the sexes. Complementarity, rather than dominance and submission, should characterise the sexual order and the social order in the future.

Like their contemporaries, therefore, Fourier, the Saint-Simonians and Tristan explored and emphasised the 'natural' differences between the sexes. The distinction between the 'masculine' and the 'feminine' was seen as a distinction between reason and emotion, between strength and love, between physical power and moral power. The originality and radicalism of these socialists lay in their attempts to open up the 'female' category and fill it with new meanings. The social significance of love, empathy and maternal nurturance was re-interpreted, so that the appropriate roles of women could be redefined.

Whereas the allocation to women of emotion and love was generally interpreted in their society as justifying women's confinement to domestic roles, therefore, the socialist vision of a new compassionate society required a wider female presence. 'Femininity' became a qualification for social participation, rather than a basis for exclusion. Since women were the representatives and guardians of compassion and morality, their liberty was necessary to release those qualities within society and allow them to flourish. Their admission to social life was essential for the creation of the ideal society which would exhibit those 'female' qualities. Proposals for new social roles for women thus served as a means for defending the social importance of the 'feminine' qualities of love and empathy. The current society based on force was contrasted with an ideal society characterised by social co-operation and harmony. The admission of women into social life provided a powerful image of the moral transformation of society, assuming a symbolic as well as a strategic significance.

However, by insisting on the distinction between men's and women's roles the theory also implied that women's potential roles were limited. It thus locked women into a particular 'female' mode of being that contrasted with its 'male' counterpart. The 'female' was often defined as superior, but in searching for the qualities and roles which distinguished it the socialists were strongly influenced by contemporary perceptions of the attributes and potential of the two sexes. While they re-examined the contents of gender categories, and attempted to open up the possibilities which those categories held for women, the more radical step of challenging the categories themselves proved impossible. Consequently, the newly-defined categories frequently threatened to revert to their more customary shapes. Conventional expectations of the sexes continually resurfaced in the theories of the men, and of some of the women too.

The relationship between the 'feminine' and the 'masculine' remained complex and ambivalent, therefore, and the subtle reassertion of masculine predominance in socialist theory and practice attested to the pervasiveness and resilience of the dominant paradigm. The socialist attack on sexual 'despotism' challenged the contemporary assumption that male power was natural and legitimate. But the alternative model of sexual complementarity often proved prescriptive and ambiguous in practice. A re-conceptualisation of women's 'nature' and social roles proved elusive, and this limited the capacity of socialist theories to redefine women's social position.

The significance of the theories of these early nineteenth-century French socialists lay in the high priority they assigned to the issue of sexual difference in the construction of the new society. The nature of relations between the sexes was identified as a crucial social variable, and one which had to be addressed in any attempt to envisage or construct that society. The socialists failed to resolve all the dilemmas which were posed by their attempt to reinterpret sexual difference and to redistribute power between the sexes. Nevertheless, their failure is ultimately less significant than their recognition that the undertaking was fundamental to the creation of a better world.

Notes

1 Introduction

1. This expression of Baudelaire's recently became the title of a study by Stéphane Michaud: *Muse et Madone. Visages de la Femme de la Révolution française aux Apparitions de Lourdes* (Paris, 1985).
2. Angela Groppi, 'Le Travail des Femmes à Paris à l'époque de la Révolution française', *Bulletin d'Histoire Economique et Sociale de la Révolution française* (1979), pp. 30–7.
3. Louise A. Tilly, 'Three faces of capitalism: women and work in French cities', in John Merriman (ed.), *French Cities in the Nineteenth Century* (London, 1982), pp. 168–70; Tony Judt, *Marxism and the French Left. Studies on Labour and Politics in France 1830–1981* (Oxford, 1986), chap. 2.
4. M. Guilbert, *Les Fonctions des Femmes dans l'Industrie* (Paris & The Hague, 1966), pp. 28–33; A. Groppi, 'Travail des Femmes', pp. 42–4; T. Judt, *Marxism*, pp. 48–51.
5. T. Zeldin, *France 1848–1945*, 2 vols (Oxford, 1973–7), I, p. 307; G. de Bertier de Sauvigny, *The Bourbon Restoration*, transl. L.M. Case (Philadelphia, 1967), p. 243.
6. Jill Harsin, *Policing Prostitution in Nineteenth Century Paris* (Princeton, 1985), pp. 114–16.
7. J.-B. Parent-Duchâtelet, *De La Prostitution dans la Ville de Paris*, 2 vols (Paris, 1836), I, pp. 103–4; II, pp. 116–17, quoted in J. Harsin, *Policing Prostitution*, pp. 121, 130.
8. G. de Bertier de Sauvigny, *The Bourbon Restoration*, pp. 254–5.
9. See Louis Chevalier, *Labouring Classes and Dangerous Classes in Paris During the First Half of the Nineteenth Century*, transl. Frank Jellinek (London, 1973). Eugène Sue was responsible for the claim that 'the barbarians are in our midst' (G. de Bertier de Sauvigny, *The Bourbon Restoration*, p. 259).
10. A. Groppi, 'Travail des Femmes', p. 39.
11. *Ibid.*, p. 40; Arlette Farge, 'L'Histoire ébruitée des femmes dans la société pré-révolutionnaire parisienne', in Christiane Dufrancatel *et al.* (eds), *L'Histoire Sans Qualités* (Paris, 1979), pp. 23–31; Michelle Perrot, 'La Femme populaire rebelle', in *ibid.*, pp. 130–49; Jane Rendall, *The Origins of Modern Feminism: Women in Britain, France and the United States, 1780–1860* (London, 1985), pp. 191–3.
12. See Joan W. Scott, 'Men and Women in the Parisian Garment Trades: Discussions of Family and Work in the 1830s and 1840s', in Roderick Floud, Geoffrey Crossick and Patricia Thane (eds), *The Power of the Past: Essays in Honour of Eric Hobsbawm* (Cambridge, 1984), pp. 67–93; M. Rebérioux, 'L'Ouvrière', in J.-P. Aron (ed.), *Misérable et Glorieuse la Femme du XIXe Siècle* (Paris, 1980), pp. 59–78, and below, chap. 5.
13. T. Zeldin, *France*, I, p. 287; Bonnie G. Smith, *Ladies of the Leisure Class*.

The Bourgeoises of Northern France in the Nineteenth Century (Princeton, N.J., 1981), pp. 57–8; A. Daumard, *La Bourgeoisie Parisienne de 1815 à 1848* (Paris, 1963), pp. 328–31.

14. B. Smith, *Ladies of the Leisure Class*, pp. 57–8; A. Daumard, *La Bourgeoisie Parisienne*, pp. 328, 375.
15. Barbara Corrado Pope, 'Maternal Education in France, 1815–1848', *Proceedings of the Third Annual Meeting of the Western Society for French History, December 1975* (Texas, 1976), p. 366; 'Revolution and Retreat: Upper-Class French Women After 1789', in Carol M. Berkin and Clara M. Lovett (eds), *Women, War and Revolution* (New York, 1980), p. 223. For a similar interpretation of the role of the bourgeois wife in mid-nineteenth century England see J.F.C. Harrison, *The Early Victorians 1823–51* (New York, 1971), chap. 4.
16. Claire Goldberg Moses, *French Feminism in the Nineteenth Century* (New York, 1984), p. 35; A. Daumard, *La Bourgeoisie Parisienne*, pp. 357–8.
17. B.C. Pope, 'Revolution and Retreat', pp. 216–20. See Patrick K. Bidelman, *Pariahs Stand Up! The Founding of the Liberal Feminist Movement in France, 1858–1889* (Westport, Conn., 1982), pp. 3–32 for an outline of the legal position of French women in the early nineteenth century.
18. B. Smith, *Ladies of the Leisure Class*, chap. 3; A. Daumard, *La Bourgeoisie Parisienne*, pp. 361–70.
19. A. Daumard, *La Bourgeoisie Parisienne*, pp. 336–40; B. Smith, *Ladies of the Leisure Class*, pp. 336–9.
20. David Landes, 'Religion and Enterprise: The Case of the French Textile Industry', in Edward C. Carpenter II, Robert Foster and John N. Moody (eds), *Enterprise and Entrepreneurs in Nineteenth and Twentieth Century France* (Baltimore and London, 1976), pp. 55–63.
21. L. Strumingher, 'L'Ange de la Maison. Mothers and Daughters in Nineteenth Century France', *International Journal of Women's Studies*, 2 (1979) 54–9.
22. B.C. Pope, 'Maternal Education', pp. 366–7; A. Daumard, *La Bourgeoisie Parisienne*, p. 325.
23. A. Daumard, *La Bourgeoisie Parisienne*, pp. 366–8; Erna Olafson Hellerstein, 'Women, Social Order and the City: Rules for French Ladies, 1830–1870', unpub. Ph.D. thesis, Uni. of California, Berkeley, 1980, chap. 2.
24. G. de Bertier de Sauvigny, *The Bourbon Restoration*, p. 244.
25. On the diversity of family life amongst the working population see Roger Price, *A Social History of Nineteenth Century France* (London, 1987), pp. 221–8; K. Lynch, *Family, Class and Ideology in Early Industrial France. Social Policy and the Working Class Family 1825–1848* (Madison, Wisc., 1988), chap. 3.
26. Austin Gough, 'French Workers and their Wives in the Mid-Nineteenth Century', *Labour History*, 42 (May 1982) 78–9.
27. *Ibid.*, 79–82; David Garrioch, *Neighbourhood and Community in Paris, 1740–1790* (Cambridge, 1986), pp. 79–83.
28. L. Strumingher, 'L'Ange de la Maison', 51–6; K. Lynch, *Family, Class*, pp. 159, 166–7; J. Rendall, *Origins*, pp. 122–5. Michelle Perrot argues strongly that this strategy was unsuccessful. See 'La Femme populaire rebelle', pp. 123–56.

29. These complexities are outlined in K. Lynch, *Family, Class*, pp. 88–100.
30. *Ibid.*, p. 114.
31. C.G. Moses, *French Feminism*, p. 24.
32. G. de Bertier de Sauvigny, *The Bourbon Restoration*, p. 243; K. Lynch, *Family, Class*, p. 121.
33. K. Lynch, *Family, Class*, pp. 140–2; 160–5.
34. Report of the Prefect of Police to the Minister for the Interior, 1838, quoted in *ibid.*, p. 159.
35. Geneviève Fraisse, *Muse de la raison. La démocratie exclusive et la différence des sexes* (Paris, 1989); Londa Schiebinger, 'Skeletons in the Closet: The First Illustrations of the Female Skeleton in Eighteenth Century Anatomy', in Catherine Gallagher and Thomas Laqueur (eds), *The Making of the Modern Body. Sexuality and Society in the Nineteenth Century* (California, 1987), pp. 42–82; Thomas Laqueur, 'Orgasm, Generation, and the Politics of Reproductive Biology', in *ibid.*, pp. 1–41.
36. Ludmilla Jordanova has pointed out the importance in eighteenth century medical discourse of the notion of woman's 'unveiling' by science. See 'Natural facts: a historical perspective on science and sexuality', in Carol MacCormack and Marilyn Strathern (eds), *Nature, Culture and Gender* (Cambridge, 1980), pp. 42–69.
37. T. Laqueur, 'Orgasm', p. 3; G. Fraisse, *Muse de la Raison*, p. 9.
38. For a detailed study of the Catholic Church's attitudes to women, see Jean-Marie Aubert, *La Femme. Antiféminisme et christianisme* (Paris, 1975).
39. *Ibid.*, pp. 52–60.
40. *Ibid.*, pp. 99–100.
41. Letter to François Lallier, 22 February 1839, quoted in S. Michaud, *Muse et Madone*, p. 46.
42. S. Michaud, *Muse et Madone*, pp. 43–5.
43. J.-J. Gaume, *Histoire de la Société domestique*, 2 vols (Paris, 1841), I, pp. 169–70, quoted in *ibid.*, p. 45.
44. S. Michaud, *Muse et Madone*, p. 32.
45. *Ibid.*, pp. 39, 40, 69.
46. *Ibid.*, pp. 39–49.
47. *Ibid.*, p. 30.
48. M. le Vicomte de Chateaubriand, *Génie du Christianisme* (Paris, 1838), p. 44. This work was first published in 1802.
49. S. Michaud, *Muse et Madone*, pp. 31–2.
50. Joseph de Maistre, *Traité sur les Sacrifices* (1831), quoted in Stéphane Michaud, 'Science, droit, religion: Trois contes sur les deux natures', *Romantisme*, 13–14 (1976) 31.
51. S. Michaud, *Muse et Madone*, p. 42; J.-M. Aubert, *La Femme*, pp. 65–8, 107–8, 130–1.
52. Arthur M. Wilson, '"Treated like Imbecile Children" (Diderot): The Enlightenment and the Status of Women', in Paul Fritz and Richard Morton (eds), *Woman in the Eighteenth Century and Other Essays* (Toronto and Sarasota, 1976), pp. 89–90; Ruth Graham, 'Rousseau's Sexism Revolutionised', in *ibid.*, p. 12.
53. Arthur M. Wilson, '"Treated like Imbecile Children"', p. 98; Jean

H. Bloch, 'Women and the Reform of the Nation', in Eva Jacobs *et al.* (eds), *Women and Society in Eighteenth Century France. Essays in Honour of John Stephenson Spink* (London, 1979), pp. 3–18; Elizabeth Gardner, 'The *Philosophes* and Women: Sensationalism and Sentiment', in *ibid.*, pp. 19–27.

54. Paul Hoffmann, *La Femme dans la Pensée des Lumières* (Paris, 1977), pp. 378, 381.
55. *Ibid.*, p. 424; L. Schiebinger, 'Skeletons in the Closet', p. 67.
56. P. Hoffmann, *La Femme*, pp. 337, 377–8, 532; E. Gardner, 'The *Philosophes* and Women', pp. 23–4.
57. T. Moreau, *Le Sang de l'Histoire. Michelet, l'Histoire et l'Idée de la Femme au XIXe Siècle* (Paris, 1982), pp. 46–8.
58. E. Gardner, 'The *Philosophes* and Women', pp. 19–27.
59. G. Fraisse, *Muse de la Raison*, p. 25.
60. P. Hoffmann, *La Femme*, p. 359.
61. Sylvana Tomaselli, 'The Enlightenment Debate on Women', *History Workshop Journal*, 20 (1985) 105–9, 119–21.
62. L.J. Jordanova, 'Natural Facts', pp. 43–53, 66–7; M. Bloch and J.H. Bloch, 'Women and the Dialectics of Nature in Eighteenth Century French Thought', in *Nature, Culture and Gender*, ed. C. MacCormack & M. Strathern, pp. 27–31; Genevieve Lloyd, *The Man of Reason. 'Male' and 'Female' in Western Philosophy* (London, 1984), pp. 61–4.
63. G. Lloyd, *The Man of Reason*, p. ix.
64. Laura W. Fleder, 'Female physiology and psychology in the works of Diderot and the medical writers of his day', unpublished Ph. D. thesis, Columbia University, 1978, pp. 151–5, 231–9; Arthur M. Wilson, '"Treated like Imbecile Children"', pp. 100–1.
65. P. Hoffmann, *La Femme*, pp. 30, 390–1, 400, 424; G. Fraisse, *Muse de la Raison*, p. 152.
66. P. Hoffmann, *La Femme*, pp. 342, 388–9; 'L'Héritage des lumières: mythes et modèles de la féminité au XIXe siècle, *Romantisme*, 13–14 (1976) 17–18.
67. G. Fraisse, *Muse de la Raison*, pp. 84–8.
68. Jean H. Bloch, 'Women and the Reform of the Nation', pp. 8, 16–17; L. Fleder, 'Female physiology', pp. 88–123.
69. P. Hoffmann, *La Femme*, p. 380; L.J. Jordanova, 'Natural Facts', pp. 58–9.
70. P. Hoffmann, *La Femme*, pp. 445–6.
71. *Ibid.*, pp. 331, 380–1.
72. *Ibid.*, pp. 344, 394–5.
73. *Ibid.*, pp. 332–5, 341.
74. G. Lloyd, *The Man of Reason*, p. 77.
75. P. Hoffmann, *La Femme*, pp. 341, 374–5.
76. *De L'Esprit des Lois*, VIII, p. 3, quoted in P. Hoffmann, *La Femme*, p. 340.
77. See G. Fraisse, *Muse de la raison*, p. 100; P. Hoffmann, *La Femme*, p. 342.
78. Yvonne Knibiehler, 'Les médecins et la "nature féminine" au temps du Code civil', *Annales E.S.C.*, 31, no. 4 (July-Aug. 1976) 824–45.

79. *Ibid.*, pp. 827–8.
80. L. Schiebinger, 'Skeletons in the Closet', p. 51.
81. P. Hoffmann, *La Femme*, p. 143.
82. P. Hoffmann, 'L'Héritage des Lumières', p. 7.
83. P.-J.-G. Cabanis, 'De l'influence des sexes sur le caractère des idées et des affections morales', quoted in P. Hoffmann, *La Femme*, p. 163, n. 39. Dr. Roussel reached a similar conclusion. See *ibid.*, p. 143.
84. *Ibid.*, pp. 143–4, 165; Y. Knibiehler, 'Les médecins', 836;
85. Y. Knibiehler, *ibid.*; P. Hoffmann, *La Femme*, p. 144.
86. T. Laqueur, 'Orgasm, Generation', p. 27; Y. Knibiehler, 'Les médecins', 832.
87. Louis Henry, 'The Population of France in the Eighteenth Century', in D.V. Glass and D.E.C. Eversley (eds), *Population in History* (London, 1965), pp. 451–2; Etienne Van de Walle, 'Motivations and Technology in the Decline of French Fertility', in R. Wheaton and T.K. Hareven (eds), *Family and Sexuality in French History* (Philadelphia, 1980), pp. 135–78.
88. Y. Knibiehler, 'Les médecins', 830, 834.
89. Quoted in P. Hoffmann, *La Femme*, p. 146.
90. *Ibid.*, p. 144.
91. Rachel G. Fuchs, *Abandoned Children. Foundlings and Child Welfare in Nineteenth Century France* (Albany, N.Y., 1984), p. 44.
92. L.J. Jordanova, 'Natural Facts', pp. 49–50.
93. J.-J. Virey, *De la Femme sous ses rapports physiologique, moral et littéraire*, 2nd ed. (Paris, 1825), pp. 228–9. J.-J. Virey was a disciple of Roussel. He published three major works on women between 1801 and 1823, as well as a number of articles. See P. Hoffmann, *La Femme*, pp. 141–52.
94. Quoted in P. Hoffmann, *La Femme*, p. 165.
95. *Ibid.*, pp. 144, 165.
96. J.-J. Virey, *De l'Education* (1802), quoted in Y. Knibiehler, 'Les médecins', 836–7.
97. Y. Knibiehler, 'Les médecins', 836.
98. Flora Tristan's reference to the 'heroic' action of Charlotte Corday, who killed Marat in 1793, is the exception. See *Les Pérégrinations d'une Paria 1833–1834* (Paris 1979), p. 34. On the roles of women in the Revolution see Paule-Marie Duhet, *Les Femmes et la Révolution 1789–1794* (Paris, 1971); Olwen Hufton, 'Women in Revolution 1789–1796', *Past and Present*, 53 (1971) 43–62; D.G. Levy and H.B. Applewhite, 'Women of the Popular Classes in Revolutionary Paris, 1789–1795', in *Women, War and Revolution*, ed. C.M. Berkin & C.M. Lovett, pp. 9–35.

2 Charles Fourier and the Nature of Women

1. Unless otherwise indicated, all citations of Fourier's published works refer to the *Oeuvres complètes de Charles Fourier*, 12 vols (Paris, 1966–8). Throughout this study printed rather than manuscript versions of sources have been cited where both are available.
2. François Marie Charles Fourier, *Théorie des Quatre Mouvements et des*

destinées générales: Prospectus et annonce de la découverte [1808], pp. 132–3. See also Flora Tristan, *Pérégrinations d'une Paria (1833–1834)* (Paris, 1838), p. xxv; Karl Marx to Ludwig Kugelman, London, December 12, 1868, in Saul K. Padover (ed.), *The Letters of Karl Marx* (Englewood Cliffs, N.J., 1979), p. 259; Rosa Luxemburg, 'Women's Suffrage and Class Struggle', in Hal Draper and Anne G. Lipow, 'Marxist Women versus Bourgeois Feminism', *The Socialist Register*, 1976, pp. 210–16 (p. 216).

3. See, for example, Nicholas V. Riasanovsky, *The Teaching of Charles Fourier* (Berkeley, Calif., 1969), p. 208; J. Rendall, *Origins*, p. 1. Neither author gives a source for this claim. To my knowledge the word 'feminism' does not occur in Fourier's writings, nor is the term included in E. Silberling's *Dictionnaire de Sociologie phalanstérienne* (Paris, 1971).

4. For a discussion of these aspects of Fourier's work, see Jonathan Beecher, *Charles Fourier: The Visionary and His World* (Berkeley, Calif., 1987), pp. 336–41; M.C. Spencer, *Charles Fourier* (Boston, 1981), pp. 98–108.

5. J. Beecher, *Charles Fourier*, p. 15.

6. C. Pellarin, *Charles Fourier. Sa Vie et Sa Théorie*, 2nd ed. (Paris, 1843), pp. 9–20; Jonathan Beecher and Richard Bienvenu (eds), *The Utopian Vision of Charles Fourier. Selected Texts on Work, Love and Passionate Attraction* (London, 1972), pp. 3–4.

7. C. Pellarin, *Charles Fourier*, pp. 30–7.

8. E. Lehouck, *Vie de Charles Fourier* (Paris, 1978), pp. 46–74; *Utopian Vision*, pp. 5–7.

9. 'Lettre de Fourier au Grand Juge' [1803], published by J.-J. Hemardinquer in 'Notes critiques sur le jeune Fourier', *Le Mouvement social*, 48 (July-Sep. 1964) 59–70.

10. *Théorie des Quatre Mouvements*, pp. 9–10.

11. For a good discussion of 'the anatomy of the passions' see J. Beecher, *Charles Fourier*, chapter 11.

12. Spencer's discussion of the problems of reading Fourier is most valuable. See *Charles Fourier*, pp. 21–9.

13. Beecher provides an overview of the scholarship on Fourier (*Charles Fourier*, pp. 1–12), although he does not mention recent feminist analyses.

14. *Théorie des Quatre Mouvements*, pp. 89, 125–30, 132–44, 172–82.

15. Charles Fourier, 'A Monsieur Victor Considerant', Archives Nationales (hereafter AN), 10 AS 21 (13), p. 18.

16. See, for instance, a draft article on women in the archives of the *Ecole sociétaire* where a pencilled note explicitly disavows 'the morals in the unpublished manuscripts of Fourier and the Sapphic practices'. AN, 10 AS 26 (27).

17. *Théorie de l'Unité Universelle* [4 vols, 1822], IV, p. 182 (this work was originally published in 1821 as the *Traité de l'Association domestique-agricole*).

18. *Théorie des Quatre Mouvements*, p. 149.

19. *Ibid.*, pp. 135–6; *Théorie de l'Unité Universelle*, III, p. 51; *Le Nouveau*

Monde Amoureux [c. 1818, pub. 1967], pp. 438–9; *Publication des manuscrits de Charles Fourier*, II, p. 173.

20. *Théorie de l'Unité Universelle*, III, p. 406; *Le Nouveau Monde Industriel* [1829], p. 200.
21. Rousseau was a major exponent of this view before the Revolution, and he remained influential into the 19th century. For a discussion see Linda Zerilli, 'Motionless Idols & Virtuous Mothers: Women, Art and Politics in France 1789–1848', *Berkeley Journal of Sociology*, XXVII (1982) 89–126.
22. *Théorie des Quatre Mouvements*, p. 147.
23. *Le Nouveau Monde Industriel*, pp. 190–1.
24. *Théorie de l'Unité Universelle*, IV, pp. 166–7, 176–80.
25. *Ibid.*, pp. 167, 180.
26. See, for example, *Théorie des Quatre Mouvements*, pp. 88, 149.
27. *Ibid.*, p. 150.
28. *Théorie de l'Unité Universelle*, IV, p. 98.
29. *Ibid.*, III, pp. 446, 568; *Publication des Manuscrits*, in *Oeuvres*, XII, pp. 271–7.
30. *Théorie de l'Unité Universelle*, IV, p. 180. Fourier also argued in the *Quatre Mouvements* that 'woman, in the state of liberty, will surpass man in all the functions of mind and body which do not require physical strength' (p. 149).
31. J. Beecher, *Charles Fourier*, p. 82.
32. *Théorie de l'Unité Universelle*, IV, p. 166.
33. *Ibid.*, I, p. 154.
34. *Publication des Manuscrits*, II, p. 202.
35. *Théorie de l'Unité Universelle*, IV, p. 240. See also *Publication des Manuscrits*, II, pp. 218–19, 229–30. The problems associated with puberty were always discussed with reference to girls only.
36. *Publication des Manuscrits*, II, p. 230.
37. *Le Nouveau Monde Industriel*, pp. 200–1.
38. *Publication des Manuscrits*, II, p. 203.
39. *Le Nouveau Monde Amoureux*, pp. 439–40. See also *Théorie des Quatre Mouvements*, p. 131. A similar view of the sexual needs of women can be found, for example, in the *Encyclopédie*, and in the medical writings of the physician Antoine Le Camus. See Laura Fleder, 'Female Physiology and Psychology', pp. 199–228; Paul Hoffmann, *La Femme dans la Pensée des Lumières*, pp. 115–17.
40. *Théorie des Quatre Mouvements*, pp. 136–7; *Publication des Manuscrits*, II, pp. 176–7.
41. *Le Nouveau Monde Amoureux*, pp. 234, 328.
42. *Publication des Manuscrits*, II, p. 229.
43. J. Beecher, *Charles Fourier*, pp. 81–4.
44. *Ibid.*, pp. 140–54.
45. *Publication des Manuscrits*, II, pp. 218–24, 229–31, 237–8.
46. J. Beecher, *Charles Fourier*, p. 151.
47. *Théorie de l'Unité Universelle*, III, p. 51.
48. *Théorie des Quatre Mouvements*, p. 128.
49. The most detailed outline of the types of (male) cuckolds can be found

in *Publication des Manuscrits*, III, pp. 253–72. Fourier outlined the three female types in *La Fausse Industrie* [2 vols, 1835–6], I, p. 564.

50. *Théorie des Quatre Mouvements*, pp. 12, 31, 287–8; *Le Nouveau Monde Amoureux*, p. 128.
51. *Le Nouveau Monde Amoureux*, pp. 8–13.
52. *Théorie des Quatre Mouvements*, p. 38.
53. Simone Debout, introduction to *Le Nouveau Monde Amoureux*, p. xiii, n. 2.
54. *Le Nouveau Monde Amoureux*, pp. 8–13.
55. *Publication des Manuscrits*, II, p. 236.
56. *Le Nouveau Monde Amoureux*, p. 9.
57. *Publication des Manuscrits*, II, p. 236.
58. *Le Nouveau Monde Amoureux*, p. 120. A large part of section 11, pp. 116–54, deals with aspects of this question.
59. *Publication des Manuscrits*, II, pp. 236–7.
60. *Le Nouveau Monde Industriel*, pp. 96–7.
61. *Théorie des Quatre Mouvements*, pp. 30–1.
62. *Le Nouveau Monde Amoureux*, pp. 456–7; *Publication des Manuscrits*, II, pp. 235–6. See also 'Tableau de l'âme humaine ou de l'homme passionnel', in Simone Debout-Oleskiewicz, 'Textes inédits de Charles Fourier', *Revue internationale de Philosophie*, 60, no. 2 (1962) 150–1.
63. *Théorie des Quatre Mouvements*, pp. 38, 46; *Publication des Manuscrits*, II, pp. 65, 237.
64. *Théorie des Quatre Mouvements*, p. 301.
65. *Le Nouveau Monde Amoureux*, p. 146.
66. *Ibid.*, p. 388.

3 Charles Fourier and the Roles of Women

1. *La Fausse Industrie*, I, p. 362.
2. *Publication des Manuscrits*, II, p. 173.
3. *Théorie de l'Unité Universelle*, III, p. 155; *Publication des Manuscrits*, in *Oeuvres*, XII, pp. 712–13.
4. *Publication des Manuscrits*, II, p. 125.
5. *Le Nouveau Monde Industriel*, p. 200; *La Fausse Industrie*, II, p. 599.
6. *Théorie de l'Unité Universelle*, IV, pp. 48–9.
7. *La Fausse Industrie*, II, pp. 598–9.
8. Maurice Garden, *Lyon et les Lyonnais au 18e Siècle* (Paris, 1975), pp. 168, 178–80.
9. O. Hufton, 'Women in Revolution', pp. 91–3; Louise Tilly and Joan Scott, *Women, Work and Family* (New York, 1978), pp. 75, 87; A. Kleinclausz, *Histoire de Lyon*, 3 vols (Lyon, 1939–1952), II, p. 179.
10. L. Tilly and J. Scott, *Women, Work and Family*, pp. 44, 46; Martine Segalen, *Love and Power in the Peasant Family. Rural France in the Nineteenth Century* (Oxford, 1983), pp. 82–94.
11. L. Tilly and J. Scott, *Women, Work and Family*, pp. 35, 44–6, 132–3; L. Strumingher, *Women and the Making of the Working Class, Lyon, 1830–1870* (St Albans, Vermont, 1977), pp. 17–18.

12. *Théorie des Quatre Mouvements*, p. 150.
13. *Publication des Manuscrits*, II, p. 173; *Théorie de l'Unité Universelle*, III, p. 174.
14. *La Fausse Industrie*, II, p. 600.
15. *Ibid.*, p. 539; *Publication des Manuscrits*, II, p. 176.
16. *Théorie de l'Unité Universelle*, III, p. 161. 'Series' was Fourier's term for a 'grouping, carefully calculated according to the exigencies of accord and discord, whereby a number of objects or people are brought together or harmonised, as in a choir' (M. Spencer, *Charles Fourier*, p. 181).
17. *Théorie de l'Unité Universelle*, IV, p. 276; *Le Nouveau Monde Industriel*, p. 200.
18. *Le Nouveau Monde Industriel*, p. 191.
19. *Théorie de l'Unité Universelle*, III, p. 489.
20. *Le Nouveau Monde Industriel*, p. 190.
21. *Théorie de l'Unité Universelle*, IV, p. 144.
22. See Martine Segalen, *Love and Power in the Peasant Family*, pp. 79–127.
23. *Le Nouveau Monde Industriel*, p. 247.
24. *Publication des Manuscrits*, II, pp. 153–4.
25. *Ibid.*, pp. 124–5.
26. *La Fausse Industrie*, I, p. 194.
27. *Le Nouveau Monde Industriel*, pp. 136, 175, 185–6; *Publication des Manuscrits*, II, p. 114.
28. *Publication des Manuscrits*, I, p. 99.
29. *Théorie de l'Unité Universelle*, IV, p. 2.
30. *Le Nouveau Monde Industriel*, p. 175.
31. *Théorie des Quatre Mouvements*, pp. 295–6.
32. *Publication des Manuscrits*, I, p. 109. See also *Théorie de l'Unité Universelle*, III, pp. 154–5; IV, p. 276.
33. *La Fausse Industrie*, II, p. 538.
34. *Le Nouveau Monde Industriel*, pp. 62, 141.
35. *Théorie des Quatre Mouvements*, p. 301. See also *La Fausse Industrie*, II, pp. 575–6.
36. *Théorie de l'Unité Universelle*, II, p. 384.
37. *Ibid.*, IV, p. 190.
38. *Publication des Manuscrits*, IV, p. 189.
39. *Ibid.*, II, p. 203.
40. *La Fausse Industrie*, II, pp. 577–84.
41. *Théorie de l'Unité Universelle*, II, p. 371. See also *ibid.*, IV, p. 558; *Le Nouveau Monde Industriel*, pp. 337–8.
42. *La Fausse Industrie*, I, p. 363.
43. My interpretation here differs from that of Catherine Francblin, who argues that Fourier regarded sexual love as divisive, and only viewed sentimental love as unifying. See 'Le Féminisme utopique de Charles Fourier', *Tel Quel*, 62 (1975) 44–69.
44. *Le Nouveau Monde Amoureux*, p. 47.
45. *Ibid.*, p. 91.
46. *Ibid.*, pp. 56, 266; *Publication des Manuscrits*, in *Oeuvres*, XII, pp. 503–4.
47. *Le Nouveau Monde Amoureux*, p. 274.

48. *Ibid.*, pp. 275, 394.
49. *Publication des Manuscrits*, in *Oeuvres*, XII, p. 265.
50. *Théorie de l'Unité Universelle*, IV, p. 219; *Théorie des Quatre Mouvements*, p. 133; *Le Nouveau Monde Amoureux*, p. 444.
51. *Le Nouveau Monde Amoureux*, p. 442.
52. *Ibid.*, p. 267.
53. *Ibid.*, p. 302.
54. *Ibid.*, pp. 388–94.
55. *Ibid.*, pp. 253–8.
56. *Ibid.*, p. 393 n. 1.
57. *Théorie de l'Unité Universelle*, I, pp. 158–9.
58. *Ibid.*, IV, p. 248.
59. *Ibid.*, p. 222.
60. *Ibid.*, pp. 248, 251–2. Leslie Goldstein also noted differences in the roles of male and female vestals in 'Early Feminist Themes in French Utopian Socialism: The Saint-Simonians and Fourier', *Journal of the History of Ideas*, XLIII, no. 1 (1982) 104–5.
61. *Théorie de l'Unité Universelle*, IV, pp. 235, 252–3.
62. *Ibid.*, p. 235.
63. *Théorie des Quatre Mouvements*, p. 141.
64. *Théorie de l'Unité Universelle*, IV, p. 254.
65. *Ibid.*, p. 251.
66. *Ibid.*, p. 250.
67. *Le Nouveau Monde Amoureux*, p. 428.
68. *Théorie de l'Unité Universelle*, IV, pp. 222–4.
69. *Théorie des Quatre Mouvements*, pp. 173–5.
70. *Théorie de l'Unité Universelle*, IV, p. 238.
71. *Ibid.*, p. 220.
72. *Ibid.*, pp. 229–30.
73. *Ibid.*, p. 224.
74. *Ibid.*, p. 238.
75. *Théorie des Quatre Mouvements*, p. 176.
76. This point was also made by C. Francblin in 'Le Féminisme utopique', 51.
77. *Théorie de l'Unité Universelle*, IV, p. 259.
78. *Ibid.*, p. 267.
79. *Ibid.*, pp. 266–70.
80. *Ibid.*, p. 270.
81. *Le Nouveau Monde Amoureux*, p. 21. The *tourbillon* was another name for the phalanx.
82. *Ibid.*, pp. 121–3.
83. *Ibid.*, pp. 78–9.
84. *Ibid.*, p. 76.
85. *Ibid.*, p. 105.
86. *Ibid.*, p. 81.
87. *Ibid.*, p. 92.
88. *Ibid.*, p. 445.
89. *Ibid.*, p. 98.

90. *Ibid.*, p. 206. On this point see C. Francblin, 'Le Féminisme utopique', 52.
91. *Le Nouveau Monde Amoureux*, p. 207.
92. *Ibid.*, p. 206n.
93. *Ibid.*

4 The Saint-Simonians Discover 'Woman'

1. On Saint-Simon's life see Sébastien Charléty, *Histoire du Saint-Simonisme* (Paris, 1931), pp. 1–23; Frank E. Manuel, *The New World of Henri Saint-Simon* (Notre Dame, Ind., 1963), and *The Prophets of Paris* (Cambridge, Mass., 1962), pp. 105–48.
2. This idea of Saint-Simon's was inscribed on the masthead of the first Saint-Simonian paper, *Le Producteur*: 'The golden age which the blindness of tradition has until now placed in the past, lies before us'.
3. G. Lichtheim, *A Short History of Socialism* (London, 1975), p. 54; F. E. Manuel, *The Prophets of Paris*, pp. 138–48.
4. F. E. Manuel, *New World*, pp. 299–301; *The Prophets of Paris*, pp. 121–9. For an account of Bichat's physiology, see John E. Lesch, *Science and Medicine in France. The Emergence of Experimental Physiology 1790–1855* (Harvard, 1984), pp. 51–63.
5. Comte Henri de Saint-Simon, *Lettres d'un Habitant de Genève à ses contemporains [1803]* (Paris, 1925), p. 90.
6. *Ibid.*, p. 54; A. Pereire, introduction to the *Lettres*, pp. xxiv–xxv; F.E. Manuel, *New World*, pp. 56–8. Note, too, Saint-Simon's description of Julie Juliand, who was his secretary, housekeeper and mistress in the 1820s: 'She is not a domestic servant, she is a worker who has considerable intelligence and a delicacy which makes her capable of filling any confidential position'. Henri Saint-Simon to Ternaud, 9 March 1823, in *Oeuvres de Saint-Simon et d'Enfantin*, 47 vols (Paris, 1965–78), I, pp. 102–3.
7. See Henri Fournel, *Bibliographie Saint-Simonienne de 1802 au 31 décembre 1832* [N.Y., 1973], pp. 34–58; S. Charléty, *Histoire du Saint-Simonisme*, pp. 26–30; Robert B. Carlisle, *The Proffered Crown. Saint-Simonianism and the Doctrine of Hope* (Baltimore and London, 1987), chap. 3.
8. Adolphe Garnier, 'Souscription européenne en faveur des grecs', *Le Producteur*, III (1826) 343.
9. 'Société des amis des arts de Paris, Bordeaux, Lyon etc. Exposition de celle de Paris en 1825', *ibid.*, 48. Henri Fournel identified the author as Allier (*Bibliographie Saint-Simonienne*, p. 59).
10. St. A.B. [Saint-Amand Bazard], 'De la nécessité d'une nouvelle doctrine générale', *Le Producteur*, III (1826) 544.
11. 'L'Industrie ou discussions politiques, morales et philosophiques', I, in *Oeuvres*, XVIII, p. 165.
12. 'Introduction', *Le Producteur*, I (1825) 6–7. This piece was written by Cerclet (*Bibliographie Saint-Simonienne*, p. 36).
13. St. A.B. 'De la Nécessité', *Le Producteur*, III (1826) 550–1. For a similar

view see A. Comte, 'Considérations sur le pouvoir spirituel', *ibid.*, I (1825) 609.

14. 'S', 'Revue littéraire', *ibid.*, II (1825) 418. Fournel identified the reviewer as Senty (*Bibliographie Saint-Simonienne*, p. 46), whom Charléty describes as a writer of political comedies and historical works (*Histoire du Saint-Simonisme*, p. 30, n. 1).

15. According to Saint-Simonian legend, Saint-Simon proposed to Mme. de Staël, seeing in her an intellect to match his own. See F.E. Manuel, *New World*, pp. 56–8; A. Pereire, introduction to *Lettres d'un Habitant de Genève*, pp. xxiv–xxv.

16. 'Extrait des journaux anglais', *Le Producteur*, I (1825) 138–9. This article was a critique of Owenite theory (no author was given by Fournel). For an account of Owenite feminism see Barbara Taylor, *Eve and the New Jerusalem. Socialism and Feminism in the Nineteenth Century* (London, 1983).

17. See S. Charléty, *Histoire du Saint-Simonisme*, pp. 64–9.

18. P. Enfantin to C. Duveyrier, August 1829, *Oeuvres*, XXVI, p. 18.

19. *Ibid.*, p. 6.

20. *Ibid.*

21. P. Enfantin to P. Buchez, 2 October 1829, *ibid.*, p. 102.

22. P. Enfantin to C. Duveyrier, August 1829, *ibid.*, p. 17.

23. P. Enfantin to P. Buchez, 2 October 1829, *ibid.*, p. 108.

24. *Ibid.*, p. 105.

25. *Ibid.*

26. P. Enfantin to E. Rodrigues, 5 September 1829, *ibid.*, p. 49.

27. See below, chap. 7.

28. P. Enfantin to P. Buchez, 2 October 1829, *Oeuvres*, XXVI, p. 106.

29. P. Enfantin to C. Duveyrier, August 1829, *ibid.*, p. 19.

30. 'Buchez au Père', September 1829, published in M.T. Bulciolu (ed.), *L'Ecole Saint-Simonienne et la Femme. Notes et Documents pour une histoire du rôle de la femme dans la société saint-simonienne 1828–1833* (Pisa, 1980), p. 67.

31. P. Enfantin to P. Buchez, 2 October 1829, *Oeuvres*, XXVI, p. 104.

32. 'Buchez au Père', September 1829, in *L'Ecole Saint-Simonienne et la Femme*, pp. 71–2.

33. *Ibid.*, p. 68.

34. *Ibid.*, p. 71.

35. P.M.L., 'Le Théologien et la Mère de Famille', *L'Organisateur*, I, 6 (19 September 1829) 2; 'Lettre d'une Mère de Famille à un Théologien', *ibid.*, I, 18 (13 December 1829) 2.

36. 'Prédication', *ibid.*, II, 11 (30 October 1830) 84.

37. [C. Lemonnier], *Religion Saint-Simonienne. Eglise de Toulouse. Avenir de la Femme* (Toulouse, 1831), pp. 7–8.

38. O. Rodrigues to P. Enfantin, undated, *Oeuvres*, II, p. 70.

39. On the circumstances surrounding Buchez's departure from the Saint-Simonian movement see A. Cuvillier, 'Un Schisme Saint-Simonien. Les origines de l'école Buchézienne (d'après des documents inédits)', *Revue du Mois*, XX (Jan.-June 1920) 494–532.

5 The Saint-Simonians Define Women's Social Roles

1. J. Vidalenc, 'Les techniques de la propagande saint-simonienne à la fin de 1831', *Archives de sociologie des religions*, 10 (July–December 1960) 8–13; S. Charléty, *Histoire du Saint-Simonisme*, pp. 45–9.
2. J. Vidalenc, 'Les techniques', 4–8; S. Charléty, *Histoire du Saint-Simonisme*, pp. 68–78, 89–94.
3. 'Prédication du 7 novembre. Aux Femmes', *L'Organisateur*, II, 13 (13 November 1830) 100.
4. Bazard-Enfantin, 'A Monsieur le Président de la Chambre des députés', *Oeuvres*, IV, p. 123.
5. 'Allocution d'Enfantin à la famille', 11 October 1831, *ibid.*, p. 111; 'Prédication Saint-Simonienne', *Le Globe*, no. 68 (9 March 1831) 272.
6. P.M.L., 'Le Théologien et la Mère de Famille', *L'Organisateur*, I, 8 (3 October 1829) 3.
7. *Ibid.*
8. *Ibid.*, 1–2.
9. 'Enseignement central. Première séance', *ibid.*, II, 24 (29 January 1831) 190.
10. P. Enfantin to T. Nugues, April 1829, *Oeuvres*, XXV, p. 194.
11. [C. Lemonnier], *Religion Saint-Simonienne. Avenir de la Femme*, p. 11. Lemonnier's fiancée, Elisa Grimailh, assisted in preparing this work, but the nature of her involvement is unclear. See [C. Lemonnier], *Elisa Lemonnier, fondatrice de la société pour l'enseignement professionnel des femmes* (Saint-Germain, 1866), p. 16.
12. G.D.E., 'Des Sentimens de famille et d'amitié', *L'Organisateur*, I, 34 (4 April 1830) 5.
13. P. Enfantin to Mme. A., August 1830, *Oeuvres*, XXVII, pp. 153–4.
14. P. Enfantin to E. Rodrigues, 5 September 1829, *ibid.*, XXVI, p. 45.
15. *Doctrine de Saint-Simon. Exposition première année 1829* (Paris, 1924), p. 476.
16. 'Exposition de la doctrine de Saint-Simon. Deuxième année (dixième séance), *L'Organisateur*, I, 39 (13 May 1830) 4; 'Prédication. Dieu', *ibid.*, II, 21 (8 January 1831) 165.
17. 'Prédication du 7 novembre. Aux femmes', *ibid.*, II, 13 (13 November 1830) 103.
18. Only Mme. de Staël was identified as a significant artist. See E. Barrault, *Aux Artistes. Du Passé et de l'Avenir des Beaux-Arts* (Paris, 1830), p. 65.
19. S. Charléty, *Histoire du Saint-Simonisme*, pp. 80–5.
20. 'Exposition de la doctrine de Saint-Simon. Deuxième année. Dixième séance', *L'Organisateur*, I, 39 (13 May 1830) 1.
21. P. Enfantin, 'Le Prêtre.-L'Homme et la Femme. Extrait du Globe du 18 juin 1831', in *Religion Saint-Simonienne. Lettre du Père Enfantin à Charles Duveyrier. Lettre du Père Enfantin à François et à Peiffer. Le Prêtre.-L'Homme et la Femme* (Paris, 1831), p. 21.
22. 'A mes filles', *L'Organisateur*, II, 14 (20 November 1830) 103.
23. 'Prédication du 5 décembre. Le Sacerdoce', *ibid.*, 18 (18 December 1830) 141–2.

24. [C. Lemonnier], *Religion Saint-Simonienne. Avenir de la Femme*, p. 16.
25. *Ibid.*, p. 12.
26. See G. Fraisse, *Muse de la Raison*, chap. 2.
27. *Doctrine de Saint-Simon. Exposition. Première année, 1829*, 2nd ed. (Paris, 1830), pp. 125–32.
28. 'Enseignement. Séance du 25 décembre. Des difficultés qui s'opposent aujourd'hui à l'adoption d'une nouvelle croyance religieuse', *L'Organisateur*, II, 19 (25 December 1830) 151–2.
29. G.D.E., 'Des sentimens de famille et d'amitié, *ibid.*, I, 34 (4 April 1830) 5.
30. [C. Lemonnier], *Religion Saint-Simonienne. Avenir de la Femme*, p. 14.
31. *Ibid.*, pp. 12–13.
32. *Ibid.*, p. 12.
33. *Ibid.*
34. P. Enfantin to P. Buchez, 2 October 1829, *Oeuvres*, XXVI, p. 100.
35. [C. Lemonnier], *Religion Saint-Simonienne. Avenir de la Femme*, p. 13.
36. L. Tilly and J. Scott, *Women, Work and Family*, chap. 4; L. Tilly, 'Three faces of capitalism', pp. 177–83; L. Strumingher, *Women and the Making of the Working Class*, chap. 2.
37. L. Tilly, 'Three Faces of Capitalism', pp. 174–85; T. Judt, *Marxism and the French Left*, pp. 44–51.
38. G.D.E., 'Des sentimens de famille et d'amitié', *L'Organisateur*, I, 34 (4 April 1830) 5–6.
39. See J. Scott, 'Men and Women in the Parisian Garment Trades', pp. 73–82.
40. *Doctrine de Saint-Simon. Exposition première année 1829*, 1924 ed., pp. 148, 163, 225, 237, 242–3.
41. 'Le Pére à F. Brack, colonel', October 1832, Fonds Enfantin, Bibliothèque de l'Arsenal (hereafter FE), 7646/422–3.
42. E. Barrault, 'Le Mariage', *Prédications*, I, pp. 431–3.
43. P. Enfantin to J. Rességuier, 17 December 1829, *Oeuvres*, II, p. 95; P. Enfantin to A. Saint-Hilaire, 17 December 1829, cited in M. Thibert, *Le Féminisme dans le Socialisme fançais de 1830 à 1850* (Paris, 1926), p. 198, n. 1.
44. P. Enfantin to C. Duveyrier, 28 April and 28 May 1830, *Oeuvres*, II, pp. 164, 171; to H. Fournel, 26 October 1830, *ibid.*, III, p. 49; to Talabot, 5 November 1830, *ibid.*, pp. 54–5.
45. S. Voilquin, *Souvenirs d'une fille du peuple ou la saint-simonienne en Egypte* (Paris, 1978), p. 110.
46. FE 7794, 'Professions de foi', 1831, 108 items; 7608, 'Correspondance du *Globe*, lettres de dames, 1831–1832', 112 items; 'Rapport de Henri Fournel sur le degré des ouvriers', 16 August 1831, *Oeuvres*, IV, pp. 80; 83, n. 1.
47. See M. Thibert, *Le Féminisme*, pp. 198–9.
48. See, for example, P. Enfantin to T. Nugues, 17 August, September and November 1828, *Oeuvres*, XXV, pp. 32–72; P. Enfantin to Madame Espert, 1829, *ibid.*, pp. 224–36.
49. 'Profession de foi de Mlle. Jenny de Roin', FE 7608/39, pp. 13–21; S. Voilquin, *Souvenirs*, p. 110.

50. S. Voilquin, *Souvenirs*, pp. 51–68.
51. FE 7608. See, for example, letters 13–14, 18, 19, 64.
52. E. Benoit to *Le Globe*, Paris, 2 February [1832], FE 7608/18.
53. 'Profession de foi de Mlle. Jenny de Roin', FE 7608/39, p. 31.
54. 'Allocution du Père Enfantin', 9 March 1831, FE 7824/10; 'Rapport de Henri Fournel sur le degré des ouvriers', *Oeuvres*, IV, pp. 80–6; 'Le Père (Bazard-Enfantin) à nos fils Simon et Lambert, à nos filles Caroline (Simon) et Marie (Talon)', *ibid.*, III, pp. 113–14. Charléty published a list of the directors of each *arrondissement* of Paris in *Histoire du Saint-Simonisme*, p. 89.
55. 'Prédication', *L'Organisateur*, II, 11 (30 October 1830) 82.
56. 'Discours sur la réalisation de la doctrine saint-simonienne', *ibid.*, II, 5 (18 September 1830) 36.
57. See A. Cuvillier, 'Un schisme saint-simonien'. This article reproduced extracts from six letters by Claire Bazard to Buchez, covering the period February to April 1830 (pp. 515–25).
58. C. Bazard to P. Buchez, late April 1830, *ibid.*, p. 525.
59. 'Discours sur la réalisation de la doctrine saint-simonienne', *L'Organisateur*, II, 5 (18 September 1830) 36; P. Enfantin to Rességuier, 27 April 1831, *Oeuvres*, III, p. 132.
60. 'Communion générale de la famille saint-simonienne, Paris, vendredi 8 juillet', *L'Organisateur*, II, 47–8 (2 and 9 July 1831) 376.
61. 'Deuxième lettre de Madame Bazard à Mme le Breton', undated, FE 7824/20.
62. [Palmyre Bazard], *Religion Saint-Simonienne. Aux Femmes. Sur leur mission religieuse dans la crise actuelle* (Paris, 1831).
63. On this newspaper see Lydia Elhadad, 'Femmes prénommées: les prolétaires saint-simoniennes rédactrices de *La Femme Libre*, 1832–1834', *Les Révoltes logiques*, 4–5 (1977) 62–88; 29–60; C. Moses, *French Feminism*, pp. 61–70.
64. Ier Numéro [1832] 8. This issue appeared with the title *La Femme Libre*. The periodical changed its name several times, but I shall use only the final title to avoid confusion. The first four issues are paginated separately, the remainder consecutively (from p. 33), in two volumes. Few issues are dated, and some articles are untitled or unsigned.
65. Jeanne-Désirée to P. Enfantin, 20 October 1832, FE 7608/43.
66. Suzanne, 'Variétés', *Tribune*, I, 164–8; 'Considérations sur les idées religieuses du siècle', *ibid.*, 187–9; Marie G., 'De l'influence des femmes en politique', *ibid.*, p. 255; Suzanne, 'Société des méthodes d'enseignement', *ibid.*, II, 53–6.
67. Marie-Reine, 'De l'instruction publique', *ibid.*, I, 146; Louise Dauriat, 'A mesdames les rédactrices de la Tribune des Femmes', *ibid.*, II, 39.
68. Letter from Angélique and Sophie-Caroline, *ibid.*, I, 92–8.
69. Marie G., 'De l'influence des femmes en politique', *ibid.*, I, 255–60; Jeanne-Désirée, 'Amélioration du sort des femmes par une nouvelle organisation du ménage', *ibid.*, 36–9; Suzanne, 'Société des méthodes de l'enseignement', *ibid.*, II, 54.
70. Marie-Reine, 'De l'esprit de l'association', *ibid.*, I, 199.
71. See, for instance, Jeanne-Victoire, 'Appel aux femmes', *ibid.*, I (no. 1),

1–3; Suzanne, 'A madame la directrice du *Journal des Femmes*', *ibid.*, I, 33–6.

72. Marie-Reine, 'Aux femmes', *ibid.*, I, 205.
73. Jeanne-Désirée, 'Amélioration du sort des femmes et du peuple', *ibid.*, 37.
74. *Ibid.*, II, 62–6; 111–17.
75. Joséphine-Félicité, *ibid.*, I, 45–6.
76. Suzanne, 'Par mes oeuvres on saura mon nom', *ibid.*, 69; *ibid.*, 86–7; Suzanne, 'Société des méthodes d'enseignement', *ibid.*, II, 9.
77. Suzanne, 'Discours adressé le 2 décembre à la famille de Paris réunie en assemblée générale', *ibid.*, I, 99.
78. 'Claire Bazard, membre du Collège, à ses fils du *troisième degré*, à l'occasion des dernières élections des femmes', *L'Organisateur*, II, 32 (26 March 1831) 245–6.
79. 'Notice historique', *Oeuvres*, III, pp. 112–13, n. 1; C. Bazard to G. d'Eichthal, March 1831, quoted in M. Thibert, *Le Féminisme*, p. 206.
80. 'Instruction de Bazard dit Bazard-Enfantin, père de la famille humaine, à Claire Bazard', 1830, FE 7824/27; 'Claire Bazard aux Pères Enfantin et Bazard', FE 7645/40.
81. 'Claire Bazard à notre Père Enfantin-Bazard', undated [1830], FE 7645/114–15.
82. 'Profession de foi de Mlle. Jenny de Roin', FE 7608/39, pp. 18–21.
83. C. Rogé to A. Saint-Hilaire, 26 May 1833, FE 7624/43; L. Crouzat to C. Démar, 18 May 1833, in V. Pelosse (ed.), *Textes sur l'Affranchissement des Femmes de Claire Démar*, (Paris, 1976), pp. 136–7; C. Démar to L. Crouzat, May-June 1833, *ibid.*, p. 50; S. Voilquin, *Souvenirs*, p. 113.
84. 'Claire Bazard à notre Père Enfantin-Bazard', FE 7645/114–15.
85. S. Voilquin, *Souvenirs*, pp. 113, 118–19.
86. P. Enfantin to A. Saint-Hilaire, 9 January 1833, *Oeuvres*, XXVIII, pp. 105–6; 25 December 1832, FE 7647/341v.
87. P. Enfantin to A. Petit, 1833, *Oeuvres*, IX, p. 30.
88. Suzanne, 'Discours adressé le 2 décembre à la famille de Paris réunie en assemblée générale', *Tribune*, I, 98–102.
89. Suzanne, *ibid.*, 107.
90. S. Voilquin, *Souvenirs*, p. 112.

6   The 'New Moral Law' and Women's Sexual Roles

1. See Antony Copley, *Sexual Moralities in France, 1780–1980: New Ideas on the Family, Divorce and Homosexuality* (London, 1989), chap. 4; Susan Mendus and Jane Rendall (eds), *Sexuality and Subordination* (London, 1989), introduction; B.C. Pope, 'Revolution and Retreat', 215–36.
2. P. Enfantin to Encely, undated, quoted in M. Thibert, *Le Féminisme*, p. 27.
3. M. Thibert, *ibid.*, p. 32, n. 1. Thibert provides a detailed analysis of Enfantin's debt to Fourier for his sexual theories on pp. 31–9.
4. 'Lettre du Père à sa Mère', August 1831, FE 7645/259.

5. *Religion Saint-Simonienne. Réunion Générale de la Famille. Séances des 19 et 21 novembre 1831* (Paris, 1831), pp. 8–9; 'Cinquième enseignement', *Oeuvres*, XIV, pp. 144–6; 'Lettre du Père à sa Mère', August 1831, FE 7645/258–60.

6. 'Lettre du Père à sa Mère', *ibid.*, 261v. For a discussion of the role of this anticipated woman, see below, chap. 7.

7. *Réunion Générale de la Famille*, pp. 6, 12. See also P. Transon, *Religion Saint-Simonienne. Affranchissement des Femmes. Prédication du ler janvier 1832* (Paris, 1832), p. 3.

8. See R.B. Carlisle, *The Proffered Crown*, pp. 158, 166.

9. *Ibid.*, pp. 154–7.

10. 'Deuxième enseignement', *Oeuvres*, VII, p. 45.

11. 'Note sur le Mariage et le Divorce, lue au Collège le 17 octobre 1831 par le Père Rodrigues', in *Réunion Générale de la Famille*, pp. 59–62; St. A. Bazard, *Religion saint-simonienne. Discussions morales, politiques et religieuses qui ont amené la séparation qui s'est éffectuée, au mois de novembre 1831, dans le sein de la Société saint-simonienne. Première partie. Relations des hommes et des femmes, mariage, divorce* (Paris, 1832), pp. 9–12; 21–2.

12. St.-A. Bazard, *Discussions morales*, p. 17.

13. *Ibid.*, pp. 15–16.

14. See James F. Traer, *Marriage and the Family in Eighteenth Century France* (Ithaca and London, 1980), pp. 72–8; B.C. Pope, 'Maternal Education in France', 366–77.

15. *Réunion Générale de la Famille*, pp. 17– 44; 184–96.

16. J. Bernard to *Le Globe*, 25 January 1832, FE 7608/20. See also a letter from Francisca Prugneaux, 27 February 1832, 7608/100.

17. E. Celnart to *Le Globe*, 5 February 1832, FE 7608/32.

18. *Ibid.*

19. On Cécile Fournel (née Larrieu) and Elisa Lemonnier (née Marie Juliette Grimailh), see M. Thibert, *Le Féminisme*, pp. 218–20; [C. Lemonnier], *Elisa Lemonnier, op. cit.*

20. See [C. Lemonnier], *Elisa Lemonnier*, pp. 16–17; C. Fournel to H. Fournel, 10 and 12 December 1831, 20 May 1832, FE 7645/411–13; 94–5.

21. E. Lemonnier to C. Lemonnier, July 1832, quoted in [C. Lemonnier], *Elisa Lemonnier*, p. 17.

22. C. Fournel to P. Enfantin, 20 May 1832, FE 7645/94–5.

23. *Ibid.*

24. C. Fournel to E. Lemonnier, 15 June 1832, FE 7727/9.

25. Cécile Fournel described her relationship to Henry in these terms in a letter to the Lemonniers, 8 October 1834, FE 7727/16.

26. S. Voilquin, *Souvenirs*, p. 118.

27. Suzanne, 'Morale', *Tribune*, I, 237.

28. *Ibid.*

29. James Henry Lawrence, alias James de Laurence, was the author of three works, an *Essay on the System of the Nairs* (1793), *Le Panorama des Boudoirs ou l'Empire des Nairs, le Vrai Paradis de l'Amour* (French edition 1814), and *Les Enfants de Dieu, ou la Religion de Jésus reconciliée avec la*

Philosophie (1831). On Lawrence, see Claire Démar, *Textes*, p. 161, n. 1, and Janet M. Todd's introduction to *The Empire of the Nairs* (N.Y., 1976).

30. J. de Laurence, *Les Enfants de Dieu*, pp. 3–4, 10–15.
31. Suzanne, 'Considérations sur les idées religieuses du siècle', *Tribune*, I, 189–90.
32. Suzanne, 'Morale', *ibid.*, 236.
33. Casaubon may not have been a full member of the Saint-Simonian movement, but her writings indicate that she read their publications and perhaps attended the public 'sermons' in Paris. The only Saint-Simonian writer she acknowledged explicitly was Claire Démar, from whom she quoted at length. See *Le Nouveau Contrat Social ou Place à la Femme* (Paris, 1834), pp. 52–5. The catalogue of the *Bibliothèque nationale* identifies the author as Mlle. Casaubon. Geneviève Fraisse names her Egérie Casaubon but gives no other information about her ('L'Usage du droit naturel dans les écrits féministes [1830–1850]', in Stéphane Michaud [ed.], *Un Fabuleux Destin. Flora Tristan* [Paris, 1985], p. 149).
34. Mme. E.A.C., *Le Nouveau Contrat Social*, p. 63.
35. Mme. E.A.C., *La Femme est la Famille*, pp. 8–10, 19–22; *Nouveau Contrat Social*, pp. 20–2. Pelosse interpreted Casaubon's views as strongly Catholic in tone (*Textes sur l'Affranchissement des Femmes de Claire Démar*, p. 224). They do reflect the Catholic influence discernible in many Saint-Simonian writings, but her views on sexual relations, her concept of God as Father and Mother, and her concept of eternal life, for instance, were explicitly Saint-Simonian.
36. Suzanne, 'Un Divorce', *Tribune*, II, 169–79; S. Voilquin, *Souvenirs*, pp. 126–35.
37. Suzanne, 'Un Divorce', *ibid.*, p. 179.
38. *Ibid.*, pp. 174–7.
39. *Ibid.*, p. 176.
40. S. Voilquin, *Souvenirs*, p. 134.
41. *Ibid.*, p. 135. See also 'Un Divorce', *Tribune*, II, 175.
42. E. Voilquin to S. Voilquin, 26 April 1833, published in 'Un Divorce', *ibid.*, 177–8; J. Parcy to S. Voilquin, undated, published in S. Voilquin, *Souvenirs*, p. 134.
43. Caroline to P. Enfantin, 24 December 1837, FE 7627/11. Punctuation added.
44. See for instance Marie-Reine, 'Aux Femmes', *Tribune*, I, 201–5. For a discussion of the *Tribune*'s presentation of these issues, see L. Elhadad, 'Femmes Prénommées', 78–88; 52–6.
45. Marie-Reine, 'Réponse à quelques objections qui nous ont été faites', *Tribune*, I, 114–15.
46. S. Voilquin, *Souvenirs*, p. 131.
47. See her *Souvenirs, passim,* and also her *Mémoires d'une Saint-Simonienne en Russie, passim,* for references to her financial straits. Further evidence is contained in letters to Enfantin between 1846 and 1864, when he and Arlès financially supported her entry into a *maison de retraite*

(FE 7791/135–44), and in a letter to Vinçard, 8 May 1873 (Bibliothèque Marguerite Durand, 901 VOI).

48. Caroline [Carbonel] to P. Enfantin, 6 February and 19 March 1837, FE 7627/8–9.
49. Claire Démar, *Ma Loi d'Avenir – 1833. Ouvrage posthume, publié par Suzanne* (Paris, 1834), in *Textes*, pp. 59–94.
50. M. Thibert, *Le Féminisme*, p. 222, n. 2, and V. Pelosse's notes on the correspondence of Claire Démar, *Textes*, pp. 24–58.
51. C. Démar to P. Enfantin, [late January-early February 1833], *Textes*, p. 44.
52. C. Démar to P. Enfantin, 29 December 1832, *Textes*, pp. 35–7; L. Crouzat to C. Démar, 18 May 1833, and C. Démar to L. Crouzat, [late May-early June 1833], *ibid.*, pp. 49–54, 134–41.
53. *Ma Loi d'Avenir*, in *Textes*, p. 71.
54. *Ibid.*, pp. 91–2.
55. *Ibid.*, pp. 68–70.
56. *Ibid.*, p. 75.
57. *Ibid.*, p. 77.
58. *Ibid.*, pp. 86–7.
59. *Ibid.*, pp. 70–1.
60. *Ibid.*, p. 83.
61. *Ibid.*, p. 65.
62. Emilie d'Eymard to P. Enfantin, [January 1833], in *ibid.*, p. 42. See also her letter to Enfantin, 29 December 1832, in *ibid.*, p. 36.
63. *Foi Nouvelle. Livre des Actes*, cited in *ibid.*, p. 148; Suzanne, 'Notice historique', *ibid.*, pp. 155; 162–5. Jules Vinçard also explained her suicide by her exalted and revolutionary outlook, in *Mémoires épisodiques d'un vieux chansonnier saint-simonien*, par Vinçard ainé (Paris, 1878), pp. 106–9.
64. C.G. Moses, *French Feminism*, p. 77. Moses also mentioned Saint-Simonian cliquishness towards recent converts, and disapproval of her relationship with Perret-Desessarts, who was ten years younger than Démar.
65. Joséphine-Félicité, *Tribune*, I, 66; Suzanne, 'Extrait du règlement qui unit les femmes nouvelles', *ibid.*, 63.
66. Christine-Sophie, 'De la Prostitution', *ibid.*, I (no. 4) 4.
67. Joséphine-Félicité, 'Affranchissement des Femmes', *ibid.*, I (no. 2) 5–6.
68. Isabelle, 'Aux Femmes', *ibid.*, I, 91.
69. See, for example, Jeanne-Désirée to P. Enfantin, 31 August 1832, FE 7608/42; P. Roland to A. Saint-Hilaire, 21 March 1834, cited in Edith Thomas, *Pauline Roland. Socialisme et Féminisme au XIXe Siècle* (Paris, 1956), p. 67.
70. Isabelle, *Tribune*, I, 130.
71. P. Enfantin to P. Duguet, 21 April 1831, *Oeuvres*, III, p. 130.
72. For examples, see S. Voilquin, *Souvenirs*, p. 189; Caroline to P. Enfantin, 24 December 1837, 3 February 1839, FE 7627/11, 15; Laure Adler, *A l'Aube du Féminisme: Les Premières Journalistes (1830–1850)* (Paris, 1979), p. 71; J. d'Ivray, *L'Aventure Saint-Simonienne et les Femmes* (Paris, 1928), p. 220.

73. A. Saint-Hilaire to P. Enfantin, June 1835, cited by L. Elhadad in her introduction to Suzanne Voilquin's *Souvenirs*, p. 38. See also C. Fournel to E. Lemonnier, 8 October 1834, FE 7727/16, where she was critical of events in Paris.
74. P. Roland to A. Saint-Hilaire, November 1833, in E. Thomas, *Pauline Roland*, p. 64; to C. Lambert, September 1833, in *ibid.*, pp. 62–3.
75. P. Roland to A. Saint-Hilaire, in *ibid.*, p. 72.
76. *Foi Nouvelle. Livre des Actes*, XI (1834) 246.
77. S. Voilquin, *Souvenirs*, pp. 258–9, 293, 304–12, 367–9.
78. See Caroline to P. Enfantin, 6 February 1837, FE 7627/8. Caroline Carbonel may also have had affairs with Charles Duguet and with Rogé before her departure for Egypt, according to a letter from Aglaé Saint-Hilaire to Enfantin, quoted in J. d'Ivray, *L'Aventure Saint-Simonienne*, p. 150. Alexandrian claimed that she had a child by Rogé, but gave no source in *Le Socialisme romantique* (Paris, 1979), p. 375.
79. See C. Lambert, 'Chronologie des principaux faits de la vie des Saint-Simoniens en Egypte', FE 7745/2; Lambert's journal, FE 7745/1; letters from S. Voilquin to P. Enfantin, 6 January and 23 January 1838, and 5 February 1839, FE 7627/60–2. Some sources suggest that Lambert was the father of Suzanne's child, but this appears to be disproved by Lambert's records. On this point see C.G. Moses, *French Feminism*, pp. 79; 258–9, n. 96.
80. C. Fournel to C. and E. Lemonnier, 8 October 1834, FE 7727/16.
81. Roland was particularly aware of the long-term implications if she became pregnant. See E. Thomas, *Pauline Roland*, pp. 64–70.
82. R. Carlisle, *The Proffered Crown*, p. 153.
83. P. Enfantin, 'Procès', *Oeuvres*, XLVII, p. 377; Pol Justus, *Liberté Femmes!!!* (Paris and Lyon, 1833), p. 15; Désessart, *Pensées politiques et religieuses d'un saint-simonien* (Paris, 1833), pp. 31–2; L.V.H., 'La Prostituée', in *Feuilles Populaires* (Paris, 1832); Haspott, *'L'Hôtel-Dieu', ibid.*
84. P. Enfantin to T. Nugues, 13 August 1832, *Oeuvres*, XXVII, p. 227; 10 September 1832, *ibid.*, vol. 28, pp. 10–11.
85. Madame E.A.C., *La Femme est la Famille*, p. 15; Joséphine-Félicité, 'Procès des Apôtres', *Tribune*, I, (no. 3) 4.
86. 'Profession de foi de Mlle. Jenny de Roin', FE 7608/39, pp. 39–40.
87. Joséphine-Félicité, 'Affranchissement des Femmes', *Tribune*, I, (no. 1) 5–7; anon., *ibid.*, I, 92–4.
88. 'Procès, *Oeuvres*, XLVII, pp. 422–3.
89. See Joanna de Groot, '"Sex" and "Race": The Construction of Language and Imagery in the Nineteenth Century', in S. Mendus and J. Rendall (eds), *Sexuality and Subordination*, pp. 89–128.
90. P. Enfantin to C. Fournel, 22 March 1833, *Oeuvres*, XVIII, pp. 5–6.
91. P. Enfantin to A. Petit, early 1833, *ibid.*, XXIX, p. 74.
92. S. Voilquin, *Souvenirs*, p. 140.
93. C. Rogé to P. Enfantin, 20 June 1845, FE 7776/52. See also J. d'Ivray, *L'Aventure Saint-Simonienne*, p. 145.
94. See J. de Groot, '"Sex" and "Race"', pp. 95–100; 104–7.
95. Gustave d'Eichthal and Ismayl Urbain, *Lettres sur la Race Noire et la Race Blanche* (Paris, 1839), p. 42.

96. *Ibid.*, p. 25.
97. *Ibid.*, p. 23.
98. Emile Barrault, *Occident et Orient. Etudes morales, politiques, religieuses pendant 1833–34 de l'ère chrétienne, 1249–50 de l'hégyre* (Paris, 1835), p. 377.
99. *Ibid.*, pp. 342–3.
100. S. Voilquin, *Souvenirs*, pp. 247–8, 269, 356–66.
101. On the conflicting meanings of 'liberty' in male political life in this period, see Edgar L. Newman, 'What the Crowd Wanted in the French Revolution of 1830', in J. Merriman (ed.), *1830 in France* (New York, 1975), pp. 17–40, and other essays in this collection. On feminist concepts of 'liberty', see M. Albistur and D. Armogathe, *Histoire du Féminisme Français*, 2 vols (Paris, 1977), II, part 2, chap. 3; C.G. Moses, *French Feminism*, chaps. 4 and 5.
102. S. Voilquin, *Souvenirs*, p. 366.

7 The 'New Moral Law', the Family and Motherhood

1. See Leslie Rabine, 'Essentialism and Its Contexts: Saint-Simonian and Post-Structuralist Feminists', *Differences: A Journal of Feminist Cultural Studies*, no. 2, (1989) 109–10.
2. 'Sixième enseignement', *Oeuvres*, XIV, p. 178; 'Huitième enseignement', *ibid.*, XVI, pp. 23–4.
3. 'Sixième enseignement', *ibid.*, XIV, p. 191; P. Enfantin to T. Nugues, 6 May 1832, FE 7649/99–100.
4. 'Notice historique', *Oeuvres*, IX, p. 55.
5. *Ibid.*, VII, p. 104.
6. P. Enfantin to A. Saint-Hilaire, 4 November 1834, *ibid.*, III, p. 9. Ivray argues that although refusing to marry Adèle Morlane, Enfantin thwarted any attempt she made to detach herself emotionally from him. See *L'Aventure Saint-Simonienne*, pp. 80–1.
7. Judith to P. Enfantin, 2 January 1838, FE 7627/12; S. Voilquin to P. Enfantin, 13 May 1838, FE 7627/64.
8. 'Sixième enseignement', *Oeuvres*, XIV, p. 191.
9. O. Rodrigues, 'Note sur le Mariage et le Divorce', in *Religion Saint-Simonienne. Réunion Générale de la Famille*, pp. 61–2.
10. O. Rodrigues, *Préface des Oeuvres de Saint-Simon. Le Disciple de Saint-Simon au Public* (Paris, 1832), pp. 11–12.
11. O. Rodrigues, *Le Disciple de Saint-Simon au Saint-Simoniens et au Public* (Paris, 1832), p. 4.
12. St.-A. Bazard, *Religion Saint-Simonienne. Discussions Morales, Politiques et Religieuses*, pp. 16, 29–30.
13. Our knowledge of the reproductive histories of the Saint-Simonian women is incomplete. Claire Bazard had an adult daughter at the time of her involvement in the movement. Cécile Fournel also had one child though she may have borne others in later life. Désirée Véret had one son (J. Maitron [ed.], *Dictionnaire biographique du mouvement ouvrier français* [Paris, 1973], II, pp. 246–7). Elisa Lemonnier bore four chil-

dren, of whom two survived infancy, as did three of Pauline Roland's four children ([C. Lemonnier], *Elisa Lemonnier*, pp. 18, 24, 35; E. Thomas, *Pauline Roland, passim*). Jeanne Deroin had three children (*Dictionnaire biographique*, II, pp. 64–6). For an analysis of attitudes towards birth control in early nineteenth-century France, see Angus McLaren, 'Some Secular Attitudes toward Sexual Behaviour in France: 1760–1860', *French Historical Studies*, VIII, no. 4 (1974) 604–25; 'Abortion in France: Women and the Regulation of Family Size, 1800–1914', *ibid.*, X, no. 3 (1978) 461–85.

14. Mme. E.A.C., *Le Nouveau Contrat Social*, pp. 41–2.
15. S. Voilquin, 'Notice historique', in C. Démar, *Textes*, p. 164.
16. *Ibid.*; Suzanne, '"Le Monde Nouveau"', par M. Ray. Duseuil', *Tribune*, I (no. 4) 8.
17. Mme. E.A.C., *Nouveau Contrat Social*, p. 66. The religious ceremonies were outlined on pp. 61–7.
18. Suzanne, 'La Justice des Hommes', *Tribune*, I, 125.
19. S. Voilquin, 'Notice historique', in C. Démar, *Textes*, p. 164; Juliette B., 'Aux Femmes', *Tribune*, I, 161–3.
20. Suzanne, 'La Justice des Hommes', *Tribune*, I, 127.
21. Suzanne, '"Le Monde Nouveau" par M. Ray. Duseuil', *ibid.*, I, (no. 4) 8; 'Considérations sur les idées religieuses du siècle', *ibid.*, I, 190.
22. Suzanne, 'Considérations', *ibid*: 'A large number of women have understood like me what potential there is in this system (modified by us)'.
23. Suzanne, 'La Justice des Hommes', *ibid.*, 125–7; *Souvenirs*, pp. 127–8.
24. P. Roland to A. Saint-Hilaire, 24 June 1834, in E. Thomas, *Pauline Roland*, p. 70.
25. Mme. E.A.C., *La Femme est la Famille*, pp. 4–5, 7.
26. *Ibid.*, p. 8.
27. For Napoleon's analogy, see Patrick Kay Bidelman, 'The Feminist Movement in France: The Formative Years, 1858–1889', Ph. D. thesis, Michigan State University, 1975, p. 10.
28. Mme. E.A.C., *Le Nouveau Contrat Social*, pp. 37–44.
29. *Ibid.*, p. 29.
30. *Ibid.*, pp. 45–6.
31. At the conclusion of *La Femme est la Famille* (p. 24), Casaubon promised to publish a brochure which would 'develop several ideas of political economy' relevant to her system. This brochure was *Le Nouveau Contrat Social*.
32. Mme. E.A.C., *Le Nouveau Contrat Social*, p. 48.
33. *Ibid.*, pp. 46–7, 62–3; *La Femme est la Famille*, p. 19.
34. Mme. E.A.C., *Le Nouveau Contrat Social*, p. 66.
35. Suzanne, 'A Mme. la Directrice du Journal des Femmes', *Tribune*, I, 35.
36. Suzanne, 'Notice historique', in C. Démar, *Textes*, p. 165.
37. S. Voilquin, *Souvenirs*, pp. 102–3; 106–8.
38. C. Lambert, 'Chronologie des principaux faits de la vie des Saint-Simoniens en Egypte', FE 7745/2.
39. S. Voilquin, *Souvenirs*, p. 394.

40. S. Voilquin to P. Enfantin, 5 February 1839, FE 7627/62.
41. Caroline to P. Enfantin, 3 February 1839, FE 7627/15. Punctuation added.
42. See her letters to Enfantin, 6 February and 24 December 1837, FE 7627/8 and 11.
43. Suzanne, '"Le Monde Nouveau" par M. Ray. Duseuil', *Tribune*, I (no. 4) 8. See also 'A Mme. la Directrice du Journal des Femmes', *ibid.*, I, 33.
44. Suzanne, 'Morale', *ibid.*, 234. See also 'La Justice des Hommes', *ibid.*, 33; S. Voilquin, *Souvenirs*, p. 68.
45. Mme. E.A.C., *La Femme est la Famille*, pp. 19–20, 24; *Le Nouveau Contrat Social*, pp. 26–31.
46. C. Démar, 'Ma Loi d'Avenir', in *Textes*, p. 94.
47. *Ibid.*
48. Suzanne, 'Notice historique', in C. Démar, *Textes*, p. 165.
49. 'Seizième enseignement', *Oeuvres*, XVII, p. 38.
50. *Ibid.*, p. 51.
51. 'Lettre du Père à sa Mère', August 1831, FE 7645/260.
52. *Ibid.*, 7645/260v. See also 'Cinquième enseignement', *Oeuvres*, XIV, p. 163.
53. P. Enfantin to C. Duveyrier, August 1829, *Oeuvres*, XXVI, pp. 7–11.
54. 'Lettre du Père à sa Mère', FE 7645/261.
55. 'Cinquième enseignement', *Oeuvres*, XIV, p. 161; 'Huitième enseignement', *ibid.*, XVI, p. 25.
56. 'Lettre du Père à sa Mère', FE 7645/261v.
57. C. Duveyrier, 'De la Femme', *Oeuvres*, XLVII, pp. 144–5, originally published in *Le Globe*, viii année, no. 12 (12 January 1832) 46–7.
58. 'Cinquième enseignement', *Oeuvres*, XIV, p. 163; 'Seizième enseignement', *ibid.*, vol. XVII, pp. 47–50; 'Les Trois Familles, par E. Barrault. Articles extraits du Globe', in *Religion Saint-Simonienne. Morale. Réunion générale de la Famille. Enseignements du Père Suprême. Les Trois familles* (Paris, 1832), pp. 192–3.
59. P. Enfantin, *Religion Saint-Simonienne. Réunion générale de la Famille. Séances des 19 et 21 novembre*, p. 6.
60. C. Fournel to E. Lemonnier, 31 July 1832, FE 7727/10; P. Enfantin, 'Cinquième enseignement', *Oeuvres*, XIV, p. 164; 'Huitième enseignement', *ibid.*, XVI, pp. 17–33.
61. A. Colin, *Aux Femmes juives* (Lyon, 1833), p. 7.
62. P. Enfantin, 'Procès', *Oeuvres*, XLVII, p. 388; C. Duveyrier, 'L'Apostolat', in *Religion Saint-Simonienne. La Prophétie. Articles extraits du Globe du 19 février au 20 avril 1832* (Paris, 1832), p. 47; E. Barrault, *1833, ou l'Année de la Mère* (Lyon, January 1833), pp. 28–9; E. Barrault, *Compagnonage de la Femme. Chant* (Lyon, 1833); C. Béranger, 'La Mairie.-Le Mariage', *Feuilles Populaires*, 2 June 1832.
63. *Religion Saint-Simonienne, Réunion générale de la famille*, p. 20.
64. *Ibid.*, p. 33; C. Fournel to A. Saint-Hilaire, 8 June 1832, *Oeuvres*, VII, p. 124.
65. Joséphine-Félicité, 'Aux Hommes', *Tribune*, I, 128–9.
66. Unita, 'Une Voix de Femme', *ibid.*, II, 153.

67. S. Voilquin, *Souvenirs*, p. 190.
68. E. Barrault, *1833, ou l'Année de la Mère* (January 1833), pp. 19, 21–2; P. Enfantin, 'Procès', *Oeuvres*, XLVII, p. 388.
69. E. Barrault, *1833, ou l'Année de la Mère* (January 1833), p. 34.
70. A. Colin, *Aux Femmes juives*, pp. 2, 8.
71. P. Enfantin to F. Brack, October 1832, FE 7646/419–24; *A Paris!* (Paris, 1832), p. 5.
72. A. Saint-Hilaire, 'Note sur le Procès', *Oeuvres*, XLVII, p. 527.
73. C. Fournel to P. Enfantin, 21 June 1833, FE, 7647/351; [M. Chevalier], *A Lyon!* (Paris, 1832), p. 8; Massol to the Saint-Simonian family in Paris, 24 May 1833, *Foi Nouvelle*, III, (1833) 47.
74. *1833 ou l'Année de la Mère. Juillet. Mission de l'Est, rédigée par Collin, Rogé, Maréchal, Charpin, Lamy* (Toulon, 1834), pp. 10–11.
75. *Ibid.*, pp. 32–3.
76. See Stéphane Michaud, *Muse et Madone*, on the rise of devotion to the Madonna and the images of women with which it was associated.
77. S. Voilquin, 'Morale', *Tribune*, I, 235; A. Colin, *Aux Femmes Juives*, p. iv.
78. E. Barrault, 'Les Trois Familles', p. 204.
79. *Ibid.*, p. 205.
80. See Mary O'Brien, *The Politics of Reproduction* (Boston, London and Henley, 1983), on the tendecy of social theorists to 'annex[e] reproductive dynamic from generic relation and relocat[e] it arbitrarily in creative intellectual intercourse between men'. (p. 18).
81. P. Enfantin, 'Treizième enseignement', *Oeuvres*, XVI, pp. 173–4. See also *1833 ou l'Année de la Mère. Juillet*, p. 12; P. Enfantin to H. Fournel, 3 March 1833, *Oeuvres*, XXVIII, p. 173.
82. 'Notice historique', *Oeuvres*, IX, p. 182.
83. P. Enfantin to E. Barrault, 8 August 1833, *ibid.*, IX, p. 57. See also E. Barrault, 'Consécration de la Matière', *Prédications*, I, p. 380.
84. E. Barrault, 'Unité de la Religion, de la Politique et de la Morale', *Prédications*, I, p. 411.
85. O. Rodrigues, *Le Disciple de Saint-Simon*, pp. 13–14.
86. 'Le Père Suprême à Michel Chevalier', 29 March 1832, in *Religion Saint-Simonienne. La Prophétie*, p. 40; P. Enfantin to C. Duguet, 17 May 1837, *Oeuvres*, XXXI, pp. 86–7.
87. 'Notice historique', *Oeuvres*, VIII, pp. 154–5.
88. Enfantin claimed to have been 'alone with the mother' at the time of Arthur's birth, and to have 'brought him into the world with [his] own hands'. See 'Notice historique', *ibid.*, VII, p. 113.
89. Hoart to the Saint-Simonians at Paris, 26 February 1832, *ibid.*, VI, p. 31.
90. 'Quatorzième enseignement', *ibid.*, XVI, p. 255.
91. E. Barrault, 'L'Oeuvre Saint-Simonien', *Prédications*, II, pp. 50–1.
92. 'Notice historique', *Oeuvres*, VI, p. 9.
93. Mary O'Brien argues that the male fondness for establishing models of intellectual continuity in human experience is a direct response to the discontinuous nature of the male experience of biological reproduction. See *The Politics of Reproduction*, pp. 59–62.

94. 'Deuxième enseignement', *Oeuvres*, XIV, pp. 72–3.
95. 'Troisième enseignement', *ibid.*, pp. 81, 104; 'Quatrième enseignement', *ibid.*, pp. 129–30.
96. 'Notice historique', *ibid.*, VII, pp. 75–9.
97. Women were admitted with other members of the Saint-Simonian 'family' on special occasions. Charléty has pointed out the similarity between the Saint-Simonian lifestyle at Ménilmontant, with its emphasis on mental and physical discipline and celibacy, and the monastic life. See *Histoire du Saint-Simonisme*, pp. 162–70.
98. C. Fournel to E. Lemonnier, 15 June 1832, FE 7727/9.
99. 'Notice historique', *Oeuvres*, VII, p. 81.
100. See S. Charléty, *Histoire du Saint-Simonisme*, pp. 205–50.
101. 'Notice historique', *Oeuvres*, VIII, p. 149.
102. E. Barrault, *1833, ou l'Année de la Mère* (January and February, 1833); Rigaud to C. Fournel and C. Rogé, October 1833, *Oeuvres*, IX, pp. 159–67; C. Duguet, *Salut au Nouveau Monde* [Paris, 1833]; *Adieux à l'Ancien Monde* [Paris, 1833]; L. Crouzat to C. Démar, 18 May 1833, in *Textes*, pp. 138–40; C. Démar to L. Crouzat, [late May–early June 1833], in *Textes*, pp. 50–1; *1833 ou l'Année de la Mère. Juillet*, pp. 1–34.
103. C. Duguet, *Adieux à l'Ancien Monde*, p. 2; C. Démar, 'Ma Loi d'Avenir', *Textes*, pp. 65–7; Cazeaux to A. Petit, 8 August 1833, FE 7624/40.
104. P. Enfantin to E. Barrault, 8 August 1833, *Oeuvres*, IX, pp. 58–60; 26 January 1833, in E. Barrault, *1833, ou l'Année de la Mère* (February), pp. 5–9.
105. P. Enfantin to E. Barrault, 8 August 1833, in *Oeuvres*, IX, p. 65.
106. P. Enfantin to Hoart, Bruneau, Rogé and Massol, September 1833, *Foi Nouvelle*, VI (1833) 105.
107. *Religion Saint-Simonienne, Réunion générale de la famille*, pp. 197–8; 'Notice historique', *Oeuvres*, V, pp. 18–20.

8 Flora Tristan and the Moral Superiority of Women

1. Flora Tristan, *Le Tour de France, Etat actuel de la classe ouvrière sous l'aspect moral, intellectuel et matériel* (Paris, 2 vols., 1980), II, p. 120.
2. See her letters to Fourier dated 21 August and 11 October 1835, and 26 April 1836, in *Flora Tristan. Lettres*, réunies, présentées et annotées par Stéphane Michaud (Paris, 1980), pp. 56–7, 59.
3. See, for example, Tristan's letters to Victor Considerant, August 1836, July 1837 and April 1844, in *Lettres*, pp. 61–4, 71, 195.
4. On Pauline Roland, see *Le Tour de France*, I, p. 43; Flora Tristan to Eugénie Niboyet, 1 March and 11 October 1836, in *Lettres*, pp. 58–9, 64–5. Tristan died at the Lemonniers' home in Bordeaux.
5. See *L'Union ouvrière*, 3rd ed. (Paris and Lyon, 1844, reprinted 1976), p. 37, where Tristan referred to Enfantin's 'public professions' of 1830–32, and commented on his *La Colonisation de l'Algérie* (Paris, 1843). She referred to *Le Globe* in *Le Tour de France*, I, p. 94.
6. Tristan provided autobiographic information in the introduction to *Les Pérégrinations d'une Paria (1833–1834)*, 2 vols (Paris, 1838). The 1 vol.

reprint of this work (Paris, 1979) omits this introduction. All references to *Pérégrinations* are to the 1979 edition, unless otherwise indicated. Other major sources on Tristan's life are Eléonore Blanc, *Biographie de Flora Tristan* (Lyon, 1845), and J.-L. Puech, *La Vie et l'Oeuvre de Flora Tristan 1803–1844* (Paris, 1925).

7. *Nécessité de faire un bon accueil aux femmes étrangères*, par Madame F.T. (Paris, 1835).
8. For a list of Tristan's newspaper articles see *Lettres*, pp. 32–3.
9. *Pérégrinations*, previously cited. See especially 1838 ed., I, pp. xxiii–iv.
10. *Méphis*, 2 vols (Paris, 1838), I, pp. 180–3; II, pp. 55–7, 289–99.
11. See *Promenades dans Londres ou l'aristocratie et les prolétaires anglais*, édition établie et commentée par François Bédarida (Paris, 1978), pp. 47–55.
12. See C.H. Johnson, 'Patterns of Proletarianisation: Parisian Tailors and Lodève Woolens Workers', in J. Merriman (ed.), *Consciousness and Class Experience in Nineteenth Century Europe* (New York and London, 1980), pp. 65–84; T. Judt, *Marxism and the French Left*, pp. 51–77.
13. *Méphis*, I, pp. 180–1.
14. *Ibid.*, p. 183.
15. See Jean Baelen, *La Vie de Flora Tristan. Socialisme et Féminisme au XIXe Siècle* (Paris, 1972), pp. 218–9.
16. *Pérégrinations*, 1838 ed., I, p. xv.
17. *Ibid.*, p. xvi; *Promenades*, p. 224; *L'Union ouvrière*, p. 98.
18. *Pérégrinations*, 1838 ed., I, p. xxx.
19. *Ibid.*, 1976 ed., pp. 30, 46.
20. F. Tristan, *Le Tour de France*, I, p. 82. See Michelle Perrot's discussion of Tristan's interest in physiognomy in 'Flora Tristan, Enquêtrice', in *Un Fabuleux Destin*, ed. S. Michaud, pp. 84–5.
21. *Pérégrinations*, p. 47.
22. *Ibid.*
23. For European feminists' utilisation of the slavery analogy see J. Rendall, *Origins*, pp. 231–2.
24. *Pérégrinations*, p. 352.
25. *Ibid.*, pp. 351–2.
26. [C. Lemonnier], *Religion Saint-Simonienne. Avenir de la Femme*, pp. 8–9.
27. *Pérégrinations*, p. 233.
28. *Ibid.*, p. 234.
29. *Ibid.*, p. 330.
30. *Ibid.*, pp. 339–40.
31. *Ibid.*, p. 335.
32. *Ibid.*, p. 343.
33. *Ibid.*, pp. 339–40.
34. *Ibid.*, pp. 334–5.
35. *Ibid.*, p. 336.
36. *Ibid.*, p. 335.
37. This point will be discussed more fully below, chap. 9.
38. See Edward Berenson, *Populist Religion and Left Wing Politics in France, 1830–1852* (Princeton, N.J., 1984), pp. 36–54; D.G. Charlton, *Secular Religions in France, 1815–1870* (London, 1963), p. 126.

39. For Saint-Simon's beliefs, see *Nouveau Christianisme. Dialogues entre un conservateur et un novateur. Premier dialogue* [1825], in *Oeuvres de Claude-Henri de Saint-Simon* (Geneva, 6 vols., 1977), vol. 2.

40. On Constant, see P. Bénichou, *Le Temps des Prophètes. Doctrines de l'âge romantique* (Paris, 1977), pp. 435–46; *Eliphas Lévi Visionnaire Romantique*, préface et choix de textes par Frank Paul Bowman (Paris, 1969). On Ganneau, see P. Bénichou, *Le Temps des Prophètes*, pp. 429–35. F.P. Bowman's 'Religion, Politics and Utopia in French Romanticism', *Australian Journal of French Studies*, II, no. 3 (1974) 307–24, also provides a useful study of the religious 'radicals'.

41. 'Never has my soul come to rest in another as gently as in his', Tristan to Charles-Joseph Traviès, 6 June 1839, in *Lettres*, pp. 99–100.

42. F. Tristan, *L'Union ouvrière*, p. xxiii.

43. Paul Chacornac, *Eliphas Lévi, renovateur de l'occultisme en France, 1810–1875* (Paris, 1926), cited in F.P. Bowman, *Eliphas Lévi*, p. 10, n. 1. Pierre Leprohon also suggests that they were lovers, or at least that Constant's writings on Tristan were evidence of frustrated desire. See *Flora Tristan* (Paris, 1979), pp. 133–4.

44. F.P. Bowman, *Eliphas Lévi*, pp. 10–12.

45. *L'Emancipation de la Femme ou le Testament de la Paria. Ouvrage posthume de Mme. Flora Tristan, complété d'après ses notes et publié par A. Constant* (Paris, 1845). Scholars have argued that this work was substantially rewritten by Constant, though there is no firm evidence of this. For a discussion of this point see J.-L. Puech, *Vie*, p. 491; P. Bénichou, *Le Temps des Prophètes*, p. 348, n. 38.

46. For Tristan's prophetic self-image, see *Promenades*, p. 319; F. Tristan to Olympe Chodzko, September 1839, in *Lettres*, pp. 110–12.

47. See P. Bénichou, *Le Temps des Prophètes*, pp. 426–7, 431–2, 436.

48. *Ibid.*, p. 430.

49. For her views on Ganneau, see F. Tristan to Charles-Joseph Traviès, 14 September 1839, in *Lettres*, pp. 108–9. The plural forms were used almost without exception in her personal correspondence from 1839.

50. In Tristan's surviving correspondence her letter to Olympe Chodzko, September 1839, provides the first example of the use of her stamp (*Lettres*, p. 110).

51. F. Tristan to Madame Laure, August 1841 (?), in *Lettres*, pp. 127–30.

52. Addendum to *L'Emancipation de la Femme*, pp. 118–9. Constant criticised this theory, accusing Tristan of seeking 'vengeance' for women (p. 119).

53. For a discussion of this point, see below, chap. 9.

54. *La Mère de Dieu*, extracts published in F.P. Bowman, *Eliphas Lévi*, pp. 127–9, 156–61; P. Bénichou, *Le Temps des Prophètes*, pp. 429–31; 435–6.

55. For example, 'Dear Son, . . . Our Mother of God is working wonders! I have already made 4 people read it; -it is in great demand . . .', F. Tristan to A. Constant, 3 March 1844, in *Lettres*, pp. 193–4.

56. *Promenades*, pp. 262–3, 269.

57. *Nécessité*, pp. 3–4, 14.

58. *L'Union ouvrière*, p. 53.

59. *Le Tour de France*, I, pp. 122, 133. Tristan expressed a similar view of

224   French Socialism and Sexual Difference

proletarian women in *Méphis*, I, pp. 155–7, 228.
60. *Pérégrinations*, 1838 ed., I, pp. xxiii–iv.
61. Puech noted Tristan's stress on the moral implications of women's oppression in *Vie*, pp. 338–9, 355–7. See also M. Thibert, *Le Féminisme*, pp. 285, 290, 299.
62. *Pérégrinations*, 1838 edition, I, p. xxv; *Promenades*, p. 262.
63. 'A Messieurs les Députés', published in *Lettres*, pp. 73–6; *Pérégrinations*, p. 74; *Méphis*, II, p. 55.
64. *Pérégrinations*, pp. 132–3; 139–41; *Méphis*, I, p. 156; II, pp. 55, 95; *Promenades*, pp. 267–70; *L'Union ouvrière*, pp. 53–5.
65. *L'Union ouvrière*, pp. 54–5.
66. *Promenades*, p. 267.
67. *Ibid.*, pp. 269–70.
68. *Pérégrinations*, 1838 edition, I, p. xiv; *Promenades*, pp. 103–4, 125, 263; *L'Union ouvrière*, pp. 44–6.
69. *L'Union ouvrière*, p. 54, n. 1; *Tour de France*, I, pp. 229–30; II, pp. 72, 124–9.
70. *Promenades*, p. 126.
71. *Ibid.*, p. 123.
72. *Ibid.*, pp. 123–6.
73. *Méphis*, I, p. 126; *L'Union ouvrière*, p. 50.
74. *L'Union ouvrière*, pp. 51–2.
75. *Promenades*, pp. 263–4.
76. *L'Union ouvrière*, p. 53.
77. *Ibid.*, p. 62.
78. *Promenades*, p. 125.
79. *L'Union ouvrière*, p. 70. For a discussion of appeals to both a single human nature and to sexual difference by nineteenth-century feminists see Geneviève Fraisse, 'L'Usage du Droit Naturel', pp. 144–56; 'Natural Law and the Origins of Nineteenth-Century Feminist Thought in France', transl. Nancy Festinger, in J. Friedlander (ed.) *Women in Culture and Politics. A Century of Change* (Bloomington, Ind., 1986), pp. 318–29.
80. *Promenades*, p. 275.
81. *L'Union ouvrière*, p. 44.

9 Flora Tristan, Socialism and the 'Reign of Women'

1. *Le Tour de France*, II, p. 140.
2. *Ibid.*, and pp. 91, 211, 168.
3. *Ibid.*, I, p. 215.
4. *Promenades*, p. 115; *Le Tour de France*, I, pp. 215–16; II, p. 149.
5. *Promenades*, pp. 52, 194; *Le Tour de France*, I, pp. 63, 90, 163, 223; II, pp. 156, 230.
6. See *Le Tour de France*, II, pp. 91, 140, and Tristan's letter to the editor of *La Phalange*, the Fourierist newspaper, August 1836, in *Lettres*, pp. 61–64.
7. *Le Tour de France*, II, p. 91. See also pp. 211, 168.

8. *Méphis*, II, p. 294.
9. *Ibid.*, I, pp. 318–19.
10. *Promenades*, p. 337.
11. *Ibid.*, p. 281.
12. 'A MM. les membres du comité de l'Union pour la correspondance', 8 April 1843, *Lettres*, pp. 153–5.
13. *L'Union ouvrière*, p. 5.
14. *Ibid.*, p. 48, n.
15. *Ibid.*, pp. 17–18.
16. *Ibid.*, p. 5.
17. *Ibid.*, p. 104.
18. *Le Tour de France*, I, p. 29.
19. *Ibid.*, II, p. 115.
20. *L'Union ouvrière*, p. 10.
21. *Méphis*, I, pp. 181, 183.
22. *Ibid.*, II, pp. 293–4.
23. Judith Grégoire to P. Enfantin, 5 August 1837, FE, 7627/10.
24. *Promenades*, p. 320.
25. *Le Tour de France*, I, p. 140.
26. *Ibid.*
27. *Ibid.*
28. *Ibid.*, pp. 123–4. Thibert also noted the differences between Tristan's concept of 'the Woman guide' and that of the Saint-Simonians in *Le Féminisme*, p. 300.
29. *Promenades*, p. 237.
30. *Ibid.*, p. 238. Jacques Valette pointed out the significance of this episode as an initiation into an illuminist sect. See 'Utopie sociale et utopistes sociaux en France vers 1848', in *1848. Les Utopismes sociaux. Utopie et action à la veille des journées de février* (Paris, 1981), pp. 48–9. Puech discusses the incident in *Vie*, pp. 103–7.
31. *Promenades*, pp. 237, 239.
32. *Le Tour de France*, I, pp. 28–9, 62; Tristan to Antoine-Laurent-Apollinaire Fée, 21 May 1843, in *Lettres*, pp. 164–5.
33. See, for example, *Le Tour de France*, II, pp. 75, 119, 132, 146.
34. *Ibid.*, pp. 19–20.
35. *Ibid.*, I, pp. 218–19; II, pp. 224–5. Tristan listed her 'spiritual children' in *ibid.*, II, p. 27.
36. *Ibid.*, I, p. 41.
37. *Ibid.*, p. 231.
38. P. Bénichou, *Le Temps des Prophètes*, p. 430.
39. *Ibid.*, p. 444.
40. *L'Union ouvrière*, pp. 53–61.
41. *Ibid.*, pp. 59–61; 64–6. For a similar account of the new role of *ménagère*, see Puech, *Vie*, pp. 350–4.
42. *L'Union ouvrière*, p. 66.
43. *Ibid.*, p. 49.
44. See J.W. Scott, 'Men and Women in the Parisian garment trades', pp. 81–2; M. Rebérioux, 'L'Ouvrière, pp. 63–6.
45. *L'Union ouvrière*, p. 62.

46. Scott makes this point in discussing the tailors, in 'Men and Women in the Parisian garment trades', pp. 70–6, and in 'Work Identities for Men and Women. The Politics of Work and Family in the Parisian Garment Trades in 1848', *Gender and the Politics of History* (New York, 1988), pp. 96–102.
47. *L'Union ouvrière*, pp. 68–9. See also pp. 43, 62, 67, etc.
48. See for example her comments on Dr. d'Amador at Montpellier: . . . although he denies the superiority of woman, he nevertheless seems to recognise and accept my own. But as an exception, he tells me each day'. (*Le Tour de France*, II, p. 140; see also I, pp. 123–4).
49. *L'Union ouvrière*, pp. 51–62.
50. *Le Tour de France*, I, pp. 204, 223.
51. See J.W. Scott, 'Work Identities for Men and Women', pp. 108–12, on idealised images of the working class family in this period.
52. *Promenades*, p. 243.
53. *Nécessité*, p. 4.
54. *L'Union ouvrière*, p. 101; *Le Tour de France*, I, p. 147.
55. In *Promenades* Tristan suggested that children might enter the *salles d'asile* at age 2 (p. 243). In *L'Union ouvrière* she proposed that the workers' palaces should receive children at the age of 6 (p. 96).
56. *L'Union ouvrière*, pp. 88–9.
57. *Ibid.*, p. xviii.
58. *Ibid.*, p. 87–8.
59. *Ibid.*, p. 88.
60. *Ibid.*, p. 89.
61. *Le Tour de France*, I, p. 123.
62. *Ibid.*, II, p. 34.
63. *Ibid.*, p. 31. Tristan mistakenly wrote that the reign of war had been that of women. This was clearly an error, as the context shows. See the editor's notes, *ibid.*, p. 37.
64. *L'Union ouvrière*, pp. 73–5. Tristan reserved for women a proportion of places on the committees as a form of positive discrimination, which would eventually become unnecessary as women were educated. They would then have equal representation with men (p. 73, n. 2). She did not imply that women had a lesser role in public affairs, as Rendall claims in *Origins*, p. 277.
65. *Le Tour de France*, I, p. 133.
66. *L'Atelier*, 3e année, no. 9 (31 May 1843).
67. Louis Vasbenter to F. Tristan, 11 June 1843, reproduced in J.-L. Puech, *Vie*, pp. 470–6 (p. 474). See also Tristan's approving comments on Vannostal, who was relatively 'advanced' on this issue, *Le Tour de France*, I, p. 38.
68. See *Le Tour de France*, I, p. 54, and the letters quoted in Puech, *Vie*, pp. 166–7; 252, n. 1.
69. *Méphis*, I, p. 181.
70. *Le Tour de France*, I, p. 231.

Bibliography

I: MANUSCRIPT SOURCES

A: Archives Nationales, Paris:

(i) *Archives Sociétaires: Série AS, la cote* 10
This is the major manuscript source for the study of Charles Fourier.
The first part of the collection (10AS 1 – 10AS 25) consists of Fourier's
manuscripts and personal papers. The second section (10AS 26 – 10AS
42) contains some documents relevant to the study of the Saint-
Simonians, particularly those Saint-Simonians who later transferred
their allegiance to the *Ecole sociétaire*. 10AS 8 and 21 on love and the
passions were particularly valuable on Fourier; 10AS 36, 41 and 42 on
the Saint-Simonians. 10AS 42 also contains letters from Flora Tristan to
Charles Fourier and Victor Considerant.
(ii) *C 2156 : Pétitions*
Included here is Tristan's petition for the re-introduction of divorce
(Dossier 133, no. 71).

B: Bibliothèque de l'Arsenal, Paris: Fonds Enfantin

The *Fonds Enfantin* is the major repository of sources relating to the
Saint-Simonian movement. The vast collection of letters and documents
is divided into four parts. My research focused on parts one and three,
which include assorted Saint-Simonian correspondence, manuscripts
relating to the Saint-Simonian venture in Egypt, the papers of Charles
Lambert, and materials on aspects of the Saint-Simonian 'dogma'.
Documents of particular relevance for this study were located in:
FE 7608 'Correspondance du *Globe*. Lettres de Dames, 1831–2'.
FE 7627: 'Correspondance, 1837–9'.
FE 7645-7: 'Archives, vols. III–V'.
FE 7727, 7776-7, 7791: 'Correspondance divers'.
FE 7745: 'Papiers Lambert'.
FE 7825: 'Dogme. Divers'

C: Bibliothèque Marguerite Durand, Paris

This feminist library contains letters by a number of the women
included in this study, such as Pauline Roland, Eugénie Niboyet,
Suzanne Voilquin and Flora Tristan, under the catalogue number 091.

D: Bibliothèque Historique de la Ville de Paris

CP 428: Dossiers d'autographes, includes some letters by Flora Tristan.

II: PRINTED PRIMARY SOURCES

A: WORKS BY CHARLES FOURIER

Mnémonique géographique, ou méthode pour apprendre en peu de leçons la géographie, la statistique et la politique, Paris, imprimerie de Charpentier--Méricourt, 1824.

Le Nouveau Monde Industriel, ou invention du procédé d'industrie attrayante et combinée en séries passionnées. . . . Livret d'annonce, Paris, Bossange père, 1830.

Oeuvres complètes de Charles Fourier, 12 vols, Paris, Editions Anthropos, 1966–8.

Pièges et charlatanisme des deux sectes Saint-Simon et Owen, qui promettent l'association et le progrès. Moyen d'organiser en deux mois le Progrès réel, la vraie Association, ou combinaison des travaux agricoles et domestiques, donnant quadruple produit, et élevant à 25 milliards le revenu de la France, borné aujourd'hui à 6 milliards un tiers, Paris, Bossange père, 1831.

Edited Selected Works

Debout-Oleskiewicz, Simone, 'Textes inédits de Charles Fourier', *Revue internationale de Philosophie,* 60, no. 2 (1962) 147–75.

'Fourier's reply to the *Gazette de France,* in which his doctrines were grossly misrepresented as being anti-Christian', in A. Transon, *Charles Fourier's theory of Attractive Industry, and the Moral Harmony of the passions . . . To which is prefixed a memoir of Fourier,* introduction by Hugh Doherty, London, Office of *The London Phalanx,* 1841, pp. 84–102.

L'Harmonie universelle et le Phalanstère exposés par Fourier. Recueil méthodique des morceaux choisis de l'auteur, 2 vols, Paris, Librairie phalanstérienne, 1849.

'Lettre de Fourier au Grand Juge', reproduced in J.-J. Hemardinquer, 'La "découverte du mouvement social": notes critiques sur le jeune Fourier', *Le Mouvement social,* 48 (1964) 60–7.

The Utopian Vision of Charles Fourier. Selected Texts on Work, Love and Passionate Attraction, ed. Jonathan Beecher and Richard Bienvenu, London, Cape, 1972.

Vers la liberté en amour. Textes choisis et présentés par Daniel Guérin, Paris, Gallimard, 1975.

B: WORKS BY THE SAINT-SIMONIANS

1: Books and Pamphlets

Barrault, Emile, *1831,* 3rd ed., Paris, au bureau de *l'Organisateur,* 1831.

——, *1833 ou l'anée de la Mère,* Lyon, Mme S. Durval, 1833.

——, *Aux Artistes. Du Passé et de l'avenir des beaux-arts,* Paris, A. Mesnier, 1830.

——, *Barrière d'Italie, 15 décembre 1832. A Paris!* [Paris, 1832].

——, *Compagnonage de la femme. Chant. Paroles de E. Barrault, musique de F. David*, Lyon, imp. de J. Perret [1833].

——, *Occident et Orient. Etudes morales, politiques, religieuses pendant 1833–4 de l'ère chrétienne, 1249–50 de l'hégyre*, Paris, Désessart, 1835.

——, *Religion Saint-Simonienne. A tous*, Paris, Librairie Saint-Simonienne, 1832.

——, (ed.), *Religion Saint-Simonienne. Recueil de Prédications*, 2 vols, Paris, au bureau du *Globe*, 1832.

Bazard, Palmyre, *Religion saint-simonienne. Aux femmes, sur leur mission religieuse dans la crise actuelle*, Rouen, imp. de D. Brière, 1831.

Bazard, Saint-Amand, *Doctrine de Saint-Simon. Exposition deuxième année. 1829–1830*, Paris, au bureau de l'*Organisateur* et du *Globe*, 1830.

——, *Religion Saint-Simonienne. Discussions morales, politiques et religieuses qui ont amené la séparation qui s'est effectuée, au mois de novembre 1831, dans le sein de la Société saint-simonienne. Première partie. Relations des hommes et des femmes, mariage, divorce*, Paris, rue des Saints-Pères, no. 26, et chez Paulin, Delaunay, Heideloff, 1832.

——, *Religion saint-simonienne. Lettre à M. le président de la Chambre des Députés*, Paris, imp. d'Everat (n.d.).

Béranger, C., *Pétition d'un prolétaire à la Chambre des Députés*, Paris, au bureau de l'*Organisateur*, 1831.

Biard, Gustave, *Religion Saint-Simonienne. Aperçu des vues morales et industrielles des Saint-Simoniens*, Blois, imp. de Dézairs, 1832.

Charton, Edouard, *Mémoire d'un prédicateur saint-simonien*, Paris, bureau de la *Revue encyclopédique*, 1832.

Chevalier, Michel, *Ménilmontant, le 23 novembre 1832. A Lyon!* [Paris, 1832].

——, *Ménilmontant, 12 décembre 1832. Au nom de Dieu, qui veut aujourd'hui l'égalité de l'homme et de la femme . . .* [Paris, 1832].

——, *Religion saint-simonienne, Evènemens de Lyon* [Paris, 1832].

——, et al., *Religion saint-simonienne. Politique industrielle et système de la Méditerranée*, Paris [imp. d'Everat], 1832.

Colin, A., *Aux femmes juives et à toutes celles qui liront cette parole, salut au nom de DIEU, PERE et MERE*, Lyon, Mme. Durval, 1833.

Collin et al. (eds), *1833 ou l'année de la Mère. Juillet. Mission de l'Est*, rédigée par Collin, Rogé, Maréchal, Charpin, Lamy, Toulon, imprimerie et lithographie de Canquoin, 1834.

David, F., *Lyon le 22 fév. 1833. Je pars pour l'Orient . . .*, Lyon [1833].

Démar, Claire, *Textes sur l'Affranchissement des Femmes (1832–1833)*, ed. Valentin Pelosse, Paris, Payot, 1976.

Désessart, *Pensées politiques et religieuses d'un saint-simonien. Sa profession de foi*, Paris, Johanneau, 1833.

Doctrine de Saint-Simon. Exposition première année 1829, 2nd ed., Paris, au bureau de l'*Organisateur*, 1830.

——, nouvelle édition publiée avec introduction et notes par C. Bouglé et Elie Halévy, Paris, Rivière, 1924.

Duguet, C., *Adieux à l'ancien monde* [Paris, 1833].

——, *Salut au nouveau monde* [Paris, 1833].

E.A.C. (Mlle. E.A. Casaubon), *La Femme est la Famille*, Paris, Gauthier, 1834.

——, *Le Nouveau contrat social, ou place à la Femme*, Paris, Delaunay, 1834.

Eichthal, G. d', and Ismayl Urbain, *Lettres sur la race noire et la race blanche*, Paris, Paulin, 1839.

Enfantin, B.P., *L'Attente*, Angers [1832].

——, *Ménilmontant, le 9 novembre 1832. Le Père à la Reine des Français*, Paris, imp. d'Everat [1832].

——, *Le Père à Fournel, apôtre*, Paris, imprimerie d'Everat, 1832.

——, *Religion Saint-Simonienne. Economie politique et politique. Articles extraits du Globe*, Paris, au bureau du *Globe*, 1831.

——, *Religion Saint-Simonienne. Lettre du Père Enfantin à Charles Duveyrier. Lettre du Père Enfantin à François et à Peiffer, Chefs de l'Eglise de Lyon. Le Prêtre-L'homme et la femme. (Extrait du Globe du 18 juin 1831)*, Paris, Everat imprimeur, 1831.

Explication de la Religion Saint-Simonienne, Nantes, imprimerie de Victor Margin, 1833.

[Haspott, E.] *Religion saint-simonienne. Aux ouvriers, par un ouvrier* [Paris, imprimerie d'Everat, 1831].

Justus, Pol, *Liberté, femmes!!!*, Paris and Lyon, Mme. Durval, 1833.

Lechevalier Saint-André, Jules, *Aux saint-simoniens, lettre sur la division survenue dans l'association saint-simonienne (20 déc. 1831)*, Paris, imprimerie d'Everat, 1831.

——, *Religion saint-simonienne. Enseignement central*, Paris, imprimerie d'Everat, n.d.

[Lemonnier, Charles], *Elisa Lemonnier, fondatrice de la société pour l'enseignement professionel des femmes*, Saint-Germain, imprimerie de L. Toinon, 1866.

——, *Religion Saint-Simonienne. Eglise de Toulouse. Enseignement de l'Athénée. Avenir de la Femme*, par Ch. L., Toulouse, imprimerie de A. Hénault, 1831.

——, *Les Saint-Simoniens!!!* [Paris, 1832].

Mercier, Jules, *A la femme*, Paris, imprimerie de Sétier [1832].

——, *Famille saint-simonienne. La Sainte canaille*, Paris, imprimerie de Sétier, n.d.

Niboyet, Eugénie, *De la nécessité d'abolir la peine de mort*, Paris, L. Babeuf, 1836.

Opinions littéraires, philosophiques et industrielles [Saint-Simon, Léon Halévy et al.], Paris, Galérie de Bossange père, 1825.

Pensées religieuses par un Saint-Simonien croyant à l'égalité de l'homme et de la femme, Angers, imprimerie de E. le Sourd, 1833.

Religion saint-simonienne. Enseignement des ouvriers. Séance du dimanche 18 décembre 1831, Paris, au bureau du *Globe*, 1831.

Religion saint-simonienne. Enseignement des ouvriers. Séance du dimanche 25 décembre 1831, Paris, au bureau du *Globe*, 1832.

Religion saint-simonienne. Feuilles populaires [Paris, 1832].

Religion saint-simonienne. La Presse. Articles extraits du Globe, journal de la doctrine de Saint-Simon, Paris, au bureau du *Globe* et de l'*Organisateur*, 1831.

Religion saint-simonienne. La Prophétie. Articles extraits du Globe du 19 février au 20 avril 1832. Ménilmontant, le 1er juin 1832, Paris, imprimerie d'Everat, 1832.

Religion saint-simonienne. Rapports adressés aux Pères Suprêmes sur la situation et les travaux de la famille [Paris? 1831?].

Religion saint-simonienne. Réunion générale de la Famille. Séances des 19 et 21 novembre. Note sur le Mariage et le Divorce; Lue au Collège de la Religion Saint-Simonienne, le 17 octobre, par le Père Rodrigues, Paris, Everat imprimeur, 1831.

Religion Saint-Simonienne. Morale. Réunion générale de la famille. Enseignemens du Père Suprême. Les trois familles, Paris, Librairie saint-simonienne, 1832.

[Rodrigues, Eugène], *Lettres sur la religion et la politique, 1829; suivies de l'Education du Genre humain, traduit de l'allemand, de Lessing*, Paris, au bureau de l'*Organisateur*, 1831.

Rodrigues, Olinde, *Aux Saint-Simoniens. (13 février 1832). Bases de la loi morale proposées à l'acceptation des femmes*, Paris, imprimerie d'Everat, 1832.

——, *Le Disciple de Saint-Simon aux Saint-Simoniens et au public*, Paris, imprimerie d'Everat, 1832.

——, *Préface des Oeuvres de Saint-Simon. Le disciple de Saint-Simon au public*, Paris, 1832.

[Rousseau, A.], *Tout pour les femmes*, Strasbourg, imprimerie de Mme. Silbermann, 1833.

Saint-Amand, Adèle de, *Proclamations aux femmes sur la nécessité des droits de la femme*, Paris, H. Fournier, n.d.

[Saint-Simon, Comte Henri de], *Lettres d'un Habitant de Genève à ses contemporains [1803], réimprimées conformément à l'édition originale et suivies de deux documents inédits. Lettre aux Européens. [Essai sur l'Organisation sociale]*, introduction par Alfred Péreire, Paris, Librairie Félix Alcan, 1925.

Oeuvres de Claude-Henri de Saint-Simon, 6 vols, Geneva, Slatkine, 1977.

——, *Oeuvres de Saint-Simon et d'Enfantin. Publiées par les membres du conseil institué par Enfantin pour l'exécution de ses dernières volontés*, 47 vols., Paris, E. Dentu, Ernest Leroux, 1865–1878.

——, *Son premier écrit; Lettres d'un habitant de Genève à ses contemporains, 1802; sa parabole politique, 1819; Le Nouveau Christianisme, 1825; précédés de fragmens de l'Histoire de sa vie écrite par lui-même, publiés par Olinde Rodrigues*, Paris, librairie saint-simonienne, 1832.

Terson, *Un Saint-Simonien au peuple de Lyon, à l'occasion des évènements d'avril, 1834*, Lyon, chez Mme. Durval, 1834.

Transon, Abel, *Religion Saint-Simonienne. Affranchissement des femmes, prédication du 1er janvier, 1832*, Paris, au bureau du *Globe*, 1832.

——, *De la Religion saint-simonienne. Aux élèves de l'Ecole polytechnique*, Paris, au bureau de l'*Organisateur*, 1830.

——, *Religion saint-simonienne – Morale du jour – La fille du Peuple*, Paris, imprimerie d'Everat [1832].

——, *Religion saint-simonienne. Prédication du 11 décembre, par Abel Transon: vue générale sur le nouveau caractère de l'apostolat saint-simonien; [Morale individuelle. Allocution prononcée . . . par P.M. Laurent]*, Paris, au bureau du *Globe*, 1831.

——, *Simple écrit d'Abel Transon aux Saint-Simoniens*, Paris, imprimerie d'Everat, 1832.

Véret, Jeanne-Désirée, *Aux femmes privilégiées, Jeanne-Désirée prolétaire, Saint-Simonienne*, n.p., n.d.

——, *Lettre au roi écrite sous l'impression des évènements des 5 et 6 juin 1832*, Paris, [1832].

Vinçard, Jules, *Aux compagnons de la femme, chant, paroles de Vinçard*, Lyon, imprimerie de J. Perret, n.d.

——, *L'Avenir est à nous*, [Paris], imprimerie de Sétier, n.d.

——, *Mémoires épisodiques d'un vieux chansonnier saint-simonien*, Paris, E. Dentu, 1878.

Voilquin, Suzanne, *Souvenirs d'une fille du peuple, ou la Saint-Simonienne en Egypte*, Paris, F. Maspéro, 1978.

——, *Mémoires d'une Saint-Simonienne en Russie (1839–1846)*, ed. Maïté Albistur and Daniel Armogathe, Paris, Editions des Femmes, 1977.

2: Edited Selected Works

Bulciolu, Maria Teresa, *L'Ecole Saint-Simonienne et la Femme. Notes et documents pour une histoire du rôle de la femme dans la société saint-simonienne, 1828–1833*, Pisa, Golliardica, 1980.

The Doctrine of Saint-Simon: An Exposition, First Year, 1828–1829, trans. George G. Iggers, New York, Schocken Books, 1972.

Henri Saint-Simon 1760–1825. Selected writings on science, industry and social organisation, trans. and ed. Keith Taylor, London, Croom Helm, 1975.

Social Organisation, the Science of Man and other Writings, ed. Felix Markham, New York, Harper Torchbooks, 1964.

C: WORKS BY FLORA TRISTAN

1: Books

Méphis, 2 vols, Paris, Ladvocat, 1838.

Nécessité de faire un bon accueil aux femmes étrangères, par Madame F.T., Paris, chez Delaunay, 1835.

Les Pérégrinations d'une Paria (1833–1834), 2 vols, Paris, Arthus Bertrand, 1838.

——, 1 vol., Paris, François Maspéro, 1979.

Promenades dans Londres, ou L'aristocratie et les prolétaires anglais, Edition établie et commentée par François Bédarida, Paris, François Maspéro, 1978 [reprint of the 1842 'édition populaire'].

L'Union ouvrière, 3rd ed., Paris and Lyon, chez tous les libraires, 1844 (facsimile, Editions d'histoire sociale, 1967).

2: Posthumous Works

L'Emancipation de la femme, ou le testament de la Paria. Ouvrage posthume de Mme. Flora Tristan, complété d'après ses notes et publié par A. Constant, 2nd ed., Paris, Guarin, 1846.

Le Tour de France, Etat actuel de la classe ouvrière sous l'aspect moral, intellectuel et matériel, texte et notes établis par Jules-L. Puech, préface de Michel Collinet, introduction nouvelle de Stéphane Michaud, 2 vols, Paris, François Maspéro, 1980.

3: Articles

'Les Couvens d'Aréquipa', *Revue de Paris*, 35 (1836) 225–48.
'Les Femmes de Lima', *Revue de Paris*, 33 (1836) 209–16.
'Lettres à un architecte anglais', *Revue de Paris*, 37–8 (1837) 134–9; 280–90.

4: Published Letters

Breton, André, 'Flora Tristan: sept lettres inédites', *Le Surréalisme même*, 3 (1975) 4–12.
Michaud, Stéphane, 'Flora Tristan: Trente-cinq lettres', *International Review of Social History*, 24, no. 1 (1979) 80–125.
Tristan, Flora, 'A M. le Directeur du *Censeur*', republished in *La Réforme*, 14 May 1844.
——, *Lettres*; réunies, présentées et annotées par Stéphane Michaud, Paris, Editions du Seuil, 1980.

5: Translated Works

Flora Tristan's London Journal: a survey of London life in the 1830s: a translation of Promenades dans Londres, by Dennis Palmer and Giselle Pincetl, London, George Prior Publishers, 1980.
The London Journal of Flora Tristan, translated and annotated by Jean Hawkes, London, Virago, 1982.
The Workers' Union, translated with an introduction by Beverly Livingston, Champaign, University of Illinois Press, 1983.

D: NEWSPAPERS

L'Atelier, 3e année, no. 9 (31 mai 1843).
Foi Nouvelle. Livre des Actes, Paris, 1833.
La Foi Nouvelle. Livre des Actes publié par les femmes, Paris, 1833–4.
Le Globe, IX-XII, Paris, 1830–32.
The New Moral World, 3rd series, I, no. 10 (5 Sep. 1840).
L'Organisateur, Paris, 1829–31.
Le Producteur, Journal de l'industrie, des sciences et des beaux-arts, Paris, 1825–6.
La Tribune des Femmes, Paris, 1832–4. This newspaper also appeared under the titles *La Femme libre*, *La Femme d'avenir*, *La Femme nouvelle* and *L'Apostolat des Femmes*.

E: CONTEXTUAL WORKS

Blanc, Eléonore, *Biographie de Flora Tristan*, Lyon, chez l'auteur, 1845.
Chateaubriand, M. le Vicomte de, *Génie du Christianisme*, Paris, chez Ledentu, 1838.
Fournel, Henri, *Bibliographie Saint-Simonienne de 1802 au 31 décembre 1832*, N.Y., Burt Franklin [1973] (reprint of the 1833 ed.).
Laurence, James de [Sir James Lawrence], *Les Enfants de Dieu, ou la religion*

de Jésus reconciliée avec la philosophie, Paris, imprimerie de Plassan et Cie., 1831.

Pellarin, Charles, *Charles Fourier, Sa Vie et Sa Théorie*, 2nd ed., Paris, Librairie de l'Ecole Sociétaire, 1843.

Reybaud, Louis, *Etudes sur les Réformateurs contemporains ou socialistes modernes*, 6 vols, Bruxelles, Société Belge de Librairie, 1844.

Reynaud, Jean, 'De la société saint-simonienne', *La Revue encyclopédique*, LIII (Jan.–Mar. 1832) 9–36.

Talon, Marie, 'Sur l'Ecole Saint-Simonienne et particulièrement sur l'appel à la femme', *Almanach des femmes* (1853), ed. Jeanne Deroin, London, J. Watson, 1853.

Virey, J.-J., *De la Femme sous ses rapports physiologique, moral et littéraire*, 2nd ed., Paris, Crochard, 1825.

III: SECONDARY SOURCES

A: WORKS ON CHARLES FOURIER, THE SAINT-SIMONIANS AND FLORA TRISTAN

1: Books and Theses

Baelen, Jean, *La vie de Flora Tristan: socialisme et féminisme au XIXe siècle*, Paris, Editions du Seuil, 1972.

Barthes, Roland, *Sade, Fourier, Loyola*, New York, Hill and Wang, 1976.

Beecher, Jonathan French, 'Charles Fourier and his Early Writings', unpublished Ph.D. thesis, Harvard University, 1967.

——, *Charles Fourier: The Visionary and His World*, Berkeley, University of California Press, 1987.

Bouglé, C., *Chez les prophètes socialistes*, Paris, Alcan, 1918.

Bourgin, Hubert, *Fourier. Contribution à l'étude du socialisme français*, Paris, Société nouvelle de librairie et d'édition, 1905.

Briscoe, James Bland, 'Saint-Simonisme and the Origins of Socialism in France, 1816–1832', unpublished Ph.D. thesis, Columbia University, 1980.

Carlisle, Robert B., *The Proffered Crown. Saint-Simonianism and the Doctrine of Hope*, Baltimore and London, John Hopkins University Press, 1987.

Carnot, Hippolyte, *Sur le Saint-Simonisme, lecture faite à l'Académie des Sciences morales et politiques*, Paris, A. Picard, 1887.

Charléty, Sébastien, *Histoire du Saint-Simonisme (1825–1864)*, 2nd ed., Paris, Paul Hartmann, 1931.

Debout, Simone, *L'Utopie de Charles Fourier*, Paris, Payot, 1978.

Debû-Bridel, Jacques, *L'Actualité de Fourier. De l'utopie au fouriérisme appliqué*, Paris, Editions du Seuil, 1975.

Desanti, Dominique, *Flora Tristan, la Femme révoltée*, Paris, Hachette, 1972.

——, *Flora Tristan: Vie, oeuvres mêlées*, Paris, Union générale des éditions, 1973.

Dijkstra, Sandra, *Flora Tristan: Pioneer Feminist and Socialist*, Berkeley, California, Center for Socialist History, 1984.

Gattey, Charles Neilson, *Gaugin's Astonishing Grandmother. A Biography of Flora Tristan*, London, Femina Books Ltd., 1970.

Goret, Jean, *La Pensée de Fourier*, Paris, Presses universitaires de France, 1974.

Grépon, Marguerite, *Une croisade pour un meilleur amour. Histoire des Saint-Simoniennes. Récit*, Paris and Brussels, éditions Sodi, 1968.

Ivray, Jehan d', *L'Aventure saint-simonienne et les femmes*, Paris, Alcan, 1928.

Lehouck, Emile, *Fourier aujourd'hui*, Paris, Denoël, 1966.

——, *Vie de Charles Fourier*, Paris, Denoël–Gonthier, 1978.

Lejeune, Paule, *Flora Tristan. Réalisations, oeuvres*, Paris, collection 'Le Peuple prend la parole', [1975].

Leprohon, Pierre, *Flora Tristan*, Paris, Corymbe, 1979.

Manuel, Frank E., *The Prophets of Paris*, Cambridge, Mass., Harvard University Press, 1962.

——, *The New World of Henri Saint-Simon*, Notre Dame, Notre Dame Press, 1963.

Michaud, Stéphane (ed.), *Un Fabuleux Destin: Flora Tristan. Actes du Premier Colloque International Flora Tristan, 1984*, Dijon, Editions universitaires de Dijon, [1985].

Poulat, Emile, *Les cahiers manuscrits de Fourier. Etude historique et inventaire raisonné*, Paris, Bibliothèque internationale de sociologie de la coopération, 1957.

Puech, Jules-L., *La vie et l'oeuvre de Flora Tristan, 1803–1844*, Paris, Marcel Rivière, 1952.

Riasanovsky, Nicholas V., *The Teaching of Charles Fourier*, Berkeley, University of California Press, 1969.

Rude, Fernand (ed.), *Bagnes d'Afrique. Trois transportés en Algérie après le coup d'Etat du 2 décembre 1851*, Paris, François Maspéro, 1981.

Schneider, Joyce Anne, *Flora Tristan: Feminist, Socialist and Free Spirit*, New York, William Morrow and Co., 1980.

Silberling, E., *Dictionnaire de Sociologie phalanstérienne*, Paris, Marcel Rivière, 1911.

Spencer, Michael, *Charles Fourier*, Boston, Twayne Publishers, 1981.

Thomas, Edith, *Pauline Roland, Socialisme et Féminisme au XIXe Siècle*, Paris, Marcel Rivière, 1956.

Thomas, Jean–Paul, *Libération instinctuelle, libération politique. Contribution fouriériste à Marcuse*, Paris, Le Sycamore, 1980.

Vergez, André, *Fourier*, Paris, Presses universitaires de France, 1969.

Walch, Jean, *Bibliographie du Saint-Simonisme avec trois textes inédits*, Paris, Vrin, 1967.

Weill, Georges, *L'Ecole Saint-Simonienne, son histoire, son influence jusqu'à nos jours*, Paris, Alcan, 1896.

Zeldin, David, *The Educational Ideas of Charles Fourier 1772–1837*, London, Cass, 1969.

2: Articles and Essays

Adler, Laure, 'Flora, Pauline et les autres', in Jean–Paul Aron (ed.), *Misérable et glorieuse la femme du XIXe siècle*, Paris, Fayard, 1980.

Altman, Elizabeth C., 'The Philosophical Bases of Feminism: The Feminist

Doctrines of the Saint-Simonians and Charles Fourier', *Philosophical Forum*, 7–8 (1975–6) 277–91.

Bouglé, C., 'Le Féminisme saint-simonien', *Revue de Paris*, année xxv, V (1918) 371–99.

Butor, Michel, 'Le féminin chez Fourier', *Répertoire IV*, Paris, Editions de Minuit, 1974.

Cuvillier, A., 'Un schisme saint-simonien. Les origines de l'école Buchézienne (d'après des documents inédits)', *Revue du Mois*, XXI (Jan.–June 1920) 494–532.

Debout, Simone, 'La Geste de Flora Tristan', *Critique*, 308 (Jan. 1973) 81–92.

——, 'Des manies au cosmos, ou le dedans et le dehors sans frontière', *Australian Journal of French Studies*, 11, no. 3 (1974) 263–87.

Elhadad, Lydia, 'Femmes prénommées: les prolétaires saint-simoniennes rédactrices de *La Femme libre*, 1832–1834', *Les Révoltes logiques*, 4–5 (1977) 62–88; 29–60.

—— and Geneviève Fraisse, *'L'Affranchissement de notre sexe*: une lecture du dedans ou du dehors', *Les Révoltes logiques*, 2 (1976) 105–20.

Francblin, Catherine, 'Le Féminisme utopique de Charles Fourier', *Tel Quel*, 62 (1975) 44–69.

Goldstein, Leslie F., 'Early Feminist Themes in French Utopian Socialism: The Saint-Simonians and Fourier', *Journal of the History of Ideas*, XLIII, no. 1 (1982) 91–108.

Gues, André, 'Histoires de Fous', *Ecrits de Paris*, 326 (1973) 66–78.

Hemardinquer, J.-J., 'La "découverte du mouvement social"', notes critiques sur le jeune Fourier', *Le Mouvement social*, 48 (1964) 49–70.

Ivray, Jehan d', 'Les femmes saint-simoniennes en Egypte', *Revue mondiale*, 1&15 June 1920, 312–25; 427–38.

Michaud, Stéphane, 'Flora Tristan. *Les Promenades dans Londres*', in *1848. Les Utopismes sociaux. Utopie et action à la veille des journées de février*, Société de l'histoire de la Révolution de 1848 et des Révolutions du XIXe siècle, Paris, Editions C.D.U. et Sédès réunis, 1981.

Moon, S. Joan, 'The *Saint-Simoniennes* and the Moral Revolution', *Proceedings of the Consortium on Revolutionary Europe*, 1976, 162–74.

——, 'The Saint-Simonian association of working class women, 1830–1850', *Proceedings of the Fifth Annual Meeting of the Western Society for French History, Las Cruces*, 1977, pp. 274–81.

——, 'Feminism and Socialism: The Utopian Synthesis of Flora Tristan', in Marilyn J. Boxer and Jean H. Quataert (eds), *Socialist Women: European Socialist Feminism in the Nineteenth and Early Twentieth Centuries*, New York, Elsevier, 1978.

Moses, Claire Goldberg, 'Saint-Simonian Men/Saint-Simonian Women: The Transformation of Feminist Thought in 1830s France', *Journal of Modern History*, 54, no. 2 (1982) 240–67.

Puech, Jules-L., 'Un précurseur de Fourier au XVIe siècle? A. Francesco Doni', *Revue d'histoire des doctrines économiques et sociales*, 2 (1923) 140–68.

——, 'Une romancière socialiste: Flora Tristan', *La Revue socialiste*, 15 Feb. 1914, 132–46.

——, 'Flora Tristan et le Saint-Simonisme', *Revue d'Histoire économique et sociale*, 13 (1925) 207–15.

Rabine, Leslie, 'Essentialism and Its Contexts: Saint-Simonian and Post-Structuralist Feminists', *Differences: A Journal of Feminist Cultural Studies*, no. 2 (1989) 105–23.

Ranvier, Adrien, 'Une féministe de 1848: Jeanne Deroin', *La Révolution de 1848*, IV, no. xxiv (1907) 317–55; V, nos. xxv, xxvi (1908) 421–30, 480–98.

——, 'Le Testament d'une Féministe de 1848: Jeanne Deroin', *ibid.*, V, no. xxx (1909) 816–23.

Spencer, Michael, 'Charles Fourier: la musique savante scande notre désir', *Australian Journal of French Studies*, 11, no. 3 (1974) 253–62.

Thibert, Marguerite, 'Saint-Simoniennes et Pacifistes: Eugénie Niboyet et Pauline Roland', *La Paix par le Droit* (1922) 196–200.

——, 'Une apôtre socialiste de 1848: Pauline Roland', *La Révolution de 1848*, XXII (1925–6) 478–502, 524–40.

——, 'Féminisme et Socialisme d'après Flora Tristan, *Revue d'Histoire économique et sociale*, 9 (1921) 115–36.

Vidalenc, J., 'Les techniques de la propagande saint-simonienne à la fin de 1831', *Archives de sociologie des religions*, 10 (July–Dec. 1960) 3–20.

Werner, Pascale, 'Des voix irrégulières: Flora Tristan et George Sand, ambivalence d'une filiation', in *l'Histoire sans qualités*, Christiane Dufrancatel *et al.*, Paris, Galilée, 1979.

Zilberfarb, Johanson, 'L'imagination et la réalité dans l'oeuvre de Fourier', *Le Mouvement social*, 60 (1967) 5–21.

B: WORKS ON SOCIALISM AND FEMINISM

1: Books and Theses

Abensour, Léon, *Histoire générale du féminisme des origines à nos jours*, Paris, Delagrave, 1921.

Adler, Laure, *A l'Aube du Féminisme. Les Premières Journalistes 1830–1850*, Paris, Payot, 1979.

Albistur, Maïté, and Daniel Armogathe, *Histoire du féminisme français du Moyen Age à nos jours*, 2 vols, Paris, Editions des Femmes, 1977.

Alexandrian, *Le Socialisme romantique*, Paris, Editions du Seuil, 1979.

Bidelman, Patrick Kay, 'The Feminist Movement in France: The Formative Years, 1858–1889', unpublished Ph.D. thesis, Michigan State University, 1975.

——, *Pariahs Stand Up! The Founding of the Liberal Feminist Movement in France, 1858–1889*, Westport, Conn., Greenwood Press, 1982.

Bouglé, C., *Socialisme français. Du 'Socialisme utopique' à la 'Démocratie industrielle'*, Paris, Librairie Armand Colin, 1932.

Cole, G.D.H., *A History of Socialist Thought*, vol. 1, London, Macmillan, 1953.

Corcoran, Paul E. (ed.), *Before Marx. Socialism and Communism in France 1830–1848*, London, Macmillan, 1983.

Dufrancatel, Christiane *et al.*, *L'Histoire sans Qualités*, Paris, Galilée, 1979.

Fournière, E., *Les Théories socialistes au XIXe siècle de Babeuf à Proudhon*, Paris, Félix Alcan, 1904.

Gould, Carol C. and M.W. Wartofsky (eds), *Women and Philosophy. Towards a Theory of Liberation*, New York, G.P. Putnam's Sons, 1976.

Hedman, Edwin R., 'Early French Feminism: From the Eighteenth Century to 1848', unpublished Ph.D. thesis, New York University, 1954.

Isambert, Gaston, *Les Idées socialistes en France de 1815 à 1848. Le Socialisme fondé sur la fraternité et l'union des classes*, Paris, Alcan, 1905.

Judt, Tony, *Marxism and the French Left. Studies on Labour and Politics in France 1830–1981*, Oxford, Oxford University Press, 1986.

Laidler, Harry W., *History of Socialism*, New York, Thomas Y. Cromwell Co., 1968.

Lichtheim, George, *The Origins of Socialism*, London, Weidenfeld and Nicolson, 1969.

Lindemann, Albert S., *A History of European Socialism*, New Haven and London, Yale University Press, 1983.

Louvancour, Henri, *De Henri de Saint-Simon à Charles Fourier. Etude sur le socialisme romantique français de 1830*, Chartres, Durand, 1913.

MacCormack, Carol and Marilyn Strathern (eds), *Nature, Culture and Gender*, Cambridge, Cambridge University Press, 1980.

Maître, Jean, *Dictionnaire biographique du mouvement ouvrier français*, vol. 2 (1789–1866), Paris, Editions ouvrières, 1973.

Mendus, Susan and Jane Rendall (eds), *Sexuality and Subordination*, London, Routledge, 1989.

Moses, Claire Goldberg, 'The Evolution of Feminist Thought in France, 1829–1889', unpublished Ph.D. thesis, George Washington University, 1978.

——, *French Feminism in the Nineteenth Century*, New York, State University of New York Press, 1984.

O'Brien, Mary, *The Politics of Reproduction*, Boston, London and Henley, Routledge and Kegan Paul, 1983.

Perrot, Michelle (ed.), *Une Histoire des Femmes est-elle Possible?*, Paris, Rivages, 1989.

Petitfils, Jean-Christian, *Les Socialismes utopiques*, Paris, Presses universitaires de France, 1977.

Picard, Roger, *Le Romantisme social*, New York, Brentano, 1944.

Rendall, Jane, *The Origins of Modern Feminism: Women in Britain, France and the United States, 1780–1860*, London, Macmillan, 1985.

Russ, Jacqueline, *La Pensée des Précurseurs de Marx*, Paris, Bordas, 1973.

Samuel, Albert, *Le Socialisme. Histoire – Courants – Pratiques*, Lyon, Chronique social, 1981.

Scott, Joan Wallach, *Gender and the Politics of History*, New York, Columbia University Press, 1988.

Sédillot, René, *Histoire des Socialismes*, Paris, Fayard, 1977.

Société de l'histoire de la Révolution de 1848 et des Révolutions du XIXe Siècle, *1848. Les Utopismes sociaux. Utopie et action à la veille des journées de février*, Paris, Editions C.D.U. et Sédès réunis, 1981.

Stein, Lorenz von, *The History of the Social Movement in France 1789–1850*, New Jersey, Bedminster Press, 1964.

Taylor, Barbara, *Eve and the New Jerusalem. Socialism and Feminism in the Nineteenth Century*, London, Virago, 1983.

Thibert, Marguerite, *Le Féminisme dans le Socialisme français de 1830 à 1850*, Paris, Giard, 1926.

Thomas, Edith, *Les Femmes de 1848*, Paris, Presses universitaires de France, 1948.

Valverde, Mariana, 'French Romantic Socialism and the Critique of Political Economy', unpublished Ph.D. thesis, York University (Canada), 1982.

2: Articles and Essays

Benenson, Harold, 'Victorian Sexual Ideology and Marx's Theory of the Working Class', *International Labor and Working Class History*, 25 (Spring 1984) 1–23.

Bruhat, Jean, 'Le socialisme français de 1815 à 1848', in *Histoire générale du Socialisme*, vol. 1, ed. Jacques Droz, Paris, Presses universitaires de France, 1972.

Draper, Hal and Anne G. Lipow, 'Marxist Women versus Bourgeois Feminism', *The Socialist Register*, 1976, pp. 210–16.

Desroche, Henri, 'Images and Echoes of Owenism in Nineteenth Century France', in Sidney Pollard and John Salt (eds), *Robert Owen Prophet of the Poor. Essays in Honour of the Two Hundredth Anniversary of his Birth*, London, Macmillan, 1971.

Fraisse, Geneviève, 'Natural Law and the Origins of Nineteenth Century Feminist Thought in France', transl. Nancy Festinger, in J. Friedlander *et al.* (eds), *Women in Culture and Politics. A Century of Change*, Bloomington, Indiana University Press, 1986.

Gans, J., 'Robert Owen à Paris en 1837', *Le Mouvement social*, 41 (Oct.–Dec. 1962) 35–45.

——, 'Relations entre socialistes de France et d'Angleterre au début du XIXe siècle, *ibid.*, 46 (Jan.–Mar. 1964) 105–18.

Montgomery, David, 'Response to Harold Benenson's "Victorian Sexual Ideology"', *International Labor and Working Class History*, 25 (Spring 1984) 24–9.

C: CONTEXTUAL WORKS

1: Books and Theses

Aron, Jean-Paul (ed.) *Misérable et Glorieuse la Femme du XIXe Siècle*, Paris, Fayard, 1980.

Aubert, Jean-Marie, *La Femme. Antiféminisme et Christianisme*, Paris, Cerf-Desclée, 1975.

Bénichou, Paul, *Le Temps des Prophètes. Doctrines de l'Age romantique*, Paris, Gallimard, 1977.

Berenson, Edward, *Populist Religion and Left-Wing Politics in France, 1830–1852*, Princeton, Princeton University Press, 1984.

Berkin, Carol N. and Clara M. Lovett (eds), *Women, War and Revolution*,

New York and London, Holmes and Meier, 1980.

Bertier de Sauvigny, G. de, *The Bourbon Restoration*, transl. L.M. Case, Philadelphia, University of Pennsylvania Press, 1967.

Borie, Jean, *Le Tyran Timide: Le Naturalisme de la Femme au XIXe Siècle*, Paris, Klincksieck, 1973.

Bowman, Frank Paul, *Le Christ romantique*, Geneva, Librairie Droz, 1973.

——, *Eliphas Lévi, visionnaire romantique. Préface et choix de textes par Frank Paul Bowman*, Paris, Presses universitaires de France, 1976.

Charlton, D.G., *Secular Religions in France, 1815–1870*, London, Oxford University Press for the University of Hull, 1963.

Chevalier, Louis, *Labouring Classes and Dangerous Classes in Paris During the Nineteenth Century*, transl. Frank Jellineck, London, Routledge and Kegan Paul, 1973.

Copley, Antony, *Sexual Moralities in France, 1780–1980. New Ideas on the Family, Divorce and Homosexuality*, London, Routledge, 1989.

Daumard, Adeline, *La Bourgeoisie Parisienne de 1815 à 1848*, Paris, S.E.V.P.E.N., 1963.

Duhet, Paule-Marie, *Les Femmes et la Révolution 1789–1794*, Paris, Julliard, 1971.

Evans, David Owen, *Social Romanticism in France 1830–1848*, New York, Octagon Books, 1969.

Fleder, Laura W., 'Female Physiology and Psychology in the Works of Diderot and the Medical Writers of his Day', unpublished Ph.D. thesis, Columbia University, 1978.

Fraisse, Geneviève, *Muse de la raison. La démocratie exclusive et la différence des sexes*, Paris, Alinéa, 1989.

Fritz, Paul and Richard Morton (eds), *Woman in the Eighteenth Century and Other Essays*, Toronto, A.M. Hakkert, 1976.

Fuchs, Rachel G., *Abandoned Children. Foundlings and Child Welfare in Nineteenth Century France*, Albany, N.Y., State University of New York Press, 1984.

Gallagher, Catherine and Thomas Laqueur (eds), *The Making of the Modern Body. Sexuality and Society in the Nineteenth Century*, Berkeley, University of California Press, 1987.

Garden, Maurice, *Lyon et les Lyonnais au 18e Siècle*, Paris, Flammarion, 1975.

Garrioch, David, *Neighbourhood and Community in Paris 1740–1790*, Cambridge, Cambridge University Press, 1986.

Guilbert, Madeleine, *Les Fonctions des Femmes dans l'Industrie*, Paris and The Hague, Mouton, 1966.

Harrison, J.F.C., *The Early Victorians 1823–51*, New York, Praeger, 1971.

Harsin, Jill, *Policing Prostitution in Nineteenth Century Paris*, Princeton, Princeton University Press, 1985.

Hellerstein, Erna Olafson, 'Women, Social Order and the City: Rules for French Ladies, 1830–1870', unpub. Ph.D. thesis, University of California, Berkeley, 1980.

Hoffman, Paul, *La Femme dans la Pensée des Lumières*, Paris, Editions Ophrys, 1977.

Jacobs, Eva *et al.*, *Woman and Society in Eighteenth Century France. Essays in*

Honour of John Stephenson Spink, London, The Athlone Press, 1979.

Kleinclausz, A., *Histoire de Lyon*, 3 vols, Lyon, Masson, 1939–52.

Knibiehler, Yvonne and Catherine Fouquet, *Histoire des Mères du Moyen Age à Nos Jours*, Paris, Montalba, 1980.

Lesch, John E., *Science and Medicine in France. The Emergence of Experimental Physiology, 1790–1855*, Harvard University Press, 1984.

Lloyd, Genevieve, *The Man of Reason: 'Male' and 'Female' in Western Philosophy*, London, Methuen, 1984.

Lynch, Katherine, *Family, Class and Ideology in Early Industrial France. Social Policy and the Working Class Family 1825–1848*, Madison, Wisc., University of Wisconsin Press, 1988.

Merriman, John (ed.), *1830 in France*, New York, New Viewpoints, 1975.

——, *Consciousness and Class Experience in Nineteenth Century Europe*, New York and London, Holmes and Meier, 1980.

——, *French Cities in the Nineteenth Century*, London, Hutchinson, 1982.

Michaud, Stéphane, *Muse et Madone. Visages de la femme de la Révolution française aux apparitions de Lourdes*, Paris, Editions du Seuil, 1985.

Moreau, Thérèse, *Le Sang de l'Histoire. Michelet, l'histoire et l'idée de la femme au XIXe siècle*, Paris, Flammarion, 1982.

Padover, Saul K. (ed.), *The Letters of Karl Marx*, Englewood Cliffs, N.J., Prentice-Hall, 1979.

Price, Roger, *A Social History of Nineteenth Century France*, London, Hutchinson, 1987.

Segalen, Martine, *Love and Power in the Peasant Family. Rural France in the Nineteenth Century*, transl. Sarah Matthews, Oxford, Basil Blackwell Publishers and the University of Chicago, 1983.

Smith, Bonnie G., *Ladies of the Leisure Class. The Bourgeoises of Northern France in the Nineteenth Century*, Princeton, Princeton University Press, 1981.

Strumingher, Laura, *Women and the Making of the Working Class, Lyon, 1830–1870*, St Albans, Vermont, Eden Press, 1977.

Tilly, Louise and Joan W. Scott, *Women, Work and Family*, New York, Holt, Rinehart and Winston, 1978.

Traer, James F., *Marriage and the Family in Eighteenth Century France*, Ithaca and London, Cornell University Press, 1980.

Vovelle, Michel, *Idéologies et Mentalités*, Paris, François Maspéro, 1982.

Zeldin, Theodore, *France 1848–1945*, 2 vols., Oxford, Clarendon Press, 1973, 1977.

2: Articles and Essays

Bowman, Frank Paul, 'Religion, Politics and Utopia in French Romanticism', *Australian Journal of French Studies*, 11, no. 3 (1974) 307–24.

Clinton, Catherine B., '"Femme et philosophe": Enlightenment Origins of Feminism', *Eighteenth Century Studies*, 8, no. 3 (1974–5) 283–99.

Devance, Louis, 'Femme, famille, travail et morale sexuelle dans l'idéologie de 1848', *Romantisme*, 13–14 (1976) 79–103.

Gough, Austin, 'French Workers and their Wives in the Mid-Nineteenth Century', *Labour History*, 42 (May 1982) 74–82.

Groppi, Angela, 'Le Travail des Femmes à Paris à l'Epoque de la Révolution française', *Bulletin d'Histoire économique et sociale de la Révolution française*, 1979, 27–46.

Henry, Louis, 'The Population of France in the Eighteenth Century', in D.V. Glass and D.E.C. Eversley (eds), *Population in History*, London, Edward Arnold, 1965.

Hoffman, Paul, 'L'héritage des lumières: mythes et modèles de la féminité au XVIIIe siècle', *Romantisme*, 13–14 (1976) 7–21.

Hufton, Olwen, 'Women in Revolution 1789–1796', *Past and Present*, 53 (1971) 43–62.

Knibiehler, Yvonne, 'Le Discours médical sur la femme: Constantes et ruptures', *Romantisme*, 13–14 (1976) 41–55.

——, 'Les médecins et "la nature féminine" au temps du Code civil', *Annales* E.S.C., 31, no. 4 (July–Aug. 1976) 824–45.

Landes, David, 'Religion and Enterprise: The Case of the French Textile Industry', in Edward C. Carpenter II, Robert Foster and John N. Moody (eds), *Enterprise and Entrepreneurs in Nineteenth and Twentieth Century France*, Baltimore and London, John Hopkins University Press, 1976.

Le Doeuff, Michèle, 'Pierre Roussel's Chiasmas: from imaginary knowledge to the learned imagination', *I & C*, 9 (winter 1981–2) 39–70.

Le Goff, Jacques, 'Les Mentalités. Une histoire ambiguë', in *Faire de l'histoire*, Paris, Gallimard, 1974, vol. 3, pp. 76–94.

McLaren, Angus, 'Some Secular Attitudes toward Sexual Behaviour in France: 1760–1860', *French Historical Studies*, 8, no. 4 (1974) 604–25.

——, 'Abortion in France: Women and the regulation of family size, 1800–1914', *ibid.*, 10, no. 3 (1978) 461–85.

Michaud, Stéphane, 'Science, droit, religion: Trois contes sur les deux natures', *Romantisme*, 13–14 (1976), 23–40.

Pope, Barbara Corrado, 'Maternal Education in France, 1815–1848', *Proceedings of the Third Annual Meeting of the Western Society for French History, December 1975*, Texas, 1976.

——, 'Revolution and Retreat: Upper-Class French Women After 1789', in Carol M. Berkin and Clara M. Lovett (eds), *Women, War and Revolution*, New York and London, Holmes and Meier, 1980.

Scott, Joan Wallach, 'Men and Women in the Parisian Garment Trades: discussions of family and work in the 1830s and 1840s', in *The Power of the Past: Essays for Eric Hobsbawm*, ed. Pat Thane, Geoffrey Crossick and Roderick Floud, London, Cambridge University Press, 1984.

Struminger, Laura, 'L'Ange de la Maison. Mothers and Daughters in Nineteenth Century France', *International Journal of Women's Studies*, 2 (1979) 51–61.

Tomaselli, Sylvana, 'The Enlightenment Debate on Women', *History Workshop Journal*, 20 (Autumn 1985) 101–24.

Van de Walle, Etienne, 'Motivations and Technology in the Decline of French Fertility', in R. Wheaton and T. K. Hareven (eds), *Family and Sexuality in French History*, Philadelphia, University of Pennsylvania Press, 1980.

Zerilli, Linda, 'Motionless Idols and Virtuous Mothers: Women, Art and Politics in France 1789–1848', *Berkeley Journal of Sociology*, XXVII (1982) 89–126.

Index